WILLIAM JENNINGS BRYAN

Also by Paul W. Glad

The Trumpet Soundeth, William Jennings Bryan
and His Democracy, 1896–1912

McKinley, Bryan, and the People

Contents

Introduction

In a lifetime of public activity William Jennings Bryan commanded attention wherever he went. Observing the effects of his compelling presence, contemporaries sought to account for his charisma. In 1896, when he first captured the Democratic nomination for the Presidency, newspaper reporters wrote endlessly about his sturdy physique, his ruggedly handsome and expressive face, his singularly powerful voice, his wit and dexterity in debate. Later, after he had grown bald and paunchy, they still turned out copy on his magnetic oratory. And in his later years they wrote, too, about the enormous energy he had expended in battling for what he believed to be righteous causes.

Bryan was, indeed, a phenomenon of American politics. Three times the Democratic party chose him as its standard-bearer—and three times he met defeat. His metier was not so much the discharge of governmental responsibility as it was the discussion of political questions. Constantly sharing every thought with his countrymen, he often seemed to have no private being; whatever the question of the moment, Bryan spoke out. Millions of Americans listened sympathetically to his views because, better than any other man of his time, he voiced the sentiments of an agrarian society. To his admirers he was "The Great Commoner," an eloquent champion of the people. Others less enamored of the traditional agrarian wisdom he expounded saw him as a fakir, a charlatan, a demagogue, or a menace. But whatever emotion he aroused, Bryan frequently pierced the consciousness of even the most phlegmatic of citizens.

As a public figure Bryan participated in scores of momentous events, yet all the variety of his experience changed him but little. The values he struggled to uphold were values derived from the milieu of his youth. From his parents he received training in the evangelical Protestantism that was to shape much of his political thinking, and from them he first imbibed the moralism characteristic of nineteenth-century America. He learned well the virtues of thrift and honesty, and the awful results of laziness and intemperance. Like any schoolboy who took to heart the lessons of his McGuffey Readers, he came to associate vice with the city and virtue with the countryside. He also saw political rivalry as part of a larger moral bifurcation. The son of an ardent Democrat, he grew up believing that the Democratic party was on the side of the angels.

To suggest that Bryan's ideas evolved out of the environment of his boyhood is not to say that he unrealistically insisted on maintaining an economic or social status quo. On the contrary he believed in progress. He thought progress inevitable in a nation governed by the majority, for majority rule provided the best means of meeting the variable needs of masses of men. Attaining prominence in an era when most of the American population was rural, the Commoner always assumed that his values were those of the majority. He never doubted that he could trust the people to bring about change consistent with the moral and religious convictions he regarded as eternal verities—provided, of course, that the people were left free and unintimidated.

What, then, could have been more understandable than Bryan's taking Thomas Jefferson as his political hero? In Jefferson's writings, particularly in the Declaration of Independence, he found a perfect statement of "the basic truths upon which a republic must rest." [1] He found, too, an idea congenial to agrarians who felt they had been badly used in a period of industrial growth, the idea that

[1] *The Commoner,* April 4, 1902.

all men were created equal in their natural rights and that those rights could be neither acquired nor surrendered.

Merely recognizing the natural rights of others was not enough, however, for Bryan learned from his religious teachers that self-sacrificing love was the most powerful force behind social progress. Charles Darwin and Herbert Spencer, with their concepts of natural selection and survival of the fittest, seemed to be suggesting that men benefited from violence and hatred. It was a retrogressive doctrine. The perfect society, to which all decent men aspired, would appear when each individual found his greatest security in the intelligence and happiness of his fellows. There the welfare of each would be the concern of all. The man who pursued only his own self-interest, as did the captain of industry, lived insignificantly no matter what his power or influence. Bryan liked to quote the paradox of Jesus: "He that saveth his life shall lose it and he that loseth his life for my sake shall find it." He saw in that teaching an "epitome of history." [2]

The Commoner's exegesis extended to international relations as well as to individual or class relations. An advocate of using arbitration to settle labor disputes, he urged the same technique in disputes between nations. "I can not conceive of any question arising between civilized nations which can not be adjusted more satisfactorily by reason than by force," he wrote Andrew Carnegie in 1911.[3] And when Bryan became Secretary of State he labored to secure treaties committing the United States to investigation of disagreements with other countries. "Is it too much to hope that as the years go by we will begin to understand that the whole human race is but a larger family?" he had asked eight years before German troops goose-stepped across the Belgian border.[4] Not satisfied with the answer he received in 1914, Bryan never abandoned the vision that reason tempered by love would prevail over force in international affairs.

[2] Bryan, "The Prince of Peace," printed in *The Commoner*, February 1, 1907.
[3] Bryan to Carnegie, April 13, 1911, Andrew Carnegie Papers (Manuscript Division, Library of Congress).
[4] Bryan, "At the Peace Congress," *Speeches of William Jennings Bryan* (New York, 1909), II, 231.

That ideas such as these should ever seem outmoded was something Bryan could not comprehend. He was, of course, aware of various dynamics at work in late nineteenth-century America. Falling agricultural prices, rapid industrialization, the emergence of monopolies, and the growth of a large urban labor force were all apparent to him. In 1896 he championed the free coinage of silver as a device for assuring the farmer a just return and a stable market, but he placed the silver crusade in a broad context. Like the Populists who were his political allies, he believed that a profound injustice lay in the direction taken by the American economy of the 1890's. He especially deplored the mergers that created gigantic business combinations, not only because he disapproved of the methods he saw tycoons using, but also because he regarded the power of the "trusts" as a threat to economic balance.

The trusts, in Bryan's view, constituted a means by which privileged groups could control prices, regulate the conditions of labor, and eliminate competitors. He envisioned their tentacles reaching out from the great cities to strangle the farmer and pick his pocket. But not only the farmer would suffer. The economic power of large business combinations could well increase to the point where such combinations would completely dominate American society. And at that point individual liberty, together with any possibility of arbitrating disputes, would disappear. The trust, then, was "a menace to the political welfare of the country, for political independence can not long exist with industrial servitude." [5] In the end, Americans would discover that large business organizations were dehumanized monsters. "When God made man He gave him a soul and warned him that in the next world he would be held accountable for the deeds done in the flesh; but when man created the corporation he could not endow that corporation with a soul, so that if it escapes punishment here it need not fear the hereafter." [6] In such manner did the Commoner caution the Chicago Association of Commerce in 1908.

During the depression of the nineties, and later in the period of

[5] Bryan, "A Remedy for the Trusts," *Public Opinion*, XXXVIII (April 29, 1905), 645.

[6] Bryan, "Commerce," *Speeches*, II, 410.

progressive reform, Bryan spoke a language that those lacking in economic power could understand. It was a language drawn out of economic permutation, sectional cleavage, and social disruption. The Commoner saw urban-rural tensions in American society as the result of intrigues among industrial leaders and manipulations by the money power. Fighting to protect an agrarian order from subversion and to assure the farmer an honorable place in a mixed economy, he spoke of the eastern seaboard in 1896 as "the enemy's country." [7] But even when he was not thinking in terms of an urban-rural or east-west confrontation, Bryan considered conflict unavoidable. Indeed, he thought it desirable. Throughout his career he believed that two parties—one democratic and the other aristocratic—would contend with each other for control of government. While he conceded that the conservative was necessary "to keep the radical from going too far," he also argued that the radical's function was "to make the conservative go at all." [8] The Commoner was no revolutionary; he preferred discussion to violence and arbitration to war. But like the Prince of Peace he glorified, he sometimes brought not peace, but a sword.

For all his social and economic criticism, however, Bryan never found fault with the new industrial technology itself. He sensed that it represented a liberating force. He understood that it offered escape from physical restrictions and demands that in pre-industrial society had been inescapable. What he objected to was the way in which the power conferred by that technology came to be exercised. Therein lay the cause of untold hardship. Concentrating on obvious injustices, Bryan never really took notice of the less obvious ways in which technology affected behavior and values throughout American society.

The machine sapped the vitality from customs and manners that had grown out of an unmechanized rural environment. It created new alternatives to the normative system imposed by a rural culture and it upset the rhythm of everyday life. Industrial areas, for example, came to know the shrill blast of the factory whistle that sharply defined the laborer's workday. Hours away

---

[7] Bryan, *The First Battle* (Chicago, 1897), p. 300.
[8] Bryan, "Radical and Conservative," *Speeches,* II, 208–209.

from the job, however the worker may have spent them, were identified as leisure time. And leisure time posed problems that Americans had never before had to face. In the period of Bryan's youth and earlier, the prevalence of husking bees, quiltings, and house-raisings bespoke the possibility of combining work and play. "If the word *recreation* is not in your vocabulary," George R. Stewart has observed, "you will probably not analyze whether you are having recreation or indulging in more serious activity when you whittle out a wooden spoon (Is this fun, utility, or folk art?), bundle with a pretty girl (Is this amusement, release of sex impulses, or the first step toward being fruitful and multiplying?), or listen to a hell-fire sermon in church (Is this the equivalent of a soap-opera, or a really practical insurance against hell-fire?)." [9]

Taught to think of play as a nonproductive result of sinful idleness, Americans of Bryan's generation perhaps felt guilty about taking part in recreational activities that the new leisure afforded. If so, a sense of guilt may help to explain the violence they sought in sports such as boxing and football. If they could not make play out of work, they could at least make work out of play. In 1894, a writer in *Harper's* Magazine thought that they pursued recreation with "all that earnestness which characterizes the American in whatever field he launches." [10]

For great numbers of people, then, leisure-time activities at the turn of the century were by no means a frivolous matter. They approached such activities with an almost fervent solemnity. The circuit Chautauqua movement, especially popular in the Middle West, reflects the seriousness with which rural folk sought to take advantage of the free time that technology brought to the farm as well as to the city. No Chautauqua organizer would ever suggest that his program was designed solely for entertainment. Every performance in the big tent had to teach a lesson or do some good, and every Chautauqua week concluded with an inspirational lecture. "My hands have labored long and steadily," read one verse of a Chautauqua psalm. "I shall give them a little rest at Chautau-

[9] Stewart, *American Ways of Life* (Garden City, N.Y., 1954), p. 211.
[10] Caspar W. Whitney, "Evolution of the Country Club," *Harper's* Magazine, XC (December 1894), 16.

qua. At the same time I shall get the brain tonic of the wholesome atmosphere there." [11] The moralistic overtones of the movement provided a means of bridging the gap between an old rural culture and a new.

Bryan was, of course, the most popular of inspirational lecturers on the Chautauqua circuit, and more than anyone else he contributed to the success of the enterprise. Yet he thought no more about Chautauqua as a by-product of technological advance than he did about relationships between the same developing technology and his own political style. Completion of a vast railway network made possible the sort of speaking and campaigning that was peculiarly his. Yet not until long after the high point of his leadership did the electronic amplifier deprive him—or any other such orator who might come along in the future—of the obvious advantage in a voice that was remarkable for its carrying power.

Whatever lay behind his opportunities, however, Bryan made the most of them. He fought for causes with a determination that never flagged. Time and time again the shrewdest and most experienced observers were ready to count him out and draft his political obituary. Time and time again the Commoner returned to do battle as a champion of the people. In 1904, when the Democratic party came temporarily under the control of its Bourbon faction and nominated the conservative Alton B. Parker, Bryan's political prestige seemed at its nadir. Twice defeated as a Presidential candidate himself, he had now even lost support of his party. Then, at one of those fervid moments that punctuated his career, he told the convention: "You may dispute whether I have fought a good fight, you may dispute whether I have finished my course, but you cannot deny that I have kept the faith." [12] Newspapermen throughout the country reported that speech as a valedictory, but by 1908 Bryan was again in control of the Democratic party. And until he finally finished his course in 1925, he was to exercise a powerful hold over an important though ever-diminishing segment of it.

Fighter that he was, Bryan tended to oversimplify the issues he

[11] Brochure, Woodbine, Iowa, Chautauqua, July 22–28, 1911, in *Chautauqua Collection,* University of Iowa, Iowa City.

[12] Bryan, *Speeches,* II, 50.

debated. Invariably taking his stand on moral grounds, he did not readily yield to compromise solutions despite his advocacy of arbitration. Regarding one set of arguments as bad and another as good, he was seldom persuaded that mutual agreement might avoid concessions to wickedness. Furthermore, although he believed that issues were created by events, he did not always understand the ways in which discussion of those issues might change with the passage of time. In his battle against the trusts, for example, he centered his attention on the iniquities of large business combinations. The Omaha *World-Herald* thought of Bryan as waging "a fight to save the Republic and its free democratic institutions from degeneration into an oligarchic despotism with the masses in hopeless industrial dependence on an arrogant plutocracy." In that struggle there was "no place for compromise, and no time to be politic." [13] Thus neither the Commoner nor his followers ever really came to grips with the transformation that took place within American capitalism during the progressive period.

Industrial capitalism in the United States did not undertake its own reformation after the manner of a repentant sinner bent upon mending his ways. But in the years before World War I, partly out of fear that criticism and the demand for reform would eventually lead to socialism, business did seek an industrial order that could be defended in progressive terms. Passage of some progressive legislation, such as the Federal Reserve Act and the Federal Trade Commission Act, could not have been accomplished without the support of industrialists and financiers. Such men found that moderate reform went a long way toward nullifying the efforts of militant radicals. Beyond this, moderate reform was also part of a more general effort to rationalize the American economy. Business and industry established associations to improve the production and distribution of goods. Scientific management of workshops had an almost mystical appeal to its enthusiastic supporters. Plant managers launched new experiments in vocational selection and guidance. In a word, the cult of efficiency came into vogue and it attracted progressives such as Herbert Croly and Walter Lippmann

[13] Omaha *World-Herald,* June 27, 1906, quoted in *The Public,* IX (July 7, 1906), 322.

as well as business and industrial leaders such as Herbert Hoover. It did not attract Bryan. In his view "no amount of economy can compensate for the evil done by a private monopoly." Suppose, he argued, using a characteristic analogy, he became convinced that he could live more inexpensively with a thousand people in a hotel than he could live at home. That would not persuade him to sell his house and move to a hotel:

No; I tell you that I would not give up the blessings of home life for all the economy hotel life could promise. I believe in the family; I believe in its sacred associations and I would not be willing to barter the home life of this nation for any economy that might be shown to result from any other kind of living; and so no economy that a private monopoly can promise will compensate for the destruction of individual independence, of the citizen's right to think as he pleases, to act as he pleases and to be his own master.[14]

In a period when American capitalism began to shift its emphasis —when its leaders talked less about seizing the main chance and more about industrial efficiency, less about getting rich quickly, and more about service to the community—Bryan still thought in terms of antagonism and cleavage. The New Era after World War I asserted the value of economic cooperation or associational activity in the name of efficiency and service, but the Commoner continued to lecture on right and wrong.

Bryan's leadership seemed to falter after World War I, then, not because he changed or because in an agrarian context his ideas were harebrained and quixotic. It faltered because industrial enterprise, and conditions of American life in general, went through a significant change in character. The student of politics cannot account for political leadership by examining only the innate qualities of men who become leaders. Leadership arises out of particular situations and the interaction of people involved in those situations. The economic conditions of the nineties, combined with the social unrest of the period, demanded a leader who could voice the protests of dissatisfied groups and integrate their forces. The

[14] Bryan, "The Wisdom of Doing Right," printed in *The Commoner,* March 11, 1904.

Commoner had never succeeded in uniting all of the discontented
—from single taxers, silverites, and socialists to Populists and progressives—but he did speak for large numbers of them. And he
continued to do so until the 1920's, when political power passed
to those who promised a New Era, an economic utopia for everyone in a society of cooperative individualists. The people whom
Bryan represented at the famous "monkey trial" in 1925 were the
last remnant of those millions who had followed him ecstatically
when he pleaded the cause of silver in 1896. They were those who
still adhered to the moralism of agrarian America and to the evangelical religious convictions that had not seemed so strange in
Bryan's youth as they did when he expounded them at Dayton,
Tennessee.

By 1925 the Commoner's following—"gaping primates from the
upland valleys of the Cumberland range" H. L. Mencken called
them—had become a laughingstock, and so had Bryan. Much of
the material written about him by sophisticated biographers such
as Paxton Hibben and Morris R. Werner teems with clichés about
his archaic ideas. Too many critics found hypocrisy and inconsistency in the Commoner when they should have looked for envi-
ronmental influence and cultural tradition. Yet not all sophisticates
in the years after World War I tried to crucify Bryan on a cross
of ridicule; many were inclined, rather, to pity him for being so
obstinate and so uncomprehending of forces at work in society.
"Unlike Duglas who took to drink when Lincoln defeated him,
Bryan took to smiles and religion . . ." wrote Edgar Lee Masters
after Bryan's death. "If he woke in another life, he surely found
no Methodist heaven, no pit ching of golden crwons around the
glassy sea, and no lamb; but he found great powers and forces
and strange wonderful proceses moving to orlds not realized; and
perahspa smiled thta he had ben such a fool and made so much
trouble for his countrymen." [15]

None of the essays I have chosen for this book takes a simplistic approach to the man who made Masters think "that life is

[15] Masters to E. R. Reese, July 27, 1925, Masters Papers (Illinois State
Historical Library, Springfield). Masters would not deign to correct the
typing errors in letters to his friends.

a strange weird thing, a joke and a tragedy combined." Some of them are more critical of Bryan than are others. Paolo Coletta examines the shortcomings of the Commoner's 1896 campaign. Richard Hofstadter writes of a Bryan who never really expected to win the Presidency and whose psychological needs were satisfied by an appreciative audience. Thomas A. Bailey sees Bryanesque vagaries as a major reason for his defeat in 1900. Richard Challener discovers an ineffective Secretary of State who lacked a capacity for subtle analysis. Merle Curti notes the inadequacies of Bryan's thinking on world peace. To Ray Ginger the Commoner's position on evolution raises questions about his rationality.

Despite the critical commentary appearing in these selections, however, each author, from John A. Garraty to Henry Steele Commager, has searched for understanding of the man and his times. When one views Bryan in a friendly environment—as does Norbert R. Mahnken in his study ·of the Commoner's empathetic relationship with the people of Oklahoma—his attractiveness is readily apparent. On the other hand, when one explores Bryan's involvement with the Prohibition movement or fundamentalism, flippancy and sarcasm may easily replace understanding. But Lawrence W. Levine neither burlesques the prohibitionists nor snickers at Bryan's prohibitionist views in his sensitive essay, and John T. Scopes writes with moderation in his recollection of the Dayton episode.

On the whole, then, the essays reveal the limitations of nineteenth-century agrarianism in a twentieth-century industrial society, but they do not·denigrate the entire world view that Bryan represented. There was, after all, much of permanent value in that view: a recognition of human rights; a faith in democracy that was the positive side of a hatred of privilege; a conviction that love and peace not only benefit society more than hatred and war but are the surest avenues to liberty and justice for all. The Commoner's mind ran toward the trite and truistic, to be sure, but such is the stuff of which benign social myths are made. Malignant alternatives advanced both in the United States and abroad during the years since his death have placed in a new perspective the beliefs by which Bryan lived. Thus to the authors of these pieces (which with two exceptions were written after World War II), the Commoner is no more accurately depicted when presented as one of H. L. Mencken's boobs than he is when apotheosized as a heaven-sent and infallible leader.

This volume is not intended to take the place of a full biography of William Jennings Bryan; its purpose is to provide a credible por-trait of a deceptively simple historical personality, a seemingly uncomplicated man who played a leading role in a complicated period. The essays fall naturally into three groups: those dealing with Bryan's background, character, and first Presidential campaign; those concerned with his period of opposition leadership from 1896 to 1912; and those that treat his tenure as Secretary of State and his later years. Although differences of interpretation are abundant, I believe that this collection furnishes a means of assessing the life of one who was *sui generis* in American political history.

PAUL W. GLAD

Madison, Wisconsin
February 1968

William Jennings Bryan, 1860–1925

William Jennings Bryan was born in Salem, Illinois, on March 19, 1860. He attended Whipple Academy and Illinois College in Jacksonville, where he soon made a name for himself as a debater and public speaker. Active in campus politics, he also took an early interest in state politics. During the summer of 1880 he helped organize the Hancock Club of Salem and took to the stump in behalf of Congressman William M. Springer. Returning to college for his senior year, he graduated first in the class of 1881. After two years' study at Union College of Law in Chicago and after gaining admission to the bar, he returned to Jacksonville, hung out his shingle, and married Mary Baird.

Although the law provided an adequate living, Bryan sought a wider field for his talents. He found it in Lincoln, Nebraska. There he formed a partnership with Union Law classmate A. R. Talbot, but the Democratic party of Nebraska soon claimed most of his attention. In 1890 he won election to Congress, where he served two terms. His Congressional career was marked by advocacy of tariff and monetary reforms. He spoke persuasively for both, but urging the free coinage of silver cost him the support of Grover Cleveland and his seat in the House. He then took a job as editor of the Omaha *World-Herald* and threw himself wholeheartedly into the silver crusade which steadily gained adherents during the depression of the nineties. Silverite control of the Chicago convention of the Democratic party in 1896—together with the dramatic "Cross of Gold" speech—assured Bryan's first nomination for the Presidency.

After a spirited campaign, which William McKinley won by a narrow margin, Bryan began a long career as leader of the Democratic opposition to Republican hegemony in national politics. Although he enlisted in the war against Spain in 1898 (taking command of the Third Nebraska Volunteers), he came out against acquisition of overseas possessions when the war was over. Running on an anti-imperialist platform in 1900, he again lost to McKinley. And for a time he appeared to have lost influence within the Democracy as well. His party nominated the conservative Alton B. Parker in 1904.

Yet Bryan was never one to leave the field of political combat in the possession of those he considered enemies of the people. By means of his oratory and his weekly newspaper *The Commoner* he constantly agitated for progressive reform and for progressive revitalization of the Democratic party. Operating outside traditional political institutions and paying scant attention to political bosses and machines, he fought his way back to the party nomination in 1908. Even though he ran well behind William Howard Taft in the election, he nevertheless continued to hold the allegiance of a significant number of Democrats. In the exciting convention of 1912 he played an important—though often overemphasized—role in the nomination of Woodrow Wilson. When Wilson assumed office in 1913, he named the Commoner Secretary of State.

Bryan headed the State Department for twenty-seven eventful months. While frequently castigated for the appointment of "deserving Democrats" to diplomatic posts and for what his critics regarded as bumpkin conduct of foreign policy, Bryan worked hard to prevent American involvement in war. He also helped the President secure much of his domestic program, particularly the Federal Reserve Act. In 1915, however, he resigned his position because he thought Wilson's policy in the *Lusitania* affair would lead to war with Germany.

During the last decade of his life Bryan continued to be active in politics. Always a moralist, he championed Prohibition as a reform that would help purify American life. But more and more his interests gravitated to religion. In his mind, World War I demonstrated the deplorable consequences of following the law of the jungle. Nietzsche with his superman and Darwin with his evolutionary hypothesis were equally the enemies of peace and brotherhood. Increasingly, therefore, Bryan became a spokesman for fundamentalists who saw Darwinism as a threat to traditional religious values. The fight against Darwin took the Commoner to Dayton, Tennessee, where he died shortly after the Scopes trial in 1925.

P.W.G.

WILLIAM JENNINGS BRYAN

✪

A Leader of the People

"The President of the United States may be an ass," wrote H. L. Mencken during the reign of Calvin Coolidge, "but he at least doesn't believe that the earth is square, and that witches should be put to death, and that Jonah swallowed the whale." The man to whom the vitriolic Mencken was comparing President Coolidge was William Jennings Bryan of Nebraska, one of the dominant figures in the progressive movement. According to Mencken, Bryan was a "peasant," a "zany without sense or dignity," a "poor clod," and, in addition, an utter fraud. "If the fellow was sincere, then so was P. T. Barnum," he sneered.

It was certainly easy enough, and tempting, for sophisticates to come to the conclusion that Bryan was a buffoon and a fake. His undignified association in his declining years with the promotion of Florida real estate and his naïve and bigoted religious views, so pitilessly exposed by Clarence Darrow during the famous "Monkey Trial" in Dayton, Tennessee, lent substance to the Mencken view of his character. So did Bryan's smug refusal, while Secretary of State under Woodrow Wilson, to serve alcoholic beverages at department receptions and dinners because of his personal disapproval of drinking, and his objection to the appointment of ex-President Charles W. Eliot of Harvard as Ambassador to China on the ground that Eliot was a Unitarian, and therefore

Reprinted from John A. Garraty, "Bryan: The Progressive, Part I," *American Heritage*, XIII (December 1961), pp. 6–11, 108–111. Reprinted by permission of American Heritage Publishing Co., Inc.

not a real Christian. "The new Chinese civilization," said Bryan, "was founded upon the Christian movement." Eliot's appointment might undermine the work of generations of pious missionaries, he implied. Bryan's unabashed partisanship—he talked frankly after Wilson's election of filling government positions with "deserving Democrats"—did not seem to jibe with his pretensions as a reformer. And his oratorical style, magnificent but generally more emotional than logical, was disappointing to thinking people. John Hay called him a "Baby Demosthenes" and David Houston, one of his colleagues in Wilson's Cabinet, stated that "one could drive a prairie schooner through any part of his argument and never scrape against a fact." Being largely a creature of impulse, Bryan was, Houston added, "constantly on the alert to get something which has been represented to him as a fact to support or sustain his impulses."

But these flaws and blind spots were not fundamental weaknesses; they should never be allowed to overshadow Bryan's long years of devoted service to the cause of reform. If there were large areas about which he knew almost nothing, there were others where he was alert, sensible, and well-informed; certainly he was not a stupid man, nor was he easily duped or misled. Although a professional politician, as his remark about "deserving Democrats" makes clear, he was utterly honest personally and devoted to the cause of the people, as he understood it.

He was perfectly attuned to the needs and aspirations of rural America. In the early nineties he was in the forefront of the fight against high tariffs on manufactured goods. Later in the decade he battled for currency reform. At the turn of the century he was leading the assault against imperialism. During Theodore Roosevelt's primacy he was often far ahead of the intrepid Teddy, advocating a federal income tax, the eight-hour day, the control of monopoly and the strict regulation of public utilities, woman suffrage, and a large number of other startling innovations. Under Wilson he played a major part in marshaling support in Congress for the Federal Reserve Act and other New Freedom measures. Whatever his limitations, his faults, or his motives, few public men of his era left records as consistently "progressive" as Bryan's.

For years he led the Democratic party without the advantage of holding office. Three times he was a Presidential candidate; although never elected, he commanded the unswerving loyalty of millions of his fellow citizens for nearly thirty years. He depended more on his intuition than on careful analysis in forming his opinions, but his intuition was usually sound; he was more a man of heart than of brain, but his heart was great.

Bryan was known as the Great Commoner, and the title was apt. He was a man of the people in origin and by instinct. He was typical of his age in rendering great respect to public opinion, whether it was informed or not. To Bryan the voice of the people was truly the voice of God. "I don't know anything about free silver," he announced while running for Congress early in the nineties. "The people of Nebraska are for free silver and I am for free silver. I will look up the arguments later." (It should be added that he did indeed "look up the arguments later." Less than a year after making this promise he arose in the House to deliver without notes a brilliant three-hour speech on the money question, a speech of great emotional power, but also fact-laden, sensible, and full of shrewd political arguments. When he sat down, the cheers rang out from both sides of the aisle.)

Bryan was born in Salem, Illinois, in 1860, a child of the great Middle West. Growing up in the heart of the valley of democracy, he absorbed its spirit and its sense of protest from his earliest years. After being graduated from Illinois College in 1881, he studied law in Chicago and for a time practiced his profession in Jacksonville, Illinois. But in 1887, stimulated by a talk with a law-school classmate from that city, he moved west to Lincoln, Nebraska. He quickly made his way in this new locale. Within a year he was active in the local Democratic organization, and in 1890, a month before his thirtieth birthday, he won his party's nomination for Congressman.

Nebraska was traditionally a Republican state, its loyalty to the party of Lincoln forged in the heat of the Civil War. But by 1890 tradition was rapidly losing its hold on voters all over the Middle

West. For the farmers of the American heartland were in deep trouble, and the Republican party seemed unwilling to do much to help them.

Tumultuous social and economic changes shaped the nation in the years after Appomattox. Within a single generation the United States was transformed from what was essentially a land of farmers into a modern industrial society, and in the process the Middle West was caught in a relentless economic vise. During the flush times of the sixties, when the Union Army was buying enormous amounts of food and fodder, and foreign demand was unusually high, the farmers of the region had gone into debt in order to buy more land and machinery. In the seventies and eighties, however, agricultural prices, especially those of such major staple crops as wheat and cotton, fell steeply. Wheat, which had sold as high as $2.50 a bushel in wartime, was down to fifty cents by the early nineties.

The impact of this economic decline was intensified by the changing social status of the farmer. Agriculture was losing its predominant place in American life. In the days of the Founding Fathers, about ninety per cent of the population was engaged in working the soil, and the farmer was everywhere portrayed as the symbol of American self-reliance and civic virtue. "Those who labor in the earth," Jefferson said, "are the chosen people of God." But as the factory began to outstrip the farm, the farmer lost much of his standing. While the old symbol remained—it was especially in evidence around election time—a new and disturbing image of the farmer as a hick, a rube, a hayseed—a comic mixture of cocky ignorance, shrewd self-interest, and monumental provincialism—began to challenge it.

Naturally the farmers resented their loss of both income and prestige, but there was little they could do about either. Price declines were largely a response to world-wide overproduction, resulting from improvements in transportation and the opening up of new farmlands in Australia, Argentina, Canada, Russia, and elsewhere. Nor did the farmers, who desired manufactured goods as much as everyone else, really want to reverse the trend that was making them a minority group in a great industrial nation.

But as they cast about for some way out of their plight, they were profoundly disturbed by certain results of the new development which did seem amenable to reform.

Industrial growth meant the mushrooming of great cities. These gave birth to noxious slums where every kind of vice flourished, where corrupt political organizations like the venal Tweed Ring in New York were forged, and where radical political concepts like socialism and anarchism sought to undermine "the American way of life." In the words of Jefferson, the farmers' hero, cities were "ulcers on the body politic."

Giant industries also attracted hordes of immigrants; these seemed to threaten the Middle West both by their mere numbers and by their "un-American" customs and points of view. Could the American melting pot absorb such strange ingredients without losing much of its own character?

Furthermore, to the citizens of Nebraska and other agricultural states, the new industrial barons appeared bent on making vassals of every farmer in America. The evidence seemed overwhelming: Huge impersonal corporations had neither souls nor consciences; profit was their god, materialism their only creed. The "interests," a tiny group of powerful tycoons in great eastern centers like Boston, New York, and Philadelphia, were out to enslave the rest of the country. Farmers worked and sweated only to see the "interests" make off with most of the fruit of their toil. Too many useless middlemen grew fat off the mere "handling" of wheat and cotton. Monopolistic railroads overcharged for carrying crops to market, unscrupulous operators of grain elevators falsely downgraded prime crops and charged exorbitant fees. Cynical speculators drove the price of staples up and down, sometimes making and losing millions in a matter of minutes, without the slightest regard for the effect of their operations on the producers whose sweat made their deadly game possible.

Conspiring with bankers and mortgage holders, all these groups combined to dictate the federal government's money policy. Population and production were surging forward; more money was needed simply to keep up with economic growth. Yet the government was deliberately cutting down on the amount of money in circulation by retiring Civil War greenbacks. On debt-ridden farmers plagued by overproduction, the effect of this deflation was catastrophic. Or so it seemed from the perspective of rural America.

While undoubtedly exaggerated, this indictment of the "interests" was taken as gospel throughout large sectors of the South and West. As a result, demands for "reform" quickly arose. The leading reformers were for the most part sincere, but few of them were entirely altruistic and many were decidedly eccentric. Participating in the movement for a variety of motives but without coming to grips with the main problem of American agriculture—overproduction—were coarse demagogues like Senator "Pitchfork Ben" Tillman of South Carolina, and unwashed characters like the wisecracking Congressman from Kansas, "Sockless Jerry" Simpson. There were professional orators like the angry Mary Ellen Lease (her detractors called her "Mary Yellin' "), and homespun economic theorists like "Coin" Harvey and "General" Jacob Coxey, who believed so strongly in paper money that he named his son Legal Tender. The excesses of such people frightened off many Americans who might otherwise have lent a sympathetic ear to the farmers' complaints; others who might have been friendly observed the antics of the reformers with contempt and wrote off the whole movement as a joke.

Since neither of the major parties espoused the farmers' cause wholeheartedly, much of the protest found its way into various third-party organizations. At first, discontented elements concentrated on opposing the government's policy of retiring the paper money put in circulation during the Civil War. To save these greenbacks from extinction a Greenback (later Greenback-Labor) party sprang up. In 1878 its candidates polled a million votes, but decline followed as currency reformers turned to other methods of inflation.

Meanwhile the Patrons of Husbandry, better known as the Grange, originally a social organization for farm families, had begun to agitate in local politics against the middlemen who were draining off such a large percentage of the farmers' profits. In the seventies the Grangers became a power in the Middle West; in state after state they obtained the passage of laws setting maximum rates for railroads and prohibiting various forms of discrimination. The operations of grain elevators were also subjected to state regulation by "Granger Laws" in states such as Illinois, Iowa, Wisconsin, and Minnesota. The Grange abandoned political activity in the eighties, but other farm organizations quickly took its place. These coalesced first into the Northern Alliance and the Southern Alliance, and around 1890 the two Alliances joined with one another to become the Populist party.

Although William Jennings Bryan was a Democrat, he had grown up amid the agitations of the Granger movement. His father had even run for Congress in the seventies with Greenback party support. The aspirations and the general point of view of the midwestern farmers were young Bryan's own. Public men, he admitted late in life to the journalist Mark Sullivan, are "the creatures of their age. . . . I lived in the very center of the country out of which the reforms grew, and was quite naturally drawn to the people's side."

And they to his, one must add. Discontented farmers in his district were on the lookout for men who understood them and their problems. In 1888 the Republicans had carried the seat by 3,000 votes; now, in 1890, Bryan swept in with a lead of 6,713.

Bryan made an excellent record in his first Congress. He was a hardworking member, studying the technicalities of the tariff question for months before making his first important speech. But he saw that the tariff was rapidly being replaced by the money question as the crucial issue of the day. When he yielded the floor after completing his tariff speech, he collared a young Texas Congressman named Joseph W. Bailey, who posed as a financial expert. Sitting on a sofa in the rear of the House chamber, he quizzed Bailey about the problem of falling prices. Bailey told him the tariff had little or no effect on the plight of the farmer; the whole difficulty arose from "an appreciation in value of gold." Interested, Bryan demanded a list of books on the subject and was soon deep in a study of the money question.

To a man like Bryan, studying the money question meant searching for some means of checking the deflationary trend that was so injurious to his farmer constituents. He quickly discovered that most farm-belt financial authorities felt this could best be done by providing for the free coinage of silver. In 1873 the United States had gone on the gold standard, which meant that only gold was accepted for coinage at the mint. By going back to bimetallism, the amount of bullion being coined would be increased, and if the favorable ratio of sixteen to one between silver and gold were established, the production of silver for coinage would be greatly stimulated.

To press for the free coinage of silver at a ratio of sixteen to one with gold seemed less radical or dangerous than to demand direct inflation of the currency through the printing of greenbacks. Silver, after all, was a precious metal; coining it could not possibly lead to the sort of "runaway" inflation that had helped ruin the South during the Civil War. Debtors and other friends of inflation could also count on the powerful support of silver-mine interests. The free-coinage issue thus had a powerful political appeal. Despite the opposition of most conservative businessmen, the silverites were able, in 1878 and again in 1890, to obtain legislation providing for the coinage of *some* silver, although not enough to check the downward trend of prices.

Within a month after his tariff speech Bryan was calling for free coinage, and he stressed the issue in his successful campaign for re-election in 1892. But the new President, Democrat Grover Cleveland, was an ardent gold-standard man, and when a severe depression struck the country early in 1893, he demanded that the Silver Purchase Act of 1890, which had raised the specter of inflation in the minds of many businessmen, be repealed by Congress at once. In this way he committed his party to the resumption of the single gold standard.

Bryan refused to go along with this policy. Threatening to "serve my country and my God under some other name" than "Democrat" unless the administration changed its mind, he resisted the repeal of the silver act in a brilliant extemporaneous speech. Cleveland carried the day for repeal, but Bryan emerged as a potential leader of the silver wing of the Democrats.

In 1894 he sought a wider influence by running for the United States Senate. In those days Senators were still chosen by the state legislatures; to be elected Bryan would need the support of Nebraska's Populists as well as of his own party. He worked hard for fusion, but Populist support was not forthcoming. Though the Democrats backed Populist candidate Silas A. Holcomb for the governorship, the Populists refused to reciprocate and ran their own man for the Senate seat. The Republican candidate therefore won easily.

At this stage the Populists were trying hard to become a truly national party. Their program, besides demanding the free coinage of silver and various land reforms desired by farmers, called for government ownership of railroads, a graduated income tax, the direct election of U.S. Senators, the eight-hour day, and a number of additional reforms designed to appeal to Eastern workingmen and other dissatisfied groups. As early as 1892 their Presidential candidate, James B. Weaver, had polled over a million votes; in 1894 the party won six seats in the Senate and seven in the House of Representatives. At least in Nebraska, the Populists were not yet ready to merge with the "conservative" Democratic organization.

Defeat for the Senate did not harm Bryan politically. He was still in his early thirties; to one so young, merely having run for the Senate brought considerable prestige. Also, he had conducted an intelligent and forceful campaign. Even so it was a defeat, certainly not calculated to lead him to the remarkable decision that he made after the Nebraska legislature had turned him down. This decision was to seek nomination for the Presidency of the United States itself!

The young man's "superlative self-assurance" (one might call it effrontery but for the fact that his daring plan succeeded) staggers the imagination. Many men within his party were far better known than he, and his state, Nebraska, was without major influence in Democratic affairs. With Cleveland and the national organization dead-set against free coinage and other inflationary schemes, Bryan's chances of capturing the nomination seemed infinitesimal. But if bold, his action was by no means foolish. Democratic voters were becoming more and more restive under Cleveland's conservative leadership. At least in Bryan's part of the nation, many thoughtful members of the party were beginning to feel that they must look in new directions and find new leaders if they were not to be replaced by the Populists as the country's second major party. Recognizing this situation before most politicians did, Bryan proceeded to act upon his insight with determination and dispatch.

First of all, he set out to make himself known beyond his own locality. Accepting the editorship of the Omaha *World-Herald* at a tiny salary in order to obtain a forum, he turned out a stream of editorials on the silver question, which he sent to influential politicians all over the country. He toured the South and West with his message, speaking everywhere and under all sorts of conditions: to close-packed, cheering throngs and to tiny groups of quiet listeners. His argument was simple but forceful, his oratory magnetic and compelling. Always he made sure to meet local leaders and to subject them to his genial smile, his youthful vigor, his charm, his sincerity. He did not push himself forward; indeed, he claimed to be ready to support any honest man whose program was sound. But he lost no chance to point out to all concerned his own availability. "I don't suppose your delegation is committed to any candidate," he wrote to a prominent Colorado Democrat in April of 1896. "Our delegation may present my name." When the Democratic convention finally met in Chicago, Bryan believed that he was known personally to more of the delegates than any other candidate.

Few delegates took his campaign seriously, however. At the convention, one Senator asked Bryan who he thought would win out. Bryan replied characteristically that he believed he himself "had as good a chance to be nominated as anyone," and proceeded to tick off the sources of his strength: Nebraska, "half of the Indian Territory, . . ." but before Bryan could mention his other backers the Senator lost interest and walked off with some of his cronies. The candidate, amiable and serene, took no offense. A majority of the delegates favored his position on silver. No one had a clear lead in the race. All he needed was a chance to plead his case.

The opportunity—Bryan called it an "unexpected stroke of luck," although he planned for it brilliantly—came when he was asked to close the debate on the platform's silver plank. When he came forward to address the jam-packed mob in the Chicago auditorium he was tense, but there was a smile on his face, and to observers he seemed the picture of calm self-confidence. He began quietly, but his voice resounded in the farthest corners of the great hall and commanded the attention of every delegate. He was conscious of his own humble position, he told the throng, but he was "clad in the armor of a righteous cause" and this entitled him to speak. As he went on, his tension evaporated and his voice rose. When he recounted the recent history of the struggle between the forces of gold and silver, the audience responded eagerly. "At the close of a sentence," he wrote later, "it would rise and shout, and when I began upon another sentence, the room was still as a church."

He spoke for silver as against gold, for the West over the East, for "the hardy pioneers who have braved all the dangers of the wilderness" as against "the few financial magnates who, in a back room, corner the money of the world."

We have petitioned, and our petitions have been scorned; we have entreated, and our entreaties have been disregarded; we have begged, and they have mocked when our calamity came. We beg no longer; we entreat no more; we petition no more. *We defy them!*

The crowd thundered its agreement. Bryan proceeded. One after another he met the arguments of the party's Cleveland wing head on. Free silver would disturb the business interests? "Gold bugs" were defining the term too narrowly. Remember that wage earners, crossroads merchants, and farmers were also businessmen. The cities favored the gold standard? Their prosperity really depended upon the prosperity of the great agricultural regions of the land, which favored bimetallism. "Burn down your cities and leave our farms," he said, "and your cities will spring up again as if by magic; but destroy our farms and the grass will grow in the streets of every city in the country."

Now Bryan was absolute master of the delegates. "I thought of a choir," he recalled afterward, "as I noted how instantaneously and in unison they responded to each point made." The crowd cheered because he was reflecting its sentiments, but also because it recognized, suddenly, its leader—handsome, confident, righteously indignant, yet also calm, restrained, and ready for responsibility. His mission accomplished, it was time to close, and Bryan had saved a marvelous figure of speech, tested in many an earlier oration, for his climax. "You shall not press down upon the brow of labor this crown of thorns," he warned, bringing his hands down suggestively to his temples; "you shall not crucify mankind upon a cross of gold." Dramatically he extended his arms to the side, the very figure of the crucified Christ.

Amid the hysterical demonstration that followed, it was clear that Bryan had accomplished his miracle. The next day, July 9, he was nominated for the Presidency on the fifth ballot.

The issue was clear-cut, for the Republicans had already declared for the gold standard and nominated the handsome, genial, and thoroughly conservative William McKinley. As a result, the Populists were under great pressure to go along with Bryan. While the Democrats had not adopted all the radical Populist demands, their platform contained a number of liberal planks in addition to that on free silver, including one calling for a federal income tax and another for stiffer controls of the railroad network. For the Populists to insist on nominating a third candidate would simply insure the election of the "gold bug" McKinley. Not every important Populist favored fusion; some were ready to concede defeat in 1896 and build their party for the future on broadly radical lines. "The Democratic idea of fusion," said Tom Watson of Georgia angrily, is "that we play Jonah while they play whale." But the rich scent of victory in the air was too much for the majority to resist. "I care not for party names," said "Sockless Jerry" Simpson bluntly; "it is the substance we are after, and we have it in William J. Bryan." Indeed, Bryan's friendly association with the Populists in earlier campaigns and his essentially Populistic views on most questions made it difficult for the party to oppose him. "We put him to school," one anti-Bryan Populist later remarked, "and he wound up by stealing the school-books." In any case, the Populist convention endorsed him; thus the silver forces united to do battle with the Republicans.

Both Bryan and McKinley men realized at once that this was to be a close and crucial contest. Seldom have the two great parties

divided so clearly on fundamental issues; a showdown was inevitable; a major turning point in American history had been
reached. Silver against gold was but the surface manifestation
of the struggle. City against countryside, industry against agriculture, East against South and West, the nineteenth century against
the twentieth—these were the real contestants in 1896.

After Bryan's nomination McKinley's manager, Mark Hanna,
abandoned plans for a vacation cruise in New England waters
and plunged into the work of the campaign. The situation was
"alarming," he told McKinley. A "communistic spirit" was abroad,
business was "all going to pieces." A mighty effort was called for.
Hanna raised huge sums by "assessing" the great bankers, oil
refiners, insurance men, and meat packers, using the threat of
impending business chaos and wild inflation to loosen the purse
strings of the tycoons. While McKinley, "the advance agent of
prosperity," conducted a dignified and carefully organized campaign from his front porch in Canton, Ohio, 1,400 paid speakers
beat the bushes for votes in every doubtful district. The Republican
campaign committee distributed more than 120,000,000 pieces
of literature printed in ten languages to carry its message to the
voters. Boiler-plate editorials and other releases were sent free to
hundreds of small-town newspapers. Hanna, Theodore Roosevelt
said, "has advertised McKinley as if he were a patent medicine!"
The Republican organization reached a peak of efficiency and thor-
oughness never before approached in a political contest; the campaign marked a methodological revolution that has profoundly
affected every Presidential contest since.

Bryan had little money, and no organizational genius like Hanna
to direct his drive. But he too effected a revolution that has left
its mark on modern campaigning. McKinley's front porch technique was novel only in the huge number of visiting delegations
that Hanna paraded across his man's lawn and the exaggerated
care that the candidate took to avoid saying anything impolitic.
It had always been considered undignified for a Presidential nominee to go out and hunt for votes on his own. Bryan cast off this
essentially hypocritical tradition at the very start. He realized that
the concerted power of business and the press were aligned against

him, and that his own greatest assets were his magnificent ability as a political orator and his personal sincerity and charm. His opponent could afford to sit tight; *he* must seek out the people everywhere if they were to receive his message. Between summer and November he traveled a precedent-shattering 18,000 miles, making more than 600 speeches and addressing directly an estimated 5,000,000 Americans. His secretary estimated that he uttered between 60,000 and 100,000 words every day during the campaign.

On the stump he was superb. Without straining his voice he could make himself heard to a restless open-air throng numbered in the tens of thousands. He was equally effective at the whistle stops, outlining his case from the rear platform of his train while a handful of country people gazed earnestly upward from the roadbed. He was unfailingly pleasant and unpretentious. At one stop, while he was shaving in his compartment, a small group outside the train began clamoring for a glimpse of him. Flinging open the window and beaming through the lather, he cheerfully shook hands with each of these admirers. Neither he nor they, according to the recorder of this incident, saw anything unusual or undignified in the performance. Thousands of well-wishers sent him good luck charms and messages of encouragement. "If the people who have given me rabbits' feet in this campaign will vote for me, there is no possible doubt of my election," he said in one speech. It was because of this simple friendliness that he became known as "the Great Commoner."

Bryan was also unfailingly interesting. Even his most unsympathetic biographer admits that he spoke so well that at every stop the baggagemen from the campaign train would run back to listen to his talk—and this despite a schedule that called for as many as thirty speeches a day.

Such a campaign is an effective means of projecting an image of a candidate and his general point of view. It is not well suited for the making of complicated arguments and finely drawn distinctions; for that the McKinley approach was far superior. Wisely, for it was clearly the issue uppermost in the minds of most voters, Bryan hammered repeatedly at the currency question. He did not avoid talking about other matters: he attacked the railroads and the great business monopolists and the "tyranny" of the Eastern bankers. He deplored the use of militia in labor disputes and of the injunction as a means of breaking strikes. He spoke in favor of income taxes, higher wages, and relief for hard-pressed mortgagees. But the silver issue was symbolic, and the Democratic position sound. There *was* a currency shortage; deflation *was* injuring millions of debtors and pouring a rich unearned increment into the pockets of bondholders. To say, as Henry Demarest Lloyd did at the time and as many liberal historians have since, that Bryan made free silver the "cowbird" of the reform movement, pushing out all other issues from the reform nest and thus destroying them, is an exaggeration and a distortion. All effective politicians stick to a small number of simple issues while on the stump; otherwise, in the hectic conflict of a hot campaign, they project no message at all. There is no reason to suspect that, if elected, Bryan would have forgotten about other reform measures and concentrated only on the currency.

For a time Bryan's gallant, singlehanded battle seemed to be having an effect on public opinion, and Republican leaders became thoroughly frightened. In addition to money, threats and imprecations now became weapons in the campaign. A rumor was circulated that Bryan was insane. *The New York Times* devoted columns to the possibility, and printed a letter from a supposed psychologist charging that he was suffering from "paranoia querulenta," "graphomania," and "oratorical monomania." "Men," one manufacturer told his workers, "vote as you please, but if Bryan is elected . . . the whistle will not blow Wednesday morning." According to *The Nation*, which was supporting McKinley, many companies placed orders with their suppliers "to be executed in case Mr. Bryan is defeated, and not otherwise." A Chicago company that held thousands of farm mortgages politely asked all its "customers" to indicate their Presidential preferences—a not very subtle form of coercion but probably an effective one. In some cases men were actually fired because of their political opinions.

By the time election day arrived the McKinley managers were so confident of victory that Hanna began returning new contributions as no longer necessary. Nevertheless, a final monumental effort was made to get out the vote. Free transportation was provided to carry citizens to and from the polls, men were paid for time lost in voting, and in doubtful districts floaters and other disreputables were rounded up and paraded to the ballot boxes. Everywhere in the crucial North Central states the Hanna machine expended enormous efforts, and in these states the decision was made. McKinley carried them all and with them the nation. In the electoral college McKinley won by 271 to 176, but the popular vote was close—7,036,000 to 6,468,000. The change of a relative handful of votes in half a dozen key states would have swung the election to Bryan.

The victory, however, was McKinley's, and conservatives all over America—and the world—echoed the sentiment of Hanna's happy telegram to the President-elect: GOD'S IN HIS HEAVEN, ALL'S RIGHT WITH THE WORLD! A watershed in the economic and social history of the United States had been crossed. The rural America of the nineteenth century was making way for the industrial America of the twentieth.

✪

The Bryan Campaign of 1896

Thoughtful men in all parties realized that Bryan's central theme throughout the campaign was his demand for general social reform, but the East proved irreconcilable. It made much of the victory of "decency" over "indecency." McKinley's carrying of the eighteen states north of the Ohio and Potomac and east of the Missouri, an area that contained 56 per cent of the population, 64 per cent of the estimated wealth, and "the most intelligent people of the land," was proof to E. L. Godkin of *The Nation* of the victory of "the great civilizing forces of the republic, as against the still surviving barbarism bred by slavery in the South and the reckless spirit of adventure in the mining-camps of the Far West." [1] Men like Theodore Roosevelt, John Hay, Whitelaw Reid, and Carl Schurz deemed the contest of 1896 more critical than that of 1861–1865. In the latter the question had been whether a democratic government could maintain itself against armed insurrection; in the former the question was whether the people could use the suffrage with an intelligent understanding of the public interest and just regard for the rights of all.

Bryan was particularly blamed for having waged a "nightmare campaign" of emotion and passion that stirred the unthinking

[1] "Significance of the Verdict," *The Nation*, 63 (November 12, 1896), 358. See also *Harper's Weekly*, October 31, November 14, 1896.

Reprinted from Paolo E. Coletta, *William Jennings Bryan, I. Political Evangelist* (University of Nebraska Press, 1964), pp. 194–212. Copyright © 1964 by the University of Nebraska Press.

masses into a frenzy not witnessed since the witchcraft craze of colonial Massachusetts. He had attracted the ignorant, discouraged, and discontented with his dreams of a magic wampum that would relieve them of debt. Throughout the campaign Roosevelt's letters teemed with references to "Bryanism" as "ugly," "criminal," "vicious," "a genuine and dangerous fanaticism." Bryanism was "a semi-socialistic, agrarian movement," he asserted, ". . . a revolt aimed foolishly at those who are better off, merely because they *are* better off; it is the blind man blinding the one-eyed." According to John Hay, "All that is left of the [Democratic] party is rank Populist. Its unquestioned leaders are the Altgelds, the Tillmans, the Debses, the moral dynamiters, whose lawlessness stops just short of the criminal courts." To Hay, Bryan was "a halfbaked glib little briefless jack-leg lawyer . . . grasping with anxiety to collar that $50,000 salary, promising the millennium to everybody with a hole in his pants and destruction to everybody with a clean shirt." [2]

Hot words were exchanged. Andrew Carnegie called Bryan a "conjurer." Hay wished to feel the "phrenological bumps" of the "glib-tongued adventurer" who promised "fairy money" for votes from the "lunatic factions." Several Chicago millionaires were quoted as saying they would use force to prevent Bryan from controlling the government were he elected. "We wouldn't be such

[2] Roosevelt to Anna Roosevelt Cowles, September 27, August 2, October 4, 1896, Anna Roosevelt Cowles, *Letters from Theodore Roosevelt to Anna Roosevelt Cowles, 1870–1918* (New York, 1924), pp. 89, 194, 195; Roosevelt to Lodge, November 26, 1896, Henry Cabot Lodge, *Selections from the Correspondence of Theodore Roosevelt and Henry Cabot Lodge, 1884–1918,* 2 vols. (New York, 1925), I, 240; Hay to Whitelaw Reid, August 31, September 23, 1896, Reid Papers (Manuscript Division, Library of Congress); editorial, *New York Tribune,* November 5, 1896; John Hay, *The Platform of Anarchy: An Address to the Students of Western Reserve University, October 6, 1896* (Cleveland, 1896); James Ford Rhodes, *The McKinley and Roosevelt Administrations, 1896–1909* (New York, 1922), pp. 22, 27–28. All important British newspapers had fiercely opposed Bryan. Their sighs of relief at the end of the campaign were incomplete, however, because they predicted that McKinley would raise the tariff rates in the near future. Moreton Frewen to Bryan, July 16, 1896, Bryan Papers (Manuscript Division, Library of Congress); "Money and the Masses in America," *Quarterly Review,* 184 (October 1896), 567–584; clippings from British newspapers in Bryan Scrapbook No. 2, Nebraska State Historical Society.

damned fools as the South was in '61. We wouldn't walk out of Washington and turn it over to that crowd!" When his conversation with a Kansas Populist turned to Bryan's chances of winning, Hanna exploded with a blood-curdling threat: "Do you think that we'd let that damned lunatic get into the White House? Never! You know you can hire half of the people of the United States to shoot down the other half if necessary, and we've got the money to hire them." He was probably letting off steam somewhat recklessly, but his feelings represented those of many of Bryan's opponents.[3]

Various Bryanites also breathed fire and swore vengeance. An Ohioan wrote him that "We have guns and powder and I promise to stand to our Party as long as I live," and appended the names of several hundred workingmen who felt the same way.[4] *"If the common people cannot win in a fair contest, then the financial question must, and will be, adjudicated by the sword!"* wrote an Illinoisan,[5] while an Alabaman declared: "We of the South, as you know, are 'natural born rebels.' We did manage to take the oath of allegiance in '65, but I register a most solemn vow never to swear allegiance to Clevelandism or McKinleyism or any other damnable ism emanating from the foul hotbed of corruption and plunder." [6] Bryan's soothing of these men reflected his pacifism; the reluctance of the American people to resort to arms in the most bitter campaign in their history revealed the solidity of their democratic institutions.

Although fulsome praise for the courage, ability, and sincerity of the "evangel of the workers and producers of the country" came from various gold Democrats, the most perceptive tribute to Bryan is found in a letter from Mrs. Henry Cabot Lodge, whose husband opposed Bryan, to Sir Cecil Spring-Rice, the British ambassador:

The great fight is won and a fight conducted by trained and experienced and organized forces, with both hands full of money, with the

---

[3] Horace A. Keefer, "The Experiences of an Unsuccessful Legislator," Mss., Commager Papers; Washington *Evening Star,* October 23, 1932.

[4] Frank Dietrich to Bryan, November 16, 1896, Bryan Papers.

[5] Robert A. Mills to Bryan, November 11, 1896, *ibid.*

[6] J. G. Heaton to Bryan, November 11, 1896, *ibid.*

full power of the press—and of prestige—on the one side; on the other, a disorganized mob at first, out of which there burst into sight, hearing, and force—one man, but such a man! Alone, penniless, without backing, without money, with scarce a paper, without speakers, that man fought such a fight that even those in the East can call him a Crusader, an inspired fanatic—a prophet! It has been marvelous. Hampered by such a following, such a platform—and even the men whose names were our greatest weapon against him, deserted him and left him to fight alone—he almost won. We acknowledged to seven millions campaign fund, against his $500,000. We had during the last week of the campaign 18,000 speakers on the stump. He alone spoke for his party, but speeches which spoke to the intelligence and hearts of the people, with a capital P.[7]

Bryan had set a new record for campaigning. Others have covered more miles in comfortable trains and reached more people by radio and television, but none has matched his physical endurance or has been able to address larger audiences. The reporters who accompanied him were impressed with his unaffected humanity, his decency, his wit, his lack of pose, his refusal to compromise with the truth as he saw it, his belief in the infallible "rightness" of the common people.[8] Thousands wrote to him for advice in solving myriads of personal problems, hundreds sent him unsolicited gifts which overflowed his home. "Sixteen to one" came in the form of a potato with 16 sprouts, a vase with 16 handles, and other ingenious ways.[9] Daughter Ruth collected 700 letters between midsummer 1896 and the end of the year that indicated that babies had been named after her father.

Thousands of letters show that Bryan won particularly the love of America's youth and aged poor. "P.S. No cross of gold, no crown of thorns," was added to many a letter, and persons of religious bent thanked God for "an able, wise, just, patriotic, Christian Hero." His trials were compared to those of Jesus. Both

[7] Stephen Gwynn, *The Letters and Friendships of Sir Cecil Spring-Rice: A Record*, 2 vols. (Boston, 1929), II, 197–198.

[8] "Rules of the Road" adopted by the journalists who accompanied Bryan, copy in Bryan Papers; Frank P. Stockbridge, "Bryan, the Great Commoner," *Current History*, 22 (September 1925), 868.

[9] William Jennings Bryan and Mary Baird Bryan, *The Memoirs of William Jennings Bryan* (Philadelphia, 1925), pp. 264–267.

had been baffled, despised, and crucified, one at the hands of silver, one by gold. Bryan told Mark Sullivan that he knew of a family that thought of him as the second Christ and that it was common to compare him with Paul.[10] Letters of praise also came from the organized bimetallists of England and Australia as well as America, and hundreds of veteran prohibitionists, Populists, and Republicans wrote him that they had deserted their own parties to vote for him, that he was "the Greatest American living," "a new Moses in the form of a Populist Yankee," "a volunteer St. George battling against the dragon of organized greed." He was "the Peerless Leader of the People," the "Wellington of the silver forces."

Bryan summed up the cause of his defeat by saying, "I have borne the sins of Grover Cleveland." [11] To a degree he was right, for millions impoverished by the "Cleveland depression" snapped eagerly at McKinley's "prosperity" argument. Without the depression, the tariff might have been the paramount issue; because of it Bryan was fated to engage in controversy over the financial system in the first national campaign in which it was the prime issue. Moreover, since Bourbon leaders deserted him, his organization was new and directed in many instances by men lacking political experience or talent or by partisans interested only in patronage, with the result that it failed adequately to discipline its farm and labor components, the very "producers of wealth" Bryan had depended upon to provide the common denominator that would have spelled his success.

Bryan was defeated by Hanna rather than by McKinley. The best estimate of Bryan's war chest is $300,000, which expenditures by local committees may have swelled to $600,000.[12] Until mid-

[10] Mark Sullivan, *Our Times: The United States, 1900–1925,* 6 vols. (New York, 1926–1935), I, 112n.

[11] Robert McElroy, *Grover Cleveland, the Man and Statesman,* 2 vols. (New York, 1923), II, 37.

[12] The silver states contributed about a fifth of Bryan's campaign chest, giving the lie to stories of boodle funds provided by English as well as American silver interests. Even if the mine owners did give the highest estimate noted, $228,000, by Paxton Hibben in *The Peerless Leader: William Jennings Bryan* (New York, 1929), p. 193, this amounts to only three cents per vote polled. Bryan had no direct connections with the silver mine owners after

September Hanna admitted that Bryan was sweeping all before him. Then he settled down to elect the man he had nominated and in a month completed his work. He gathered about him a committee of forty-five whose wealth ranged from a low of $2,000,000 to a high of $125,000,000. Their contributions, those by corporate interests, and sums shaken out of bankers, businessmen, life insurance companies, public utilities, and other employers of labor amounted to about $7,000,000, while total national and local expenditures may have approached $16,000,000.[13] Thus he system-

his second Congressional campaign. A mine owner, Marcus A. Daly, made the single largest contribution to his campaign fund, of $50,000, but Bryan's Papers reveal that he declined to give the additional $300,000 requested of him by James K. Jones and Arthur Pue Gorman. Such silver mine owners as Eben Smith, Simon Guggenheim, and S. A. Josephi denied the existence of any organization of silver miners that sought to foster Bryan, and diligent research has discovered none. From research in the State Historical Society of Colorado, Nevada State Historical Society, and Library of the University of California, H. Wayne Morgan concluded that there is "no evidence whatever in these places indicating that Bryan was in the pay of the Western silverites." He cogently added that any such evidence would probably have been destroyed long ago (letter to the author, August 22, 1958). Distressed by Senator Thurston's charge that he was in the pay of the silver barons—for which charge Senator Teller and ex-Senator William Stewart called Thurston a liar and won a retraction—Bryan published his account book, which showed that since leaving Congress he had received only $150 a month while with the Omaha *World-Herald,* some income from his law partnership, and pay for speeches arranged by lecture bureaus, and challenged the Republican National Committee to make an official charge so that he could prove his innocence. Public appeals for funds issued by Jones and various newspapers brought in only small amounts. The *New York Journal* raised the largest public subscription, $40,000, toward which Hearst himself gave $15,000. See *The New York Times,* August 17–19, 1896; Omaha *Bee,* August 8, 10, 1896; Omaha *World-Herald,* August 15, 19–21, 1896.

[13] Omaha *World-Herald,* September 7, 1896; John Hay to William McKinley, August 3, 1896, McKinley Papers; *The Commoner* (Lincoln, Nebraska), April 27, May 4, 1906; Herbert Croly, *Marcus Alonzo Hanna* (New York, 1912), pp. 206, 217–221; Louise Overacker, *Money in Elections* (New York, 1932), pp. 1, 21–28, 107–108. E. H. Harriman gave $35,000; Marshall Field $10,000; Standard Oil $250,000; the Beef Trust $400,000; John Wanamaker his "customary" $10,000; and John Hay contributed $1,000 a month from August to November. In the course of the life insurance investigations of a decade later, the directors of the New York Life, Mutual, and Equitable insurance companies confessed that they had given of their policy holders' funds to defeat free silver. New York State Legislature. Joint Committee on Investigation of Life Insurance. *Armstrong*

atized and nationalized the fat-frying tactics of Corporal James Tanner and Senator Matthew S. Quay and capped the alliance between politics and big business which had flourished since the Civil War and remained undisturbed until Bryan challenged it. Bryan eloquently preached the rights of the poor, dreamed of equality, and refused to employ the forces of political corruption that strove for his patronage and might have elected him. Hanna, who frankly championed plutocracy, pitted cold cash against him and won. Theodore Roosevelt later asserted that Bryan frightened capital too much, that those who feared him threw themselves into the arms of those who opposed him.[14]

Hanna defeated Bryan in every detail of campaign management. In a campaign peculiarly one of education, Bryan distributed about 10,000,000 copies of speeches on silver by himself and others; Hanna issued 120,000,000 copies of 275 pamphlets and speeches. Lithographs, cartoons, and posters advertised McKinley as the "Advance Agent of Prosperity," or, as in the cartoons of W. A. Rogers in *Harper's Weekly,* depicted Bryan as an unrestrained populist, anarchist, blasphemer, and Anti-Christ. The Democrats provided some "boiler plate" for both the weekly and the daily press. Hanna furnished so many of these patent insides that each week 5,000,000 families received 13,000 newspapers containing material unfavorable to Bryan.

While Bryan shouldered the greatest part of the Democratic speaking campaign, Hanna paid "colporteurs" to do missionary work among the farmers of the Middle West and provided an "Old Soldiers' Touring Special" to enable Union generals Alger, Howard, Stewart, and Sickles to declaim on the theme of "strength in the Union and the hell with the Democrats." McKinley, a veteran, had the advantage over Bryan in the North, especially with the then 350,000 members of the G.A.R. Hanna also made special appeals to teachers and clergymen to popularize the threat to their professions posed by free silver. While more evidence is needed to prove the point, it is probable that the Roman Catholic vote shifted

---

Committee. Testimony, Exhibits and Report, 1905, 7 vols. (Albany, 1906), I, 639, III, 2062; Overacker, *Money in Elections,* pp. 107, 180–181.

[14] Theodore Roosevelt, *Autobiography* (New York, 1913), pp. 273–274.

from the Democratic to the Republican party.[15] Hanna had ten good speakers for one of Bryan's, and Bryan's did not always help him. Tillman, whom the East called "a filthy baboon," spoke in thirty states but lent color to the Republican charge that lawlessness was the ruling element in the Democratic party and helped defeat Bryan. Nor did Altgeld help, for the East regarded him, too, as one of Bryan's "evangels of Anarchism." [16] The most eloquent Democratic speakers, Bryan excepted, were Cockran and Schurz, both of whom opposed Bryan, and Hill refused to stump for him.[17]

Bryan was like a private citizen waging war on a daily newspaper. About half the Democratic and Independent press opposed him.[18] He had no friendly newspaper in Chicago, and James J. Hill bought the St. Paul *Globe,* the only Democratic newspaper in the upper Mississippi Valley, and made it a gold organ. Teller failed to bring the Scripps-McRae league over to Bryan, and the publications of the educational silver organizations, like the *National Bimetallist,* were smothered by gold Democratic papers and Hanna's subsidized sheets. Gustav Schwab estimated that 503 of the 581 German-language newspapers opposed Bryan.[19]

Bryan went to the people. Hanna brought the people to McKin-

[15] C. Vann Woodward, *Tom Watson, Agrarian Rebel* (New York, 1938), p. 422.

[16] Francis B. Simkins, *Pitchfork Ben Tillman, South Carolinian* (Baton Rouge, 1944), pp. 338–339. Altgeld, Stone of Missouri, Tillman, Weaver, Bland, Teller, Towne, George F. Williams, Homer S. Cummings, and Edward Carmack were Bryan's major stump speakers. Others who helped were Shively, Turpie, and Matthews in Indiana; Blackburn in Kentucky; Hogg and Reagan in Texas; Vest in Missouri; Tom Johnson in Ohio; John W. Daniel and Carter Glass in Virginia; Adlai E. Stevenson and Clarence Darrow in Illinois; Henry G. Davis in West Virginia; and William E. Borah, Republican, of Idaho.

[17] Hill to Judge Hamilton Ward, September 12, 1896, George S. Bixby Papers (New York State Library, Albany).

[18] Except for Hearst's *New York Journal* and McLean's Cincinnati *Enquirer,* Bryan had little support north of Mason and Dixon's line and east of the Mississippi. Hearst in California, Thomas M. Patterson in Denver, Charles H. Jones in St. Louis, and the Salt Lake *Tribune* provided most of his Western support, and the New Orleans *Times-Democrat* and the Atlanta *Constitution* his Southern. The Atlanta *Journal,* owned by Hoke Smith, who had resigned from Cleveland's cabinet in September, supported him as the party's nominee but rejected his platform.

[19] Schwab cited in "A Notable Bolt of Newspapers," *American Review of Reviews,* 14 (August 1896), 142.

ley, expenses paid. Obdurately refusing to allow extemporaneous addresses in his presence, McKinley would stand on his front porch and face a field of leaping yellow ribbons. The head of each delegation would read a carefully prepared speech that had been submitted beforehand, revised, and returned. Then McKinley would reply from a manuscript, not without a stumble or two, but always dignified, always commonplace and dull but proper, safe, sober, and always, says Herbert Croly, "with a high respect for the proprieties of political life." [20]

Bryan put on a one-man steeplechase. Hanna provided the populace with circuses bigger and better than those of Blaine's "plumed knights." On Chicago Day, October 9, 100,000 men with golden badges, hats, caps, and shoes marched in honor of "sound money" for five hours before a crowd of half a million. In the evening came a counter demonstration of only 40,000 workingmen.[21] In New York, on the Saturday before election, 110,000 men marched for gold in the largest demonstration since the disbanding of the veterans in Washington in 1865. Employers either "suggested" that their men march or plainly told them to march or lose their jobs. All day long New York resounded to the singing of "We'll hang Billy Bryan on a sour apple tree as we go marching on," while below their breath the workers sang:

> You ask me why 'tis thus
> That I make this outward show,
> Because my millionaire employer
> Says "Bryan men must go."
> And I have got a wife at home
> With little ones to feed,
> And must appear to think and vote
> To suit the goldbugs' greed.[22]

The most effective tactic used to defeat Bryan was the coercion of productive labor. Orders labeled "Cancel if Bryan Wins" and "Double this Order if McKinley Wins" or made "contingent" upon

[20] Croly, *Hanna*, p. 215. See also Charles S. Olcott, *The Life of William McKinley*, 2 vols. (Boston, 1912), I, 318, 321.
[21] Omaha *World-Herald*, October 10, 1896; G. W. Steevens, *Land of the Dollar* (New York, 1897), pp. 186–192.
[22] *New York Journal, The New York Times*, November 1, 1896.

McKinley's election directly affected industrialists and workers alike. Hundreds of workers wrote Bryan that their employers warned them that they would close their shops if he were elected or that Bryan men need not return to work if Bryan were elected. Some workers who favored Bryan were fired and blacklisted; others were forced to contribute money to the Republican campaign fund. Particularly bitter complaints reached Bryan about detectives assigned to "work on the workers" on the railroads.[23] "The brutality of the methods is almost incredible," said Professor Edward A. Ross.[24]

Political blackmail was probably a more potent argument with workers than all the benefits gold men set forth for an "honest" currency. "Our defeat is due to the fact that hungry stomachs know no law," a factory hand wrote Bryan.[25] "For daring to speak, and write, one letter in the [Philadelphia] Evening Telegraph alone, made a difference in my business of at least 25 per cent. Many old friends and acquaintances remaining away and still doing so," reported a grocer,[26] revealing that support for Bryan could result in social ostracism as well as reduced profits.

Farmers were subjected to similar pressures, and Bryan declared that "the coercion practiced by large financiers upon the small ones, and by the small ones upon borrowers, was far reaching in its extent." [27] Banks and loan companies blackmailed their borrowers by refusing to extend credit or to renew loans that fell due or by demanding the immediate collection of debts held by those who favored silver. Banks that held the notes of the industrial and commercial firms of a town dictated to both employer and employee by threatening to call in loans, declining to discount even the best commercial paper, and refusing ordinary accommodations.[28] Champ Clark was once denied the right to cash a personal

[23] The New York Times, August 2, 1896; Omaha World-Herald, November 15, 1896; Philip S. Foner, History of the Labor Movement in the United States, 2 vols. (New York, 1955), II, 341.
[24] San Francisco Examiner, September 27, 1896.
[25] M. J. Pareneau to Bryan, November 7, 1896, Bryan Papers.
[26] R. W. Jennings to Bryan, November 11, 1896, ibid.
[27] William Jennings Bryan, The First Battle (Chicago, 1896), p. 617.
[28] Wilson Hutchins to Bryan, November 11, 1896, J. W. Hemsted to Bryan, November 11, 1896, George W. Bird to Bryan, November 11, 1896,

check because he supported Bryan.[29] The Eastern insurance companies, which held many Western mortgages, also sent agents to contact every borrower and to offer a five year extension of loans at low interest rates if McKinley were elected. Tens of thousands found the temptation too great to resist.[30] Even stocks were quoted "cum McKinley." One exchange, for example, quoted Postal Telegraph shares at 80½ "regular" and 83 "cum McKinley." [31] Only three members of the New York Stock Exchange favored Bryan.[32]

In every Presidential election except that of 1932 in which the Democrats staked their case on hard times, something happened about August to raise prices, satisfy the farmers, and still the revolt of rural Republicans. The price of wheat rose from 47 cents a bushel in 1894 to 53 cents in August 1896 and to a three-year high of 84 cents in December. The reason lay with crop failures abroad, but the price of wheat had been used since the Civil War as a barometer of agricultural discontent, and Bryan had assiduously cultivated its intimate connection with the price of silver. The failure of the price of silver to follow that of wheat in the fall of 1896 effectively burst his contention. Many farmers thought the rise in the price of wheat presaged a general upturn in prices and voted accordingly.[33] Of the wheat-growing states, Bryan won

---

P. Burton to Bryan, November 24, 1896, Bryan Papers; Omaha *World-Herald*, July 24, 30, August 1, 1896.

[29] Morris R. Werner, *Bryan* (New York, 1929), p. 142.

[30] For example, see George L. Kinney to Bryan, November 11, 1896, George W. Bird to Bryan, November 11, 1896, and James V. Bouvier to Bryan, December 15, 1896, Bryan Papers.

[31] *The Nation*, November 5, 1896.

[32] James V. Bouvier to Bryan, December 15, 1896, Bryan Papers.

[33] *Thirty-ninth Annual Report of Trade and Commerce of Chicago, for the Year Ending December 31, 1896*, pp. 9, 12; Wilfred E. Binkley, *American Political Parties, Their Natural History* (New York, 1943), pp. 315–316; Alexander Dana Noyes, *Forty Years of American Finance, 1865–1907* (New York, 1909), pp. 264–265; James A. Barnes, "Myths of the Bryan Campaign," *Mississippi Valley Historical Review*, 34 (December 1947), 392–394. See also Edward Atkinson, "Our Grain Farmers the Creditors of the World," *Harper's Weekly*, September 12, 1896, and the penetrating analysis by Gilbert C. Fite, "Republican Strategy and the Farm Vote in the Presidential Campaign of 1896," *American Historical Review*, 65 (July 1960), 787–806.

only three—Nebraska, South Dakota, and Kansas—and he lost the corn-producing states of the Middle West.

Bryan made other egregious mistakes in his canvass. The nomination of Sewall was a mistake, for Sewall failed to hold the East and irked Watson. Bryan probably should have declined to run with Watson, who hurt him by reaffirming the important Populist principles omitted from the Chicago platform and by appealing for a sectional alliance between the South and West.[34] Moreover, Bryan could not make fusion work. In the South, Marion Butler ditched the Democracy and fused with the Republicans. In the West, Teller complained of unfair Democratic treatment of the silver Republicans, and fusion arrangements finally made in twenty-six states involved various legal battles and fierce fights over local patronage which in the end detracted from Bryan's strength.[35] Since Bryan would have gained votes where he needed them by dropping Sewall and taking Watson, he did not act out of mere expediency; yet he persistently ignored Watson. He did not acknowledge his aid in stumping the West and he disagreed with his methods. It was not until 1907 that he thanked him and offered a weak apology for the discourteous and possibly dishonest treatment of him by Jones in 1896.[36]

Bryan erred in permitting Jones to head the Democratic National Committee. Jones had no unusual facility for touching the hearts of the poor or the pockets of the rich, was from a safely Democratic state, did nothing to bring out the vote, and failed to reject the endorsement of Bryan by such organizations as Tam-

[34] Watson rebuffed all offers of reconciliation, including a purported Cabinet post tendered by Tillman, if he retired. Sewall to Bryan, July 25, August 31, 1896, Bryan Papers; John D. Hicks, *The Populist Revolt: A History of the Farmers' Alliance and the People's Party* (Minneapolis, 1931), pp. 368–369; Woodward, *Watson,* pp. 316–325.

[35] Omaha *Bee,* August 10, September 3, 1896; Bryan to James K. Jones, February 21, 1898, Bryan Papers; Josephus Daniels, *Editor in Politics* (Chapel Hill, 1941), pp. 171–178; Elmer Ellis, *Henry Moore Teller* (Caldwell, Idaho, 1941), pp. 277–280, 285–286, 303; Hicks, *Populist Revolt,* pp. 357–359; Alex M. Arnett, *Populist Movement in Georgia* (New York, 1922), pp. 202–204, 209–210.

[36] Bryan to Watson, January 24, 1907, Woodward, *Watson,* p. 323; Bryan, *First Battle,* pp. 622–623; Eugene H. Roseboom, *A History of Presidential Elections* (New York, 1957), pp. 316–317.

many, whose leaders should have been jailed for their criminal activities. He bungled badly both in permitting the naming of Sewall and in his dealings with the Populists at St. Louis, and his treatment of the Populists, rather than Bryan's, made complete fusion impossible. A rabid Southerner, he let it slip that he hated the very thought of Watson, that the Populists of the South were "a bad lot, a discreditable class out for nothing but the spoils," and that they should "go to the Negroes, where they belong." [37] Despite additional violations of party discipline, Bryan refused to dismiss him. On the other hand, Bryan rejected Jones's sage advice to concentrate on the Middle West and the doubtful states and went "skylarking" in the East, which Jones believed already lost.

Aware of his extraordinary effectiveness as a speaker, Bryan adopted the normally futile experiment of electioneering from rear platforms. He was heard by perhaps three million persons, but he failed to take into account the curiosity that moves men, and his touring did not disprove the principle that elections are won not by oratory but largely by effective organization of a sufficient number of minority groups into a majority. In a Western state a stranger approached him, saying, "I have ridden fifty miles to hear you speak tonight. I have always read every speech of yours that I could get hold of. I would ride a hundred miles to hear you make a speech. And, by gum, if I wasn't a Republican I'd vote for you." [38] Bryan often retold this incident in accounting for his success and failure—he attracted people but not votes. His "heart to heart" appeal won a number of undying friendships. What he lacked was the group diplomacy needed to win the minds of millions.

Bryan's understanding of the money question was imperfect, and in taking free silver as his paramount issue he campaigned on too narrow a front. He erred in saying that the supply of silver had not exceeded that of gold between 1870 and 1896, and he

[37] *The New York Times,* August 4, 8, 1896; Omaha *Bee,* August 7, 30, 1896, *The Nation,* August 6, 1896; W. J. Bryan, "Memorandum on James K. Jones," Bryan Papers; Willis J. Abbot, *Watching the World Go By* (Boston, 1933), p. 179.

[38] Daniel C. Roper, *Fifty Years of Public Life* (Durham, N.C., 1941), p. 87.

overlooked the reduction in the price of silver caused by mechanical and chemical advances. His belief that the remonetization of silver would bring prices and values back to where they had been in 1873 was based on the quantitative theory of money alone—he disregarded credit and the velocity of circulation and the fact that in 1896 at least 80 per cent of our international trade was transacted with gold standard countries. The restoration of bimetallism would have worked some injustice, for the debtor and creditor of 1873 and 1896 were not necessarily the same, and it would have benefited the holders of long-term rather than of short-term loans. Moreover, how could both farmers and workers be aided by free silver? Until his mortgage is paid off, and annually until the harvest is garnered, the farmer tends to be a debtor, whereas the laborer, paid weekly or monthly, need not be a debtor and is less affected than the farmer by the long-term appreciation of the currency. Nevertheless, Bryan was basically right; in the 70 per cent decline in the price level that occurred between 1865 and 1896 he had an excellent base for an economic reform program, and he clearly saw that depressions were inherent in the price system rather than in the economic system as such; yet to many of his opponents silver was not the issue at all—the issue was "Altgeld's policies of free riot, free spoils, and free injustice." It is quite likely that Bryan was defeated more because he reflected Altgeld's attack upon the executive and judicial power than because he sponsored silver, a single practical issue which did not give full expression to the reformation of *principles* demanded by Democratic and Populist liberals.

Bryan was right in demanding economic justice in the name of the millions harmed by a grossly inequitable banking and currency system, the appreciation of gold,[39] and the concentration of wealth

[39] The decline in the gold price of silver is better expressed by saying that the gold dollar of 1873 had become a two-dollar dollar in 1893 than by saying that the silver dollar of 1873 had become a 50-cent dollar. Taking the gold dollar of 1873 as 100 in its purchasing power over wholesale goods, the 1893 dollar was a 140-cent dollar and that of 1896 a 164-cent dollar. Alonzo B. Hepburn, *History of the Currency of the United States* (New York, 1915), p. 433; J. G. Hodgson (comp.), *Stabilization of Money* (New York, 1933), pp. 56–64; Edwin Walter Kemmerer, *Money: The Principles of Money and Their Exemplification in Outstanding Chapters of Monetary History* (New York, 1935), pp. 361–364, 368.

in the hands of a few, but he was wrong in method. He used free silver as a text for sermons on discontent designed to create a popular demand for reform via a revitalized Democracy, yet he failed signally to sponsor the more effective remedies he had proposed in his speech of August 16, 1893, in which he had at least hinted at a managed currency, a federal reserve system of banking, and the insurance of bank deposits. Free silver without further changes in the banking and currency systems such as occurred under Woodrow Wilson and Franklin D. Roosevelt would not have been a miraculous contrivance to relieve debtors of their burdens and restore the nation to prosperity. Indeed, inflation of the currency alone, by encouraging production, would have aggravated the problem of too many farmers already producing too much. Moreover, the mere anticipation of the relief of financial stringency by the influx of gold discovered in 1896 in Alaska, Australia, and South Africa worked against him, as did the trend toward a favorable balance of international trade.[40]

As an extreme nationalist and "little American," Bryan held Britain largely responsible for America's troubles and believed the unfounded story so widely promulgated in Populist and silver Democratic literature that an international gold conspiracy had bribed American Congressmen to demonetize silver so that they could keep gold at a premium and use their wealth to buy up productive enterprise during times of depression.[41] His belief, said some, was on a par with that of thousands of less well educated men who thought "16 to 1" meant that their silver dollars would somehow multiply by sixteen when he was elected. As a young engineer named Herbert Hoover put it, Bryan's 16 to 1 was his

[40] Cecil Spring-Rice to Henry Adams, August 24, 1896, Gwynn, *Spring-Rice*, I, 209–210; Joseph Sibley to Bryan, November 11, 1897, Bryan Papers. The per capita circulation fell from $24.28 in 1894 to $21.10 in 1896. Four years later it had increased to $25.75 because of the new gold influx, which exceeded the rate of population growth. If the year 1899 is considered 100, the value of farm products rose to 106.4 in 1900 and to 133 in 1905. Theodore Saloutos and John D. Hicks, *Agricultural Discontent in the Middle West, 1900–1939* (Madison, Wis., 1951), p. 21. Generally good industrial times marked the years 1897 to 1907.
[41] Richard Hofstadter, *The Age of Reform: From Bryan to F.D.R.* (New York, 1955), pp. 74–76; Henry Nash Smith, *Virgin Land: The American West as Symbol and Myth* (Cambridge, Mass., 1950), esp. pp. 126–298.

"first shock at intellectual dishonesty as a foundation for economics." [42] There is no direct evidence that Bryan was intellectually dishonest, but his conclusions on the money question, his suspiciousness of Eastern, metropolitan, and British ideas and actions, and the reasons he adduced for the depressed status of the American farmer point to his having eschewed the treatises of scholarly economists and read instead such books as William A. Peffer's *The Farmer's Side,* Ignatius Donnelly's *Caesar's Column,* Hamlin Garland's *Main Travelled Roads* and essays such as "Under the Lion's Paw," James B. Weaver's *A Call to Action,* and especially Mrs. S. E. V. Emery's *Seven Financial Conspiracies Which Have Enslaved the American People,* all written by Middle Westerners and all published between 1888 and 1892. [43]

Bryan was capable of concentrated study, and he had a retentive memory, but he was not a widely read man. He immersed himself in the Bible, the writings of Jefferson, and the history of the Democratic party. His speeches on the tariff and the income tax remain classic appeals to the intellect; those on the money question reveal imperfect knowledge of the business, mercantile, and financial world. Had he wished, he could have mastered areas in science, philosophy, literature, or language, but he was "too busy" to study them, and he had no training in the appreciation of the fine arts. But he had three qualities that marked him for leadership—love for people as individuals, power to interpret popular demands, and unique capacity to give voice to popular passion. He mirrored the mind of the average man, particularly of the provincial and isolationist farmers of the Middle West and South who had sought reform via Grange, Greenback party, Alliance, and populism. Without greater intellectual insight than they, he also reflected the suspiciousness and hostility of the "producing classes" to forces and movements they feared because they did not understand. By

[42] *The Memoirs of Herbert Hoover: I. Years of Adventure, 1874–1920* (New York, 1951), p. 28.

[43] Mrs. Emery's conspiracies included the "exception clause" of 1862, the National Bank Act of 1863, the retirement of the greenbacks, the Credit Strengthening Act of 1869, the refunding of the national debt in 1870, the "Crime of 1873," and the abolition of fractional paper money in 1875.

nature he was more a preacher and exhorter than a politician and statesman; he was a missionary who sought to change men, a political evangelist. He threw himself wholeheartedly and with consuming passion into "causes." He refused to dodge issues. He made a sentimental appeal because of his fight for the little fellow and because there was no such thing as an "off year" in his fight against special privilege. He appealed, too, because of his grace of person, unimpeachable moral character, courage, sincerity, honesty, forcible imagery in speech, pure and mellifluous language, and his professing of Christianity. Yet friend and foe alike agreed that he sought "yes" and "no" answers to complicated questions, that he deduced conclusions before his argument was complete yet held them sacred, that he was so sure of the correctness of his methods that he was not susceptible to argument. He was a purist without a redeeming vice except a voracious appetite. Above all he was profoundly Western and agrarian. No one owned or controlled him. More commonplace than original in conception, he reflected the thoughts that animated the millions and uncannily identified himself with the mass sense of need, with the common man's hopes and fears. He would curb the power of great corporations, divest the industrial system of the abuses of monopoly capitalism, sunder the proved alliance between big business and reactionary politicians, apportion the national income so that the agricultural community would no longer feel a sense of blighting frustration before the financial and political power in the East, and restore the moral and civic virtues he believed embodied in a simple rural economy.

In this sense Bryan could be called a liberal and a progressive. He resented predatory wealth, not wealth itself. In another sense, however, he was the rankest of conservatives, for he resented industrialism and urbanism and perpetuated the myth of Protestant-Yankee agrarianism. He sought to avoid for the American farmer the ills the Industrial Revolution visited upon the English and European peasant. To him, the man who tilled the soil or engaged in otherwise "honest" labor was the most important of America's producers of wealth. The family farm was the "Gibraltar of security" that furnished the nucleus of democratic and egalitarian society. Rather than noting their conflicts, he believed that the

farmer, laborer, and small businessman were blood brothers in
economic interest, and he insisted upon vigorous government action
to restore not only political democracy but the equality of opportunity, or economic democracy, without which political democracy
cannot truly exist. In the long run, his demand for an interventionist government was the major reason for objection to him on the
part of the devotees of the *laissez faire* policy of the day.

When it is said that Bryan "spoke as if he had just had a spiritual visitation from Jefferson," [44] the import is upon his looking
upon Jefferson as an eloquent exponent of democracy as the American political ideal. Both were sincere and enthusiastic believers in
the rights of humanity. Both advocated the maximum of personal
liberty, opposed the concentration of industry, disliked urban life,
and eschewed the trappings of aristocracy and riches. Both confused liberty and equality and believed that the latter could be
obtained simply by the destruction of special privilege.

As his followers looked upon him as a reincarnated Jefferson,
so Bryan looked upon Jefferson's political principles as a code that
was fundamental and unchangeable. Herein lay his tragedy, for in
leading the third great revolt against plutocracy, or monopoly capitalism, he proved himself to be a political fundamentalist when
the times called for change. He overlooked the fact that subsistence
farming had shifted largely to commercial farming. The farmer
whom he had apotheosized in his "Cross of Gold" speech and for
whom he would rebuild Jefferson's Arcadia had made possible
large-scale industry and the rise of the city, but he farmed for
money rather than just to make a living; he was now a farmer-
businessman who produced too much and was caught in the mech-
anism of distribution in a world market controlled by the law of
supply and demand. By 1896 the value of industrial exports alone
exceeded that of America's farms, and between a third and a half
of America's people lived in cities—in sum, Bryan fell short in
seeking largely to redress the grievances of the agrarian minority
in an industrialized nation.

Like Jefferson's, Bryan's objectives were more important than

[44] Merrill D. Peterson, *The Jefferson Image in the American Mind* (New
York, 1960), p. 230.

the methods each used;[45] like Jefferson's, Bryan's influence was "on the spirit of the people and their attitude toward their institutions rather than on the formation of the institutions themselves." [46] Popular sovereignty had ended in the rule of the political machine. Bryan's cure was more popular sovereignty, enough to control the machine. Individualism had ended in the tyranny of the corporation. His cure was more individualism, enough to permit representative government to protect the rights of man rather than of money. Progress, he said, "is measured not so much by the discovery of new principles as by the more perfect assimilation of old principles." Thus like Jefferson, Bryan believed that the greatness of America lay not in the strength of government but in the government's release of the individual talents and energies of its people, and in the right of the ability of the people to govern themselves.[47] As has been suggested, however, he stood the Jefferson of the Kentucky Resolutions and the Jackson of the Maysville Road veto and hard money "on their heads" by shaking his party clear of its fear of the national government and advocating that it become interventionist, that it serve the people rather than merely govern them.[48]

Although only thirty-six years old in 1896, Bryan had captured the leadership of a great political party. He found it demoralized; he reorganized it and gave it new life. He drew heretofore incoherent reform forces into a national progressive movement. He infused these forces with a new spirit, a consciousness of power, and a hope of victory to challenge the control of the businessman and his political henchman who had ruled the country since the Civil War. In defending the tenets of a frontier already living on borrowed time he provoked a social revolt so savage that it ap-

---

[45] Carl Becker, "What Is Still Living in the Political Philosophy of Thomas Jefferson?" *American Historical Review,* 48 (July 1943), 691–706.

[46] David S. Muzzey, *Thomas Jefferson* (New York, 1918), p. 70.

[47] Merrill D. Peterson, "Thomas Jefferson and the National Purpose," *Proceedings of the American Philosophical Society,* 105 (December 1961), 517.

[48] Carl N. Degler, *Out of Our Past: The Forces That Shaped Modern America* (New York, 1959), pp. 336–337.

peared to threaten a civil war over a new balance of class power. He failed because he ran on a new issue, and no new party in America ever succeeded in winning the Presidency in its first campaign. The dynamics of the era gave much greater leverage to the directors of corporations than to individual entrepreneurs. Rather than use the ballot box to demand paternalism or interventionism, the people decided to retain *laissez faire*. Rather than create a welfare state in which the government would redistribute the national wealth on an equitable basis, the voters determined to keep the Hamiltonian system as better fitted to an industrial rather than agricultural economy.

Though defeated, Bryan's crusade for social justice was not wasted. The adoption of income and inheritance taxes, abolition of government by injunction, approval of the labor boycott, sharp reduction in the tariff, strict control of banks, railroads, and industrial corporations attempting or exercising monopoly control, changes in the currency and banking system that benefited the agrarian community, sweeping changes in the order and procedure of the House of Representatives, the direct election of Senators, direct primaries and direct legislation, and modifications of the Supreme Court's powers were all accomplished within a generation of 1896. All that was reasonable in Bryanism—and in populism— was eventually granted.

The significance of the election of 1896 lay not in the temporary defeat of the New Democracy but in the breaking of the backbone of the agrarian resurgence. Tangential effects included the death of the labor-populist alliance and the withdrawal of organized labor from political action for more than a decade. So long as the New England, Middle Atlantic, Central, and North Central sections united in supporting the Republican party, they would control the electoral college and thereby the Presidency. The influence of the small farmers and pioneers of the West and South, which had elected Jefferson and Jackson, would henceforth pale before the combined power of the more prosperous rural interests and the commercial and industrial interests of the town and city. America's farmers and wage workers would receive little help from government until they formed strong self-interest blocs in Congress and forced recognition of their demands. Thomas E. Watson was one of the few perceptive men who tasted the irony of Bryan's phrase "The First Battle," for the election of 1896 was the last battle, the "last aggressive stand of agrarian provincialism against capitalist industrialism." [49] Henceforth the business-minded farmer sought government aid in the form of parity, export debentures, equalization fees, and crop allotments rather than by repeating Jeffersonian rhetoric.

In his statement of November 6 to the bimetallists of the United States, Bryan revealed himself still insufficiently aware of the impact upon the country of the agricultural, commercial, and industrial revolutions of the nineteenth century. He retained his faith in the eventual righting of their wrongs by "the people." Bimetallism had been overcome, not vanquished, by small pluralities and was now stronger than ever. Let the roll call be sounded for the next engagement! Let all bimetallists renew their allegiance to the cause! Right shall yet triumph! Agitation of the truth must result in the remedying of abuses! The election meant that the people wanted to continue the experiment of the gold standard for four years more— but as sovereigns they could make a change in 1900. To his followers nothing was more certain than that he would run again in 1900. "The fight has just begun. We have enlisted for the war. We look for you to blaze the way," Josephus Daniels wired him, and John Clark Ridpath noted that Jefferson marked the first stage of historic Democracy, Jackson the second, and Bryan the third.[50]

---

[49] Woodward, *Watson*, p. 330.

[50] Daniels to Bryan, telegram, November 4, 1896, Bryan Papers; John Clark Ridpath, "Three Epochs of Democracy and Three Men," *The Arena*, 19 (May 1898), 543–563.

✪

The Democrat as Revivalist

A man can be born again; the springs of life can be cleansed instantly. . . . If this is true of one, it can be true of any number. Thus, a nation can be born in a day if the ideals of the people can be changed.—WILLIAM JENNINGS BRYAN

Those who know American revivalism are familiar with the story of the skeptic who comes to the camp meeting to scoff and stays to be converted. Bryan's great "Cross of Gold" speech at the Democratic convention of 1896 had the same galvanic effect. One of his followers who was sitting in the gallery reported the behavior of a near-by gold Democrat who had been sneering at every friendly reference to the silver cause. When Bryan finished his appeal the gold Democrat "lost control of himself and literally grabbed hold of me and pulled me up from a sitting to a standing position on my chair. He yelled at me, 'Yell, for God's sake, yell,' as Bryan closed his speech."

The Great Commoner was a circuit-riding evangelist in politics; the "Cross of Gold" speech, with its religious imagery, its revivalist fervor, its electric reaction upon the audience, was a miniature of his career. Many who laughed at the gospel of his first years in politics came in time to accept much of it as commonplace. Bryan himself, emerging suddenly from obscurity at an hour when the people were in an angry mood, framing his message for a simple constituency nursed in evangelical Protestantism and knowing little

From *The American Political Tradition, and the Men Who Made It,* by Richard Hofstadter. Copyright 1948 by Alfred A. Knopf, Inc. Reprinted by permission.

literature but the Bible, helped to lead a Great Awakening which swept away much of the cynicism and apathy that had been characteristic of American politics for thirty years.

Bryan was equally at home in religion and politics. In his lecture "The Prince of Peace," which he gave many times and in almost every corner of the world, he declared:

I am interested in the science of government, but I am more interested in religion. . . . I enjoy making a political speech . . . but I would rather speak on religion than on politics. I commenced speaking on the stump when I was only twenty, but I commenced speaking in the church six years earlier—and I shall be in the church even after I am out of politics.

Unfortunately Bryan's political leadership and social philosophy were as crude as the theology of his evangelical brethren.

Charles Willis Thompson once remarked that "Bryan's hold on the West lay in the fact that he was himself the average man of a large part of that country; he did not merely resemble that average man, he was that average man." In this Bryan was different from the other great leaders of the progressive era. Theodore Roosevelt, with his leisure-class background and tastes, Wilson with his professorial reserve, La Follette with his lonely stubbornness and his craftsmanlike interest in the technical details of reform, were singular men. They sensed popular feelings; Bryan embodied them.

Bryan's typical constituent was the long-suffering staple farmer of the West and South. This farmer had broken the prairie or survived the rigors of Reconstruction. His wheat or cotton had fed and clothed the growing industrial population of the cities; exported to Europe, his produce had bought the foreign capital that financed American industrial expansion. For thirty years, since 1865, he had kept his eyes on the general price level, watching it sink downward almost without interruption until at last the dollar had trebled in value. This meant slow agony for the farmer; he was a debtor, and his long-term debts were appreciating intolerably. A debt that he could have paid in 1865 with 1,000 bushels of wheat now cost him 3,000 bushels. To one who owes money and finds it hard to come by, economic hardship appears in its simplest guise as a shortage of money. If money was scarce, the farmer concluded, then the logical thing was to increase the money supply. The silver campaign of 1896 was a struggle between those who wanted money cheap and those who wanted it dear.

But in 1896 free silver ranked among the heresies with free love. Except in the farm country, wherever men of education and substance gathered together it was held beneath serious discussion. Economists in the universities were against it; preachers were against it; writers of editorials were against it. For almost forty years after the campaign was over, the single gold standard remained a fixed star in the firmament of economic orthodoxy, to doubt which was not merely wrong but dishonest. (As late as 1933, when Franklin D. Roosevelt took the United States off the gold standard, Lewis W. Douglas was heard to moan: "Well, this is the end of Western civilization.")

In fact, however, the logic of the silver inflationists was not so wrongheaded as Bryan's orthodox contemporaries believed. Some eminent authorities look back upon the single gold standard as a vicious *idée fixe,*[1] and few will deny that there was a profound need for currency reform in 1896. The farmers were indeed being milked by the interests, in part through contraction of the currency. Accused during the election campaign of fighting for a dishonest dollar, Bryan had by far the better of the argument when he replied that "A dollar approaches honesty as its purchasing power approaches stability."

But free-silverites went on to the disastrous conclusion that currency was the great cause of their miseries, and that currency reform would end them. The many ways in which farmers were victimized by tariffs, railroads, middlemen, speculators, warehousers, and monopolistic producers of farm equipment were all

---

[1] John Maynard Keynes found in the gold standard one of the major causes of the modern world tragedy. In *The General Theory of Employment, Interest, and Money* he stated: "Under the system of domestic *laissez faire* and an international gold standard such as was orthodox in the latter half of the nineteenth century, there was no means open to a government whereby to mitigate economic distress at home except through the competitive struggle for markets."

but forgotten; yet these things had been subjects of much sound agitation in the Bryan country not long before; to revive them would have been neither novel nor strange. In 1892, before the depression brought popular discontents to fever pitch, General James B. Weaver, campaigning on a well-rounded platform of reform issues, had polled over a million votes for President on the Populist ticket. The time seemed ripe for a many-sided attack on abuses that had flourished since the Civil War. Instead, the growing demand for free silver so completely overshadowed other things in the minds of the people as to fix them on a single issue that was at best superficial. This neglect of other facets of reform caused Henry Demarest Lloyd, one of the most intelligent and principled reform spokesmen, to complain:

> Free silver is the cow-bird of the reform movement. It waited until the nest had been built by the sacrifices and labour of others, and then it laid its eggs in it, pushing out the others which lie smashed on the ground.

In defense of the free-silver politicians it must be said that they only stressed the issue that the farmers themselves greeted most responsively. "During the campaign of 1892," writes John D. Hicks in *The Populist Revolt,* "the Populists had learned that of all the planks in their platform the silver plank had the widest appeal." And not only to the farmers—it was the only fund-raising issue the Bryan-Altgeld Democrats had; it attracted the Western silver mine owners who, eager to enlarge their market, gave liberally to the cause, distributed 125,000 copies of W. H. Harvey's plausible free-silver pamphlet, *Coin's Financial School,* and supplied Bryan with most of his meager campaign resources.

Bryan was content to stress free silver to the exclusion of everything else, and thus to freeze the popular cause at its lowest level of understanding. No one can read his campaign speeches in *The First Battle* without being struck by the way the free-silver obsession elbowed all other questions out of the way. It was the only time in the history of the Republic when a candidate ran for the Presidency on the strength of a monomania. At Hartford Bryan asserted warmly: "Of all the instrumentalities which have been conceived by the mind of man for transferring the bread which one man earns to another man who does not earn it, I believe the gold standard is the greatest." In the "Cross of Gold" speech he claimed that "when we have restored the money of the Constitution all other necessary reforms will be possible; but . . . until this is done there is no other reform that can be accomplished."

There seems to have been an element of expediency in Bryan's original acceptance of free silver. "I don't know anything about free silver," he told an audience during his campaign for Congress in 1892. "The people of Nebraska are for free silver and I am for free silver. I will look up the arguments later." Many other politicians have gone through just such an intellectual process, but Bryan's simplicity was unique: he saw nothing to be ashamed of in such a confession. The cause of the people was just; therefore their remedies must be sound; his duty was simply to look up the arguments. That he came to believe earnestly in free silver can hardly be questioned, for his capacity to convince himself, probably the only exceptional thing about his mind, was boundless. "It is a poor head," he once declared, "that cannot find plausible reason for doing what the heart wants to do."

"Of all the men I have seen at close range in thirty-one years of newspaper service," Oswald Garrison Villard has written, "Mr. Bryan seemed to me the most ignorant." The Commoner's heart was filled with simple emotions, but his mind was stocked with equally simple ideas. Presumably he would have lost his political effectiveness if he had learned to look at his supporters with a critical eye, but his capacity for identifying himself with them was costly, for it gave them not so much leadership as expression. He spoke for them so perfectly that he never spoke to them. In his lifelong stream of impassioned rhetoric he communicated only what they already believed.

If Bryan failed to advance a well-rounded program for his farm followers in 1896, he did still less for labor. Aside from one uninspiring address in which he assailed government by injunction—a nod to the Pullman strikers—he did not go far out of his way to capitalize the bitter working-class discontent of the campaign year.

Subsequently he was friendly toward labor, but he never sponsored a positive program of labor legislation, and it is doubtful that he had any clear conception of the trials of working-class existence. When he first ran for Congress, he told an audience of farmers that he was "tired of hearing about laws made for the benefit of men who work in shops." In 1896 he won the support of the A.F. of L., then a struggling organization of some 270,000 members, although such labor leaders as Gompers were well aware that "the cause of our ills lies far deeper than the question of gold or silver." In Mark Hanna's estimation Bryan's appeal was too narrow: "He's talking Silver all the time, and that's where we've got him." Bryan ran stronger in the industrial cities of the East than he did in the East generally, but his labor support was too weak to win him any of the heavily populated states.

Bryan's social philosophy, which can be reconstructed from speeches made from 1892 to 1896, was not a grave departure from the historic ideology of the Democratic party. Protesting against the drift of government from the popular will, he set down his faith in Jeffersonian principles in the most forthright terms:

I assert that the people of the United States . . . have sufficient patriotism and sufficient intelligence to sit in judgment on every question which has arisen or which will arise, no matter how long our government will endure. The great political questions are in their final analysis great moral questions, and it requires no extended experience in the handling of money to enable a man to tell right from wrong.

The premise from which Bryan argued was that social problems are essentially moral—that is to say, religious. It was inconceivable that the hardworking, Bible-reading citizenry should be inferior in moral insight to the cynical financiers of the Eastern cities. Because they were, as Bryan saw it, better people, they were better moralists, and hence better economists. In after years when he bustled to the support of the antievolution laws with the argument that he was defending the democracy of Tennessee, he was simply carrying this variety of political primitivism to its logical end.

The second principle of Bryan's philosophy was summarized in the old Jacksonian motto that he often quoted: "Equal rights to all and special privileges to none." Like the men of 1828, Bryan felt that he represented a cause that was capable of standing on its own feet without special assistance from the government. The majority of the people, he declaimed, who produced the nation's wealth in peace and rallied to its flag in war, asked for nothing from the government but "even-handed justice." "It is the duty of government to protect all from injustice and to do so without showing partiality for any one or any class."

Several writers have argued that Bryanism marked the beginning of the end of *laissez faire* in the United States, but this is true only in the most indirect and attenuated sense. The Democratic platform of 1896 called for no sweeping restrictions of private enterprise; none of its planks required serious modification of the economic structure through government action.[2] Most of its demands, on the contrary, can be summed up in the expression: "Hands off." The call for a return to bimetallism was a call for the removal of a restriction on silver coinage imposed as late as 1873, not for some thoroughly novel policy. The labor planks asked only that the federal government keep its hands off labor disputes and leave them to state authority—a victory for John P. Altgeld over Grover Cleveland. The income tax plank was not accounted a means of redistributing wealth on any considerable scale, but merely of forcing the plutocracy to pay for its own services. It was the great merchant, not the farmer, who needed a navy, cried Bryan, echoing the Jeffersonians of old; it was the capitalist, not the poor man, who wanted a standing army "to supplement the local government in protecting his property when he enters into a contest with his employees." Then let the merchant and the capitalist pay their share in maintaining the army and navy. The spirit of the agrarians, throughout defensive rather than aggressive, was aptly expressed by Mary E. Lease when she said that the people were "at bay," and by Bryan himself when he proclaimed: "We do not come as ag-

[2] The Populist platform, which included proposals for unemployment relief, public works, and government ownership, was more positive in its demands. Bryan deftly dissociated himself, without being too specific, by stating that there were some planks in the Populist platform of which he did not approve.

gressors. . . . We are fighting in defense of our homes, our families and our posterity."

In Bryan's mind the purpose of "the first battle" was to preserve classic American individualism. In one of the most frequently quoted passages of the "Cross of Gold" speech he tried to assimilate the cause of the people to American traditions of enterprise—to restore it, in effect, to respectability by underlining its bourgeois aspirations:

When you come before us and tell us that we are to disturb your business interests, we reply that you have disturbed our business interests by your course. We say to you that you have made the definition of a business man too limited in its application. The man who is employed for wages is as much a business man as his employer. The attorney in a country bank is as much a business man as the corporation counsel in a great metropolis; a merchant at the crossroads store is as much a business man as the merchant of New York; the farmer who goes forth in the morning and toils all day—who begins in the spring and toils all summer—and who by the application of brawn and muscle to the natural resources of the country, creates wealth, is as much a business man as the man who goes upon the Board of Trade and bets upon the price of grain.

When he came to New York to deliver his acceptance address he declared in words strikingly similar to Jackson's bank message:

Our campaign has not for its object the reconstruction of society. We cannot insure to the vicious the fruits of a virtuous life; we would not invade the home of the provident in order to supply the wants of the spendthrift; we do not propose to transfer the rewards of industry to the lap of indolence. Property is and will remain the stimulus to endeavor and the compensation for toil. We believe, as asserted in the Declaration of Independence, that all men are created equal; but that does not mean that all men are or can be equal in possessions, in ability, or in merit; it simply means that all shall stand equal before the law. . . .

After one hundred years of change in society the Jeffersonian-Jacksonian philosophy was intact. To those who accept that philosophy, this will appear as steadfastness of faith; to those who reject it, as inflexibility of mind.

II

Ridiculed and condemned by all Eastern respectability in 1896, denounced as an anarchist, a socialist, a subverter of religion and morals, the victim of every device that wealth and talents could bring to bear, Bryan has gained a place among the celebrated American rebels. But in an important psychological sense he was never a rebel at all—and this is a clue to the torpor of his mind. What was lacking in him was a sense of alienation. He never felt the excitement of intellectual discovery that comes with rejection of one's intimate environment. The revolt of the youth against paternal authority, of the village agnostic against the faith of his tribe, of the artist against the stereotypes of philistine life, of the socialist against the whole bourgeois community—such experiences were not within his ken. Near the end of his life his own party laughed him off the stage, but that came too late to be instructive.

Politicians cannot be expected to have the traits of detached intellectuals, but few men in any phase of life have been so desolately lacking as Bryan in detachment or intellectuality. While he was eager to grapple with his opponents in the political arena, he was incapable of confronting them in the arena of his own mind. His characteristic mental state was not that of a man who has abandoned the assumptions of his society or his class after a searching examination, but rather of one who has been so thoroughly nurtured in a provincial heresy that it has become for him merely another orthodoxy. Colonel House relates that Bryan often told him "that a man who did not believe in the free and unlimited coinage of silver at 16 to 1 was either a fool or a knave." Bryan was rooted in a section of the country where his panaceas were widely taken as gospel; even the substantial citizenry of the West gave him a following. As he complacently observed in *The First Battle* concerning the men who helped him launch the Nebraska Democratic free-silver movement in 1894, "They were all men of standing in the State and most of them men of considerable property." He referred to the East as "the enemy's country." When he went to battle for the Western farmer, therefore, it was not in the spirit of a domestic quarrel in which one's object is to persuade, but of a war against a foreign power in which an exchange of views is impossible. He could no more analyze the issues of his day than the Confederates could realize the obsolescence of slavery.

Intellectually, Bryan was a boy who never left home. His father, Silas Bryan, was a Baptist and a Democrat of Southern origin, who carved out a successful career in the "Egypt" section of Illinois, became a judge in the state courts, owned a large house, and provided his family with the stale culture and niggardly comfort that usually result when ample means are used to achieve puritan ends. In 1872, when Bryan was twelve, Silas Bryan ran for Congress with the endorsement of the Greenback party. The father believed in the supremacy of the Anglo-Saxon race, the value of education as an instrument of success, democratic opportunity, the God of the Old Testament, and an expanded currency. The son never found reason to question these convictions: there was no ideological tension in the Bryan household. William Jennings did break with his father's church to join the Presbyterians, abandoning his ambition to become a Baptist minister because he was frightened by the strenuous dunking of the baptismal ceremony, but he learned that his conversion had hurt Silas Bryan's feelings only long after his father was dead.

From his father's home Bryan was sent to Whipple Academy and Illinois College at Jacksonville, Illinois. His six years there did nothing to awaken his mind. The faculty of Illinois College consisted of eight men, and its curriculum carried no subject except mathematics and classics beyond an introductory course. During his years of attendance Bryan withdrew eighteen books from the college library (which was closed to students all but a few hours of the day), and they were chiefly fiction. (Bryan especially liked the novels of Charles Dickens.) The president of the college, Julian Monson Sturtevant, was the author of a textbook, *Economics,* which defended free trade and bimetallism. "The President of the College," Bryan declaimed happily, "is for free trade, our ex-President is for free trade, and *I myself* am for free trade." After what Bryan had heard in his father's home and absorbed from Sturtevant, the protective tariff and monometallism seemed outlandish.

For two years after leaving college Bryan read law at the Union College of Law in Chicago and in the office of Lyman Trumbull, after which he returned to Jacksonville, married the daughter of a prosperous storekeeper, and for five years practiced law without distinction. Smarting with realization of his mediocrity as a lawyer, Bryan fled westward and settled in Lincoln, Nebraska, where he soon edged into politics under the protective wing of J. Sterling Morton, the Democratic political agent of the railroads. He was fond of saying that he had entered politics by accident, but in a franker mood he once confessed: "Certainly from the time I was fifteen years old, I had but one ambition in life, and that was to come to Congress. I studied for it. I worked for it, and everything I did had that object in view."

In 1890, with the backing of the business and liquor interests of Omaha, he won a seat in Congress. Two years later, after many months of arduous study, he made an impressive antitariff speech in the House, which focused national attention upon him. Then, quickly perceiving the decline of the tariff as a political issue, and observing the rapid rise of populism, which was especially strong in his own state, he took up free silver. Nebraska districts had been rearranged; Omaha was no longer in his bailiwick; Bryan now "looked up the arguments" on silver as he had on the tariff, negotiated financial backing from the Utah and Colorado silvermine operators, and won re-election from a more rural constituency. In 1893 he made another spectacular speech in Congress against repeal of the Sherman Silver Purchase Act, of which almost a million copies were distributed by silver mine owners. The following year he tried for election to the Senate, but the legislature spurned him, and he turned to an ill-paid position as editor of the Omaha *World-Herald,* which had been procured by his patrons among the silver interests. With cool nerve and considerable skill, he set to work to make the *World-Herald* an instrument of his Presidential ambitions, which then seemed fabulously premature to everyone but himself.

Bryan's political career after 1896 was a long, persistent search for an issue comparable in effect to free silver, and an equally persistent campaign to keep himself in the public eye. In 1899 anti-imperialism seemed a likely issue. Democratic and Populist opponents of expansion were planning to block annexation of the Philippines by rejecting the peace treaty with Spain in the Senate. To Bryan, fighting in this way as an organized minority seemed wrong; the people themselves must decide—and the issue must be exploited in a campaign. Assuming that an anti-imperialist platform in 1900 would appeal to the idealism of the American people, as the cause of Cuba had before the war, he managed to persuade just enough Democratic Senators to permit the treaty to pass. He proposed to win a mandate for Philippine independence in the election. This was the most grotesque miscalculation of his life. Anti-imperialism would have been a much more live issue if the treaty had been rejected and the question of annexing the Philippines was still hanging fire. Once the treaty was ratified, the people were quite content to let the matter rest. Bryan found anti-imperialism such a sterile issue during his 1900 campaign that he turned increasingly to others—antitrust and free silver—but prosperity had returned and he was unable to excite the electorate as before.

Bryan's attempt to revive the stale free-silver issue during the campaign also backfired. The world production of gold, stimulated by the new cyanide extraction process and the discovery of fresh deposits, had risen markedly, and the price level had also gone up, but when followers like the sociologist E. A. Ross pointed out to Bryan that the new gold supplies had relieved the money shortage and undermined the cause of silver, the Commoner was unimpressed. Considerations of practical economics, Ross recalls, meant little to him. "He . . . merely suggested how to parry arguments based upon them brought out by our opponents. . . . I saw that Mr. Bryan was no realist." From a strategic standpoint, Bryan was worse than wrong, he was impractical. By insisting on the free-silver plank in the 1900 platform he may have lost whatever chance he had of winning some of the Eastern states, while he did not need the issue to win the West or the South. "Bryan," quipped Thomas B. Reed, "had rather be wrong than president."

In 1902 Bryan took a trip abroad and observed state ownership of utilities as it was practiced in European countries. Thrown aside by his party in 1904 in favor of the conservative Alton B. Parker, he continued to press for a more radical program, including government ownership and operation of the railways. And yet, after Theodore Roosevelt's overwhelming victory, he visited the Rough Rider at the White House, greeting him with the words: "Some people think I'm a terrible radical, but really I'm not so very dangerous after all." To the *New York Tribune* he wrote: "It is time to call a halt on Socialism in the United States. The movement is going too far." Then in the summer of 1906, returning from a grand tour of the world, he went back to government ownership of railroads. He had now achieved a synthesis: government ownership would be a way of avoiding socialism:

The man who argues that there is an economic advantage in private monopoly is aiding socialism. The socialist, asserting the economic superiority of the monopoly, insists that its benefits shall accrue to the whole people, and his conclusion cannot be denied if his assertion is admitted. The Democratic party, if I understand its position, denies the economic as well as the political advantage of private monopoly and promises to oppose it wherever it manifests itself. It offers as an alternative competition where competition is possible, and public monopoly wherever circumstances are such as to prevent competition.

Like free silver in 1900, government ownership of railways did not take with the voters. Preparing for his third Presidential nomination in 1908, Bryan scurried to haul down his flag, promised that he would not "force government ownership upon the country against the will of the people," and testified in a letter to the *Wall Street Journal* that he was in "no hurry about government ownership." Instead he campaigned on the trust question, proposing a rule-of-thumb system of curbing big business that must have caused apoplexy in hundreds of clubrooms.[3] The campaign was rather list-

[3] According to Bryan's formula, when a corporation engaged in interstate commerce came to control as much as 25 per cent of the business in its field of enterprise it must obtain a federal license; the provisions of this license would guarantee the public against watered stock and prevent the corporation from controlling more than 50 per cent of the traffic in its product or products.

less, and the mammoth Taft beat the Commoner more soundly than McKinley had in 1896 or 1900.

And yet, while Bryan had the smallest percentage of the total vote received by any Democratic candidate except Parker for the past sixty years, his ideas were about to reach the peak of their influence. Theodore Roosevelt, during both his terms, had been appropriating one after another of Bryan's smaller issues. Progressive Democrats, held in cohesion by the Bryan influence, were to harass Taft in collaboration with the progressive Republicans. Finally, in 1912 Bryan was to help swing the Democratic nomination to Woodrow Wilson. The Commoner, always defeated, had, in the course of a sixteen-year quest for issues, effectively turned public attention upon one reform after another; and many of his proposals had had a core of value. Mary Bryan, completing her husband's *Memoirs* in 1925, listed with understandable pride the Bryan projects that had become law: the federal income tax, popular election of United States Senators, publicity in campaign contributions, woman suffrage, a Department of Labor, more stringent railroad regulation, currency reform, and, in the states, the initiative and referendum.

Bryan accepted his perennial defeats with a good humor that seems extraordinary, in the light of the earnestness of his campaigns and the vituperation that was heaped upon him. There is good reason, however, to doubt that at heart he ever really expected to win. He had risen overnight from comparative obscurity to become a major Presidential candidate—a thrilling and profoundly gratifying experience. He was grateful that he could run at all, that he could run again, and yet again, that he could earn a good and easy living at the Chautauquas, that he could constantly command national attention, thrill millions with his fine voice, throw a Democratic convention into an uproar with a barbed phrase. For Silas Bryan's son who had once seemed on the verge of failure in the law, this was ample achievement. As prices turned upward and the temper of his following eased, Bryan grew fat and genial, and on occasion passed jests about the futility of his campaigns. It was never success that he demanded, but an audience, and not until audiences began to laugh at him did he become the bitter and malignant old man of the Scopes trial.

III

When Woodrow Wilson reluctantly appointed him Secretary of State, Bryan held a leading office for the only time in his career and the State Department at last had a head who was committed to oppose imperialism and dollar dipomacy. But those who remembered his earlier career wondered what this might mean in practice. Bryan had been a most eloquent Christian pacifist, and yet when the Spanish War came he had fulfilled his idea of "service" by enlisting in the First Nebraska Volunteers, rising to a colonelcy, and camping with his troops in a sinkhole near Jacksonville, Florida, until the war was over. The inconsistency between his participation in the war and his discipleship of the Prince of Peace seemed not to trouble him. (Paxton Hibben remarked that the Commoner "appeared unable to grasp that the sole business of a soldier is to kill. To Bryan the function of a soldier was to be killed —he saw war a game to be won by sacrifice hits.")

Bryan in power was like Bryan out of power: he made the same well-meant gestures, showed the same willingness under stress or confusion to drop ideas he had once been committed to, the same inability to see things through. His most original enterprise was to promote a series of international arbitration treaties, a task that he undertook with moral earnestness such as had not been seen in his department for many years. These treaties provided that when disputes arose between contracting parties, there should be a "cooling-off" period to permit animosities to wane, followed by arbitration. He had great hopes for the treaties; they would help materially to dissipate the danger of war. "I believe there will be no war while I am Secretary of State," he declared fervently in 1913, "and I believe there will be no war so long as I live."

Bryan's inability to hold steadily to a line of principle was nowhere so well illustrated as in his imperialist policies in the Caribbean, where, as Selig Adler has shown, he was "chiefly responsible for a distinct acceleration of American penetration." Wilson, harassed by the Mexican question and the problems of neutrality, gave Bryan a substantially free hand in Caribbean policy, and the former anti-imperialist, in dealing with Nicaragua, Haiti, and Santo Domingo, was fully as aggressive as his Republican predecessors. Root, Knox, or Hay could have been no more nationalistic or jealous of the prerogatives of American capital in the face of foreign penetration. Apropos of the Haitian situation, Bryan wrote to Wilson, April 2, 1915:

As long as the [Haitian] Government is under French or German influence American interests are going to be discriminated against there as they are discriminated against now. . . . The American interests are willing to remain there with a view of purchasing a controlling interest and making the Bank a branch of the American bank . . . providing their Government takes the steps necessary to protect them. . . . I have been reluctant to favor anything that would require an exercise of force there, but there are some things that lead me to believe that it may be necessary to use as much force as may be necessary [*sic*] to compel a supervision which will be effective.

Bryan also wanted to father a sweeping policy of financial intervention in Latin America, which he outlined in two memoranda to Wilson in 1913. He proposed to counteract the influence of European creditors of Latin-American nations by having the United States government go to their "rescue." The United States would make available the funds necessary for the education, sanitation, and internal development of these nations, and relieve them of the necessity of applying to private financiers in other countries, thus making "absolutely sure our domination of the situation." This would so increase the nation's influence in Latin America "that we could prevent revolutions, promote education, and advance stable and just government." In proposing to wave aside private interests and make economic penetration a state function, Bryan, in the words of Samuel Flagg Bemis, anticipated "the formula of the newer dollar diplomacy of our day." Wilson, however, was not impressed by Bryan's plans.

With the advent of the World War Bryan was the one major figure in the Wilson administration who represented a genuinely neutral point of view. A Midwesterner and an old opponent of the international gold power, Bryan did not look at Britain with the soft eyes of the middle- and upper-class East. His great aim was not to further the Allied cause, but to maintain such relations with both sides as would make possible American arbitration. For his persistent criticism of administration policies Wilson's biographer, Ray Stannard Baker, has found him "the statesman of largest calibre" among Wilson's advisers. Urging mediation upon the President in September, 1914, Bryan wrote prophetically:

It is not likely that either side will win so complete a victory as to be able to dictate terms, and if either side does win such a victory it will probably mean preparation for another war. It would seem better to look for a more rational basis for peace.

When American bankers brought pressure upon the administration to allow them to make large loans to the Allies, Bryan was primarily responsible for choking off the project. Money, he pointed out, was the worst of all contrabands because it could command all other goods; such economic commitments to the Allies would be inconsistent with the spirit of neutrality and would ultimately lead to war. Events proved him right, but he characteristically refused to hold to his position and quietly gave his consent when it was proposed to jettison his original ban on loans. Just as he had gone back on anti-imperialism, pacifism, and government ownership of railways, so he backed down on the loans question.

It was neither courage nor sincerity but simply steadfast and self-confident intelligence that Bryan lacked. The steady drift of the United States away from neutrality caused him untold anguish. When Wilson began a long train of controversy with Germany by permitting American citizens to travel on British vessels that were likely to be sunk by U-boats, Bryan alone perceived the folly of the stand. The question, as he put it, was "whether an American citizen can, by putting his business above his regard for his country, assume for his own advantage unnecessary risks and thus involve his country in international complications." He also urged acceptance of the German proposal that relaxation of submarine warfare be exchanged for relaxation of the British food blockade against Germany, but the idea received no sympathy in Britain. "Why be shocked," he then asked Wilson, "at the drowning of a few people, if there is to be no objection to starving a nation?" Troubled by Wilson's protests to Germany over the sinking of the *Lusitania,* he resigned, June 8, 1915.

Bryan decayed rapidly during his closing years. The postwar era found him identified with some of the worst tendencies in American life—Prohibition, the crusade against evolution, real-estate speculation, and the Klan. For the sake of his wife's health he moved to Florida, where he became a publicity agent for the real-estate interests, in which capacity his incurable vulgarity stood him in good stead—"What is our vision of what Magic Miami should be?" He collected such magnificent fees for his real-estate promotion and his Prohibition lectures that he was able to bequeath a small fortune. His last political appearance took place at the Democratic convention of 1924 in New York City, when the party was racked with conflict over the famous resolution denouncing the Ku Klux Klan by name, and the delegations from the Bryan country were filled with Klan supporters. It was a magnificent opportunity for a man who had read Jefferson on tolerance to give a great lecture on bigotry. Instead, fearing more than anything else a further decline in his influence, Bryan delivered a weak appeal not to rend the "Christian Church" nor destroy party unity. Of the Klan he said: "We can exterminate Ku Kluxism better by recognizing their honesty and teaching them that they are wrong." Fat, balding, in wrinkled clothes, taxed by the heat, bereft of the splendid voice that had made him famous, he was unequal to the merciless heckling from the galleries, and when he descended from the platform after a ludicrous effort to promote compromise candidates, he told Senator Heflin with tears in his eyes that he had never in his life been so humiliated.

When the convention, in a stalemate between Al Smith and William Gibbs McAdoo, nominated John W. Davis, a lawyer for Morgan and Standard Oil, Bryan, who had once scourged the Morgan forces in a party conclave, lent his brother Charles to the Davis ticket as Vice-Presidential nominee and supported Davis in the campaign. Bryan's old principles were represented that year by Robert M. La Follette on an independent progressive ticket, but

La Follette got no support from the man whose followers had so often united with him in Congressional fights. The Commoner could no more think of leaving the Democratic party than of being converted to Buddhism. He had never failed to support a Democratic nominee. The party, he confessed to the 1924 convention, was a great passion of his life; he owed it an unpayable debt, for it had taken him out of obscurity, a young, penniless man, and had lifted him to exalted heights, three times honoring him with nominations.

But even in the Democratic party, Bryan knew, his influence was on the wane. He was an agrarian leader, whose strength lay in his appeal to a certain type of Protestant mind in the hinterland; the growing urbanism of the country was submerging him. He was not forgotten by his old followers, but as he wrote an acquaintance in 1923, "the wets are against me and they have the organization and the papers in all the big cities of the north. I cannot get before the public."

As his political power slipped away, Bryan welcomed an opportunity to divert himself with a new crusade and turned with devotion to his first interest. To one correspondent he wrote:

While my power in politics has waned, I think it has increased in religious matters and I have invitations from preachers in all the churches. An evidence of the change is found in the fact that my correspondence in religious subjects is much larger than my correspondence in political subjects. My interest is deeper in religious subjects because I believe that the brute theory has paralyzed the influence of many of our preachers and undermined the faith of many of our young people in college.

He once explained that he thought himself fit to be a leader in the fight against evolution because he had had a measure of success in his life that would dispel all doubts as to his "mental ability." He began to give lectures to the college youth of the nation bearing the message: "No teacher should be allowed on the faculty of any American university unless he is a Christian."

Bryan's presence for the prosecution at the trial of John Thomas Scopes for teaching evolution in Tennessee surprised no one who had been following his talks. The Scopes trial, which published to the world Bryan's childish conception of religion, also reduced to the absurd his inchoate notions of democracy. His defense of the antievolution laws showed that years of political experience had not taught him anything about the limitations of public opinion. The voice of the people was still the voice of God. The ability of the common man to settle every question extended, he thought, to matters of science as well as politics and applied equally well to the conduct of schools as it did to the regulation of railroads or the recall of judges or the gold standard. In prosecuting Scopes the people were merely asserting their right "to have what they want in government, including the kind of education they want." Academic freedom? That right "cannot be stretched as far as Professor Scopes is trying to stretch it. A man cannot demand a salary for saying what his employers do not want said. . . ."

So spoke the aging Bryan, the knight-errant of the oppressed. He closed his career in much the same role as he had begun it in 1896: a provincial politician following a provincial populace in provincial prejudices. From all corners of the country, but especially from the old Bryan territory, came messages of encouragement. "MY DEAR BROTHER BRYAN," wired an admirer from Smackover, Arkansas, "FIGHT THEM EVOLUTIONS UNTIL HELL FREEZES OVER AND THEN GIVE THEM A ROUND ON THE ICE." When a few weeks after the trial's close Bryan's heart gave out, there was profound grief among those who had followed him faithfully from the fight against gold to the fight against the ape. Fiery crosses were burned in his memory, and one of his constituents celebrated him as "the greatest Klansman of our time." A cruel and inaccurate characterization, it underscored the fatal weakness of a man who at sixty-five had long outlived his time.

PAOLO E. COLETTA

✪

Imperialism and the Treaty of Paris

One of the commonplaces of history is that the intervention of William Jennings Bryan resulted in the ratification of the Treaty of Paris by the United States Senate. It is the purpose of this paper to suggest that, while Bryan did influence a number of Senators, approval of the treaty resulted less from his efforts than from an overpowering public demand for colonial expansion and from superb leadership by such Republican Senators as Henry Cabot Lodge, Mark Hanna, and Nelson W. Aldrich, including the making of a number of "deals" by which opponents of the treaty were won to its support.

A perusal of the metropolitan newspapers for 1898 and 1899 and of the literary, military, commercial, and religious press of those years reveals that editors and feature writers never tired of describing the glories of empire. Their concepts, embodied in phrases like "manifest destiny," "the logic of events," and the "white man's burden," helped engender a public opinion overwhelmingly favorable to "imperial fatalism." Although anti-imperialist leagues mushroomed in all major cities, particularly in New England,[1] they proved powerless to stop the "movement of a race"

---

[1] F. H. Harrington, "The Anti-Imperialist Movement in the United States, 1898–1900," *Mississippi Valley Historical Review*, XXII (1935), 211–230; Erving Winslow, "The Anti-Imperialist League," *Independent*, LVI (May 18, 1899), 1347–1350, and "The Anti-Imperialist Position," *ibid.*, LVI

Reprinted from Paolo E. Coletta, "Bryan, McKinley, and the Treaty of Paris," *Pacific Historical Review*, XXVI (May 1957), pp. 131–146.

that gave the United States a new sense of international importance and opened up a new era of history based on altruism and commercialism. Strangely for one who wished his heart to beat in unison with the political pulse of the people, William Jennings Bryan insisted upon countering the inevitable.

As early as June, 1898, Bryan prayed that a war undertaken in the cause of humanity would not degenerate into one of conquest.[2] "Military lockjaw" kept his ample mouth sealed during the war, but his correspondence indicates that he had a plan to follow once he was discharged from the army.[3] President William McKinley, meanwhile, undecided with respect to Philippine policy, utterly ignored the question of the government of the Philippines in his annual message of December 3. At that time the administration lacked sufficient strength to ratify the treaty; and Lodge and Theodore Roosevelt, major architects of the "large policy," were plainly worried.[4]

Four schools represent the major divisions of thought on imperialism. Republicans in general favored expansion. Republicans in opposition, led by men like Andrew Carnegie and Senators George F. Hoar and Walter Mason, would defeat the treaty or amend it by deleting the provision that the United States acquire the Philippines. Democrats in general, and Southern Democrats in particular, favored expansion. Bryan headed a minority school that would ratify the treaty in order to end the war, stop the bloodshed, and detach the Philippines from Spain, and then grant the Filipinos independence by Congressional resolution.

To Bryan, expansion *per se* was antagonistic to the ideals America had cherished since the days of the Declaration of Independence. Expansion implied that the United States would become involved

---

(Mar. 25, 1899), 699. Excellent summaries of opinion on expansion may be found in *Public Opinion* for 1898 and 1899 and in Walter Millis, *The Martial Spirit* (1931), Julius W. Pratt, *Expansionists of 1898* (1936), and A. K. Weinberg, *Manifest Destiny* (1935).

[2] Omaha *World-Herald,* June 15, 1898.

[3] Bryan to Mrs. Bryan, Sept. 5, Oct. 12, 26, 1898. Bryan Papers (Manuscript Division, Library of Congress).

[4] H. C. Lodge to Theodore Roosevelt, Dec. 7, 1898. Roosevelt to Lodge, Dec. 12, 1898, H. C. Lodge, *Selections from the Correspondence of Henry Cabot Lodge and Theodore Roosevelt: 1884–1918* (1925), I, 368.

in the quarrels of Europe and Asia, thereby scrapping the Monroe Doctrine, and in wars for the subjugation of alien races. Most important, colonialism meant the abandonment of the vital principle of government only by the consent of the governed. On these grounds, which reflected his attachment to an isolationist foreign policy and to basic American principles of government, Bryan had ample warrant to oppose ratification. But how could he avoid expansion by supporting a treaty that provided for the acquisition of the Philippines? What appears a dichotomy in his thinking becomes clear upon restatement of his purpose. If the treaty were ratified, Spain would be pushed out of the picture and the United States alone would be in control of Filipino destiny. We would then take the Philippines only long enough to permit the American Congress to resolve that they should be free.

Two days after his discharge from the army on December 12 Bryan was in Washington demanding that the treaty be approved and that the Congress then resolve upon the nation's policy on expansion, a procedure that made it appear that he had forfeited the leadership that had carried him within sight of the White House in 1896. However, on imperialism he followed Democratic doctrine as espoused from Jefferson to Cleveland, and by his early objection to imperialism he was more of a molder of public opinion in 1899 than he was in 1896. Stanch Republican Andrew Carnegie, for example, wrote him that he stood at his side. Indeed, Carnegie saw Bryan as a formidable candidate in 1900 if he would drop free silver and campaign on only one issue, "the saving of the Republic from departure from its foundation principles." [5]

On December 17 Bryan returned from a conference with Carnegie in New York for another consultation with anti-imperialist leaders in Washington, for the scene of action had shifted from the battlefield to the Senate. On December 18, when the peace commissioners left Paris, Senator George Gray, the only Democrat on the commission, stated frankly that the United States had committed a grave blunder in annexing the Philippines and that the Democratic party had a perfect right to charge McKinley for the

[5] Carnegie to Bryan, Dec. 15, 18, 1898, Bryan Papers.

blunder. He would vote for the treaty, however, in order to end the war and avoid chaos. Most Republicans greeted the treaty as a great victory. "Not to confirm it," said Cushman K. Davis, chairman of the Senate Committee on Foreign Relations, "would be a crime against history," and commission chairman William Day declared that "it marked the beginning of the fulfillment of the greatest epoch in American history."

On the nineteenth, when Platt of Connecticut spoke on Vest's resolution that no power is given to the federal government to acquire territory to be held and governed permanently as colonies, the informal debate on ratification got under way. The formal debate, from January 4 to February 6, 1899, while one of the most interesting in American history, proceeded in profound ignorance of the real situation in the Philippines and of the true character and aspirations of its people. Had an unequivocal declaration been made prior to the ratification of the treaty that the Filipinos would be granted independence, the armed conflict that followed might have been prevented, but as yet the government had no power to make such a declaration. McKinley defended his position on expansion in various speeches. Then, three days before he received the peace treaty itself, he suddenly proclaimed American sovereignty over the Philippines on the basis of military conquest and ordered American troops from Manila to the island of Panay.

Bryan failed to see the incongruity of being on McKinley's side and argued that the treaty was a solemn obligation that must be enforced. He stated that his zeal for his prewar reforms had not abated but that he accepted two new issues—opposition to McKinley's demand for a reorganized army of one hundred thousand men, an issue henceforth called "militarism," and anti-imperialism. McKinley had asked, "Who shall haul down the flag that floats over our dead in the Philippines?" Bryan replied:

The flag is a national emblem and is obedient to the national will. . . . When the American people want it raised, they raise it, when they want it hauled down, they haul it down. . . .
Shall we keep the Philippines and amend our flag? . . . Shall we add a new star, the blood star, to indicate that we have entered upon a

career of conquest? . . . Or shall we adorn our flag with a milky way composed of a multitude of minor stars representing remote and insignificant dependencies?

No, a thousand times better to haul down the stars and stripes and substitute the flag of an independent republic than to surrender the doctrines that gave glory to "Old Glory." . . .[6]

Bryan hoped that the question of imperialism would be settled quickly, so that he could campaign in 1900 on the money and trust issues. "Just now I am talking against imperialism," he told Carnegie, "not because I have changed my mind on the other questions but because this attack of the imperialists must be met *now* or never." [7] When the Senate received the treaty and McKinley's request for its approval, Bryan began a barnstorming tour against imperialism on the theme that the mission of the United States was to liberate those who were in bondage, not to place shackles upon those who were struggling to be free. He found the people still excited by the war and talking about what they *would* do. They would reason better once they cooled off, he said, and then talk about what they *ought* to do. McKinley was appealing to them while they were intoxicated by military triumph; he would appeal to them when they were sober. To the abstract principles of the Declaration of Independence and the Constitution he added religious and moral arguments, asserting that the conflict between right and might would continue until a day was reached when the love of money would no longer sear into the national conscience and hypocrisy would no longer hide the hideous features of avarice behind the mask of philanthropy. The saying "Preach the gospel to every creature" does not have a "Gatling gun attachment." [8] He denied that we must govern the Filipinos for their own good and that we needed the profits obtainable from trading with them, and he found the President's "religious duty" argument pitifully weak, saying, "When the desire to steal becomes uncontrollable in an individual he is declared to be a kleptomaniac and is sent to an

[6] Omaha *World-Herald*, Dec. 23, 1898.

[7] Bryan to Carnegie, Jan. 30, 1899, Carnegie Papers (Manuscript Division, Library of Congress).

[8] Omaha *World-Herald*, Jan. 7, 1899.

asylum; when the desire to grab land becomes uncontrollable in a nation we are told that the 'currents of destiny are flowing through the hearts of men' and that the American people are entering upon their manifest mission." [9]

Despite the efforts of antiexpansionists within and without the Senate, Carnegie estimated that the treaty would lose by two or three votes. Bryan's advocacy of ratification had disorganized matters, however, and several Senators were "shaky" about voting it down. Only by coming to Washington, said Carnegie, could he learn that he had the power to defeat the treaty; at least he should wire his friends to defeat it. Bryan demurred, replying, "Have tried to convince others but have not tried to control them. Your plan is dangerous; my plan is safe. . . . If the people are against us, the minority of the Senate cannot save us." [10] Finally, on January 24, 1899, Augustus O. Bacon, of Georgia, introduced a four-part resolution, the last part of which Bryan acknowledged would prevent the impending rebellion and implement his policy. It read:

. . . the United States hereby disclaim any disposition to exercise sovereignty, jurisdiction, or control over said islands, and assert their determination, when a stable and independent government shall have been duly erected therein entitled to recognition as such, transfer to said government, upon terms that shall be reasonable and just, all rights secured under the cession by Spain, and to thereupon leave the government and control of the islands to their people.[11]

Bryan demanded an immediate statement of American policy. If, as McKinley said, American forces were being used to help the Filipinos achieve independence, well and good; if the army merely displaced Spain as a master, however, then the United States owed the Filipinos an explanation. If Americans believed in the doctrine of the consent of the governed, the treaty must be ratified; if not, Democrats would oppose a government not based on such consent. As for the twenty millions involved, we could either obtain that

---

[9] *New York World, Omaha World-Herald,* Jan. 8, 1899.

[10] Carnegie to Bryan, Jan. 19, 1899, Bryan Papers; Bryan to Carnegie, Jan. 11, 1899, Carnegie Papers.

[11] *Congressional Record,* 55 Congress, 3 Session, Vol. 32, Part 1, p. 561.

amount from the Filipinos in return for their independence or consider it a contribution to the cause of liberty.

Lodge worried about the trend of the debates, for each day's delay increased American difficulties in the Philippines. On January 12, the Senate began to debate the treaty in executive session. Leaks invalidated secrecy, and various Senators openly announced how they intended to vote. McKinley deemed the situation critical enough to appoint a commission to advise him on a Philippine policy, while Hoar sought to establish that policy by introducing a resolution calling for Philippine independence. Senator Wilkinson Call, of Florida, wired Bryan: "Your friends think you ought to be here aiding Carnegie and others to amend treaty." Bryan replied:

I believe that the fight should be made in favor of a resolution declaring the nation's policy. To reject the treaty or amend it throws the matter back into the hands of the executive. . . . The resolution declaring policy might be passed before the treaty is ratified or it might be attached to the bill appropriating the twenty millions of dollars.[12]

Lodge estimated that all the Democrats but two would vote against the treaty. But even if some of them did not vote the way they talked, he added, "I think we shall come out all right . . . by the sheer force of events." Roosevelt asked Senator Platt to have the New York legislature resolve in favor of the treaty. "The Senator is really against the Philippines," he wrote Lodge, "but he stands by the President. . . ." Lodge replied that such a resolution would help but that the result was still doubtful. "On the surface they have more than a third, but they have some very weak supporters, and it is quite in the cards that we shall ratify all right," he concluded.[13]

Carnegie and Call had not overstated the strength of the proponents of the treaty, who were doing their heavy work behind the scenes and gathering in the votes. On January 20, Henry M. Teller, who disagreed with Bryan on "unqualified independence"

[12] Call to Carnegie, Dec. 29, 1898, Jan. 5, 12, 1899, Carnegie Papers; Call to Bryan, Jan. 12, 1899, Bryan to Call, Jan. 12, 1899, Bryan Papers; Bryan to Carnegie, Jan. 13, 1899, Carnegie Papers.
[13] Lodge to Roosevelt, Jan. 21, 25, 1899, Roosevelt to Lodge, Jan. 23, 1899, Lodge, *Correspondence*, I, 387, 399.

for the Philippines, described the status of the struggle in the Senate in detail to Bryan. Gorman, of Maryland, had apparently aligned all but five or six of the Democrats in opposition to ratification. The Republicans, feeling securely in command of the situation, talked about preventing rejection of the treaty by two methods, by postponing the vote until the new Senate met or by having McKinley withdraw the treaty and then resubmit it. "I have not written this because I think you can change the situation here. I do not believe it can be done by any one or by all of us," Teller concluded.[14]

While Bryan pressed the attack from the stump, Carnegie declared that McKinley's success in getting the treaty ratified depended upon a word from Bryan. But Bryan did not control the Senate in the degree Carnegie suggested. James K. Jones, of Arkansas, the first Democratic Senator to break with him over the treaty, told him that the Republicans would accept Democratic help to ratify the treaty and then merely scoff at suggestions that the treaty be nullified by Bryan's proposition of a resolution granting the Filipinos independence.[15]

The third week in January was a critical one, for on January 23 Aguinaldo proclaimed the Philippine Republic and General Otis cabled of an expected rupture. On the twenty-fifth Bacon demanded a vote on his resolution and the Foreign Relations Committee set the date for the vote on the treaty for February 6. Two weeks of executive sessions on the treaty would intervene.

Although apprised of the ugly situation in the Philippines, McKinley clung to the hope that violence would be avoided and that Aguinaldo would not embarrass him while the treaty was in its most critical stage. But Aguinaldo did not want the "large share" in the Philippine government McKinley had promised; he wanted complete independence. McKinley ordered Otis to occupy all strategic points before they fell into Aguinaldo's hands, but Aguinaldo already held them. During the night of February 4 an exchange of shots between sentries of the Nebraska First, ironically, and a Filipino patrol developed into a general engagement in

[14] Teller to Bryan, Jan. 20, 1899, Bryan Papers.
[15] Jones to Bryan, Jan. 24, 30, 1899, Bryan Papers.

which both American and Filipino lives were lost.[16] According to
the administration, the Filipinos had fired first, broken the truce
recently established, and thus freed the United States from further
obligation. Some believed that Aguinaldo had resorted to hostilities
in order to prevent the impending ratification of the treaty, a step
supposedly applauded by Bryan and other anti-imperialists. There
is no evidence to warrant the latter charge. Proponents of the treaty
asserted that the news from Manila made ratification certain, while
the anti-imperialists praised American skill and valor but marked
the paradox of American soldiers helping to obtain freedom from
the Cubans and denying it to the Filipinos. The revolt proved a
catalyst; now the wavering Senators must make up their minds.

Bryan did not believe that the Filipino attack would affect the
outcome of ratification. Those who sought to conquer must expect
bloodshed, he said. A resolution promising independence would
probably prevent further trouble. Until the nation's policy was determined, however, American soldiers would of course defend
American interests.

The vote on the treaty was fifty-seven to twenty-seven, just one
more vote than the necessary two thirds. Was Bryan responsible
for the ratification of the treaty and for fastening upon the nation
the imperialism he so heartily denounced? If so, was he also responsible for the Filipino war? Was he "the most interesting and
the least explicit person" in the whole episode;[17] the "baffling
figure" who was delivering his party and his country "into the
hands of the skillful politicians of expansion and imperialism," [18] the
one who "secretly" urged his followers to ratify the treaty? [19] He
himself denied that he was responsible for the change of a single
vote,[20] flatly contradicting the conclusion of Paxton Hibben that
by his influence he "cajoled and dragooned seventeen Democrats

[16] Colonel John M. Stotsenburg to McKinley, Feb. 4, 5, 1899, Admiral
George Dewey to McKinley, Feb. 4, 5, 1899, McKinley Papers (Manuscript
Division, Library of Congress); *Annual Report of the War Department*
(1899), pp. 1–167, 334–528.

[17] Nathaniel Stephenson, *Nelson W. Aldrich* (1930), pp. 159–160.

[18] Walter Millis, *The Martial Spirit* (1931), p. 403.

[19] Claude M. Fuess, *Carl Schurz, Reformer* (1932), p. 359.

[20] *The New York Times,* Sept. 7, 1900.

and Populists . . . into approving the Spanish treaty." [21] No one knows the exact number of Senators Bryan influenced: Carnegie found seven, Julius Pratt fifteen, Hoar eighteen, Garraty "more than a dozen." [22]

On the Saturday before the vote, Lodge counted fifty-eight in favor, with four of these doubtful. Henry Heitfeld (Pop., Idaho) was the first to come over to Lodge, leaving only three doubtfuls, McLaurin, McEnery, and John P. Jones. Half an hour before the opening of the executive session on Monday, February 6, McLaurin came over. McEnery joined up five minutes before roll call, while Jones withheld his vote until after roll call. Thus the proponents of the treaty had their fifty-seven votes. [23]

What about the supposed influence of Bryan with the ten Democrats who voted yea? Morgan and Pettus, of Alabama, Gray and Kenney, of Delaware, and Clay, of Georgia, had announced their support of the treaty by mid-January, when McEnery, McLaurin, and Sullivan were already known as doubtfuls. Gray thought there was ample time to determine Philippine policy after ratification, although Richard Olney and Hoar suggested that some of the fuel Lodge burned in his "engine room" cooking up a federal judgeship for him soon thereafter influenced him. [24] Faulkner, although chairman of the Democratic Congressional Campaign Committee in 1894 and 1896, was in high favor with McKinley and voted yea in order to support him. Lindsay was an expansionist; Clay dis-

---

[21] Paxton Hibben, *The Peerless Leader: William Jennings Bryan* (1929), p. 222.

[22] Andrew Carnegie, *Autobiography of Andrew Carnegie* (1920), p. 352; John A. Garraty, *Henry Cabot Lodge, a Biography* (1953), p. 201; George F. Hoar, *Autobiography of Seventy Years* (1903), II, 322; Julius W. Pratt, *Expansionists of 1898* (1936), p. 357, and *A History of the United States Foreign Policy* (1955), p. 390.

[23] The party line-up, including those paired, stood: yeas, 40 Republicans, 10 Democrats, 4 Populists, 1 Silver Republican, 1 Silverite, and 1 Independent; nays, 22 Democrats, 2 Republicans, 1 Silverite, and 2 Populists. The political affiliation of Senators follows that in the *Congressional Directory* for December 1899. For difficulties in ascertaining political affiliations, see Elmer Ellis, *Henry M. Teller* (1941), pp. 315–316.

[24] Olney to Cleveland, March 22, 1899, Cleveland Papers (Manuscript Division, Library of Congress); *New York Tribune,* Jan. 20, 1899; Garraty, *Lodge,* p. 201.

claimed Bryan's influence.[25] Sullivan, of Mississippi, sided with Bryan and voted for ratification in order to end the war and proceed with the solution of the Philippine problem.

This leaves McEnery and McLaurin. McEnery apparently was corralled by the persuasive Aldrich and then won over by the promise of the appointment of a federal judge of his choice. Promise of support for his resolution granting Philippine independence "in due time" undoubtedly influenced him. McLaurin was so changeable in his views and disposition that his integrity, even his rationality, were at times questioned. After speaking against ratification, he suddenly swung to the Republican side. Mrs. McLaurin stated that he was converted on the night before the vote by the news of the Filipino vote. He was really won over by the promise of the post office patronage of his state and pledges of support for his resolution calling for the eventual independence of the Philippines.[26]

Of the Populists, silver Republicans, and the lone silverite who voted yea, Bryan may have influenced William V. Allen and John P. Jones but not the others—Butler, Harris, Cannon, Teller, Stewart, and Kyle.[27] On the day before the vote, Bryan wired Allen: "Chicago *Chronicle* says you contemplate making speech charging Senators with opposing treaty in order to injure me. Please leave me out of the discussion entirely unless others attack me and then only to defend my right to think and speak as I please like any other citizen." [28] During the morning hours on the sixth, Allen told his colleagues that he did not presume to represent Bryan and that assertions made that he did so were "utterly unfounded, sinister, and false." [29] Pettigrew later wrote a violent disclaimer that Bryan

[25] *Congressional Record,* 55 Congress, 3 Session, Vol. 32, Part 2, p. 1484.

[26] *Ibid.,* Part 1, pp. 638–641, Part 2, p. 1783; *New York Herald, New York Journal,* Feb. 7, 1899; *Review of Reviews,* 19 (1899), 267; Samuel Telfair, Jr., "Bryan and the Spanish American Treaty" (MS thesis, Columbia University, n.d., courtesy of Prof. Henry S. Commager); Nelson W. Aldrich Papers; Manuscript Division, Library of Congress (used by permission of Mr. Winthrop Aldrich).

[27] Merle E. Curti, "Bryan and World Peace," *Smith College Studies in History,* XVI (1931), 122.

[28] Bryan to Allen, Jan. 5, 1898, Henry S. Commager Papers.

[29] *Congressional Record,* 55 Congress, 3 Session, Vol. 32, Part 2, pp. 1479–1484.

had influenced his vote. Indeed, he maintained that Bryan did not change a single vote.[30] Others have held Bryan almost solely responsible for ratification. According to Hoar, Bryan got all that were needed of his followers to force the treaty through the Senate, making lawful our ownership of the Philippines and, according to high constitutional authorities, making it McKinley's duty to reduce them to submission. That act was a declaration of war against the Filipinos. "And for that war Mr. Bryan is more responsible than any other single person since the treaty left the hands of the President." Hoar credited Bryan with influencing seventeen Senators but failed to name them.[31]

Gorman's opposition to ratification stemmed less from conviction than from jealousy of Bryan and hope that the expansion issue would sidetrack the Chicago platform and lead to the Presidential nomination for himself. The Democrats and antiexpansionist Republicans had the treaty defeated, he said, until Bryan personally appealed to the Democratic Senators. He privately flayed Bryan and demanded that his renomination be prevented, yet he categorically denied that he opposed the treaty for personal political reasons.[32]

Perhaps with tongue in cheek, Tillman denied that "politics" had determined the vote of the Senators. Several Republicans had joined the Democrats in opposing imperialism. Tillman would have been glad to see the treaty ratified because ratification promised to bring disaster to the Republican party. But he had learned that Aldrich was now pushing the McEnery resolution "for the purpose of redeeming a pledge." Moreover, he had never heard so many speakers give more cogent reasons for not voting for the treaty and then voting for it anyway. "So at least a great many votes that have gone to the treaty . . . have been cast by men who have been in great doubt as to their duty, and have at least yielded rather to pressure than to any conscientious or calm consideration of the

[30] Richard F. Pettigrew, *Imperial Washington* (1922), pp. 270–271.
[31] Hoar, *Autobiography*, II, 321–324.
[32] Gorman to Dr. George L. Miller, Jan. 3, 1900, John R. Lambert, *Arthur Pue Gorman* (1953), p. 272; Josephus Daniels, *Editor in Politics* (1941), p. 282; Weinberg, *Manifest Destiny*, p. 299.

result," he concluded.[33] Pettigrew buttressed Tillman, saying, "I do not believe Mr. Bryan's visit changed the result, although several Democrats, who made speeches against it, voted for the treaty. The only effect of his visit was to give an excuse for Democrats, for a cash consideration, to sell out to Aldrich and vote for the treaty." [34] Several years later, when the Senate debated the Philippine tariff, Spooner reminded the Democrats that they had made possible the acquisition of the islands. Tillman disclaimed that Bryan's influence had been decisive. "You know," he shouted, shaking his finger at the Republican majority, "how these votes were secured." He had been assured by Republican sources, he declared, that "improper influences were used in getting votes." Questioned, he stated that the federal patronage of South Carolina had been parceled out since ratification. When McLaurin heard this, he called it a "willful, malicious and deliberate lie." Tillman sprang at his former protégé with tigerlike ferocity and landed a blow just above his eye. McLaurin met the attack courageously, hitting Tillman on the nose in the first exchange of fisticuffs in the Senate in fifty years.[35]

Much credit for convincing three of the four doubtfuls goes to Lodge. He wrote Roosevelt that "it was the closest, hardest fight I have ever known," and he modestly gave credit to Aldrich, Chandler, Hanna, Elkins, Hansbrough, and Carter, not to Bryan. He also complimented Gray for coming out "in a splendid way." "We were down in the engine room and do not get flowers, but we did make the ship move," he told Roosevelt.[36] Aldrich had proved exceedingly active in a desk-to-desk campaign, and the chauvinist Chandler had worked loyally to ratify the treaty.[37] Hanna wrote McKinley on February 7: "In securing the votes of McEnery and McLaurin yesterday I made myself your representative to the

[33] Congressional Record, 55 Congress, 3 Session, Vol. 32, Part 2, pp. 1529–1530.

[34] Pettigrew, Imperial Washington, p. 271.

[35] Sam Hanna Acheson, Joe Bailey, the Last Democrat (1932), pp. 155–156; Francis B. Simkins, Pitchfork Ben Tillman, South Carolinian (1944), pp. 8–9.

[36] Lodge to Roosevelt, Feb. 9, 1899, Lodge, Correspondence, I, 391–392.

[37] Pettigrew, Imperial Washington, pp. 204–205; Leon Burr Richardson, William E. Chandler, Republican (1940), pp. 570–571, 583–585.

extent of a personal plea, so if either should call at the White House today don't fail to express your appreciation of their acts." [38] When Cushman Davis congratulated McKinley on the ratification of the treaty, he said, "When you see Senator Elkins have him tell you about the struggle. I do not believe we could have secured ratification without him." [39] Pettigrew was so outraged by what he saw that he complained to Davis of "the open purchase of votes to ratify this treaty right on the floor of the Senate," including the "purchase" of one Democrat who had remained doubtful until the final session.[40] Lodge also knew of at least one Democrat who was offered a large bribe for a yea vote.[41] Gorman, too, was upset by "the way Hanna and his friends are working this treaty through the Senate. . . . All the railroad influence, which is being worked through Elkins, all the commercial interests and every other interest which can be reached are bringing pressure on Senators in the most shameful way. Some of the things they are doing transcend the bounds of decency." [42]

Erving Winslow, of the Anti-Imperialist League, believed that Bryan's visits to Washington strengthened the proponents of the treaty, yet no major metropolitan newspaper gave Bryan credit for ratification. We are also confronted with his own statement that he tried "to convince but not to control"; Teller's comment, "I have not written you . . . because I think you can change the situation here"; and Pettigrew's disclaimer of his influence. Yet evidence of partisan bias in the vote is so presumptive that when added to other contemporary evidence it becomes almost a certainty. It is impossible to divine how many Senators voted for the treaty for political reasons rather than for its merits. Rejecting the treaty meant rejecting the Philippines, repudiating McKinley, and throwing the treaty back into the uncertainties of international diplomacy. The action of the Senate was therefore not a fair test of its sentiment.

[38] McKinley Papers.
[39] *Ibid.*
[40] Pettigrew, *Imperial Washington,* p. 206.
[41] Lodge to Roosevelt, Feb. 9, 1899, Lodge, *Correspondence,* I, 391–392.
[42] Arthur W. Dunn, *From Harrison to Harding: A Personal Narrative, Covering a Third of a Century, 1888–1921* (1922), I, 282.

On the clear-cut issue of the annexation of the Philippines alone the expansionists would quite certainly have failed to muster a two-thirds majority.

Much credit for the ratification of the treaty must be given to McKinley. His views were probably unaffected by consideration for the ultimate welfare of the Filipino, but his narrowly partisan administration had created a condition in the Philippines which, even if unpremeditated, certainly influenced various Senators. That he saw political expediency in expansionism is readily understandable. Extensive patronage arrangements and promises of good committee assignments were made in his name, and the work of Hanna, Lodge, and Elkins has been recognized as even more effective than that of Bryan.[43] Moreover, resolutions favoring expansion passed by several state legislatures may have helped sway the Senators, as did the feeling of popular indignation provoked by the Filipino revolt, for opposition to the President's plan obstructed the army and was, in a sense, treason.

Although Roosevelt gave credit "partly to the Senate, partly to Providence, and partly to the Filipinos," [44] it was McKinley who had halfway won the Senate by appointing to the Peace Commission the chairman of the Committee on Foreign Relations, its next ranking majority member, and its ranking Democrat, and he had also impressed his views upon the country with tours of the Middle West and South late in 1898. Carnegie, for one, denied that the Philippine burden was chargeable to the war. He told Carl Schurz, "This is the President's own Pandora's box—this New Year gift to his country, for which he is alone responsible." [45] Lodge visited the White House frequently during the ratification fight and found McKinley "extremely anxious" but showing "great firmness of strength." Had the treaty been rejected, he would have called an extra session in the next twenty-four hours.[46] McKinley thus held the trump card all along, for the new Senate would have lacked

---

[43] *New York Journal*, Feb. 4, 1899; Hoar, *Autobiography*, II, 322–323; Garel A. Grunder and William E. Livezey, *The Philippines and the United States* (1951), p. 49; Weinberg, *Manifest Destiny*, p. 291.

[44] Roosevelt to Lodge, Feb. 7, 1899, Lodge, *Correspondence*, I, 390.

[45] Carnegie to Schurz, Feb. 10, 1899, Carnegie Papers.

[46] Lodge to Roosevelt, Feb. 9, 1899, Lodge, *Correspondence*, I, 392.

seven men who opposed the treaty. "Bryan let his friendliness for McKinley, his desire to do the right and good thing, and his love of peace euchre him into an embarrassing situation," concluded one of Bryan's biographers.[47] According to Merle Curti, "What Mr. Bryan actually did was to crown McKinley's success." [48]

Bryan remained convinced that his stand was correct. He was pleased with the passage of the treaty, for "ratification converts a foreign question into a domestic one. It takes the fate of the Filipinos out of the hands of diplomats and places it in the hands of Congress." Now the people could voice their opposition to the permanent control of the islands and crystallize opinion in favor of their independence.[49]

The Senate and McKinley decreed otherwise. There were before the Senate seven resolutions, Vest's denying the power of the United States to acquire overseas territory and six seeking to define Philippine policy. The authors of three of the latter, Bacon, Mason, and McEnery, had prodded the Senate for weeks to discuss their resolutions. After ratification, they redoubled their efforts, with the result that for another week the debate on expansion continued, with some hints dropping as to how and why the treaty had passed. Right after the vote on the treaty Aldrich moved to consider the McEnery resolution. Various amendments were proposed, including one by which Bacon's resolution would be added to McEnery's. On the next day Mason noted a manifest disposition not to have a vote, and Tillman intimated that some sort of agreement had been reached or pledge made to McEnery and McLaurin prior to the vote on the treaty. Allen had heard about such a pledge and inferred that it was made on the Republican side, and no Republican denied that such was the case. Gorman wrote Carnegie on February 9: "The result only shows the power of an Administration in controlling votes in the Senate. If the peculiar circumstances surrounding this case shall ever be generally known, it will be found that they excel anything which has heretofore occurred . . ." and Mason told the steel king, "The trade was made for four votes and

[47] J. C. Long, *Bryan, the Great Commoner* (1928), p. 131.
[48] Curti, "Bryan and World Peace," p. 132.
[49] Omaha *World-Herald*, Feb. 7, 10, 15, 1899.

on an absolute agreement to pass the McEnery resolution." Words
cannot be more specific.[50]

Another hint of pressure lies in Hanna's letter of February 9 to
McKinley: "When I got to the Senate today I heard that Senator
Lindsay was prepared to make a speech in favor of his resolution
in regard to the future relations with the Philippines. I wrote him
a note asking him to see you before doing so. Therefore if he calls
you will know what it is for." Furthermore, when Bacon and Mason
renewed their demands for a vote on their own resolutions, the
Senators appeared to be under restraint. Finally, on Mason's request for unanimous consent, the vote was set for February 14.
When a tie occurred on the vote to add Bacon's resolution to
McEnery's, Vice-President Hobart broke it by voting on the negative side. Party lines divided. While there was a preponderant
Democratic vote for the Bacon amendment, which would have
established Bryan's policy, the Republicans put over the McEnery
resolution, which was merely a pious hope expressed by twenty-six
Senators. Since the latter never reached a vote in the House, Philippine annexation was not accompanied by any formal declaration
of policy.[51]

Undismayed, Bryan continued his demand for a speedy declaration of a Philippine policy. We must reveal our purpose *before* the
Filipinos laid down their arms and not make the laying down of
their arms the condition upon which we would declare our purpose,
he asserted. The Filipinos were not inspired to insurgency by those
Senators who had opposed ratification; rather they fought because
the United States refused to announce its intention, because they
could see that they had accomplished nothing but an exchange of
masters, he declared. Then, on February 22, in a terse and epi-
grammatic speech entitled "America's Mission," he condemned the
immorality of imperialism and established the proposition that imperialism would be an issue in 1900 unless settled before then.

The conclusion that Bryan demanded the ratification of the

[50] Gorman to Carnegie, Feb. 9, 1899, Mason to Carnegie, Feb. 8, 1899,
Carnegie Papers.
[51] *Congressional Record,* 55 Congress, 3 Session, Vol. 32, Part 2, pp. 1154–
1848.

treaty in order to obtain a new "paramount" issue in 1900 is simply incorrect. He was a man of peace, one deeply fed by faith in Christian ethics and individualistic democracy. Unaware that McKinley had not exhausted diplomatic means of getting Spain to free Cuba, he had blessed America's going to war in the name of self-determination for an underdog. Nonetheless he had unequivocally declared his opposition to imperialism at a very early date; and he certainly would have opposed ratification if he had sincerely believed that ratification would impel the United States on a career of imperialism that would have completely negated his own moral outlook. He could have prevented ratification and the acquisition of the Philippines, and had he been a mere politician he should have opposed ratification because McKinley demanded it. The fact is that he did not need or want a new issue. He had issues enough, and he defied those Democrats who demanded that he make expansion another. He was wise enough to see that he could not enter the lists in 1900 with a party divided on a popular issue, and he fervently hoped that ratification would settle forever the question of imperialism and leave him free to campaign in 1900 on the issues left unsettled since 1896. Not until the Kansas City convention did he acquiesce in making expansion "paramount" and silver subsidiary. That he would have refused to run at all had not "16 to 1" been restated explicitly in the platform sufficiently attests to his devotion to his first love, silver.

Bryan's tactics with respect to the treaty backfired. Instead of the fast action needed to avoid armed conflict in the Philippines the Republican leaders stalled and threatened to have the treaty go over to the next session. If the treaty had failed, the whole problem would have been thrown back into McKinley's hands or into those of another peace commission. Firm believer in the people's capacity to solve all problems aright, Bryan wanted the people, not the executive, to pass judgment. The Senate passed the treaty but not a resolution stating the nation's purpose to grant the Philippines independence. Caught short, Bryan had no recourse but to submit a *fait accompli* to the people. Despite his making imperialism paramount in 1900, he was defeated.

Thus triumphed McKinley's shortsighted policy, one immediately responsive to the momentary whim of the people, one pregnant with reward for his party, one which the American public forgot in a few short years. Although the election of 1900 was not a mandate on imperialism,[52] Cushman Davis prated that "we did a great—a very great—thing for our country at Paris" and averred that the re-election of McKinley was "a vindication of his verdict" on expansion.[53] Bryan agitated for another fifteen years before his demand for a return to fundamental principles was in part answered by the Jones bill of the Wilson administration.[54] Toward the end of his life he wrote that he had "never regretted the position taken; on the contrary, I never showed more statesmanship than I did when I insisted upon the termination of the war and the making of the promise embodied in the Bacon resolution." [55] Not until he had been a decade in his grave, however, did the nation, once more under Democratic leadership, finally promise a full return to the basic democratic mission of the United States as he had defined it in 1898. In the long run, history upholds Bryan rather than McKinley.

[52] Thomas A. Bailey, "Was the Election of 1900 a Mandate on Imperialism?" *Mississippi Valley Historical Review*, XXIV (1937), 43–52.

[53] Royal Cortissoz, *The Life of Whitelaw Reid* (1921), II, 265.

[54] Bryan's consistent attitude is revealed in his *Commoner;* correspondence with President Wilson, Woodrow Wilson Papers (Manuscript Division, Library of Congress); and letter to Charles Burke Elliott of Nov. 5, 1915, in Elliott, *The Philippines to the End of the Military Regime* (1916), p. 378. See Roy Watson Curry, "Woodrow Wilson and Philippine Policy," *Mississippi Valley Historical Review*, XLI (1954), 435–452, and William Jennings Bryan and Mary Baird Bryan, *The Memoirs of William Jennings Bryan* (1925), pp. 465–466.

[55] Bryan, *Memoirs*, p. 121.

THOMAS A. BAILEY

○

The Election of 1900[1]

For a number of years a considerable body of historians has assumed that imperialism was the "paramount" issue in the campaign of 1900, and that McKinley's triumphant re-election was a generous endorsement of his policy of expansion. The origins of this interpretation are not difficult to trace. First of all, McKinley won by the largest popular plurality that a Presidential candidate had yet polled; and the party in power invariably but illogically interprets re-election as a blanket endorsement of all its deeds and misdeeds. Secondly, the Democratic platform stated unequivocally that imperialism was both the "burning" and the "paramount" issue. In his letter of acceptance Bryan stood squarely on this pronouncement, as did his running mate, Adlai E. Stevenson.[2] But

[1] This paper was read at the Chattanooga meeting of the American Historical Association, December 1935. It is based primarily upon the correspondence of Carl Schurz, Grover Cleveland, W. J. Bryan, Theodore Roosevelt, J. C. Spooner, W. E. Chandler, Henry White, and W. A. Croffut—all in the Library of Congress. Croffut was secretary of the Anti-Imperialist League. The McKinley MSS. in the Library of Congress yielded little. The editorial observations of ninety American newspapers (twenty-four of which were consulted directly, the others second-hand through magazines of opinion or other newspapers) proved useful.

[2] *Chicago Record*, September 18, 28, 1900.

Reprinted from Thomas A. Bailey, "Was the Presidential Election of 1900 a Mandate on Imperialism?" *Mississippi Valley Historical Review*, XXIV (June 1937), pp. 43–52. Reprinted by permission of the Organization of American Historians.

unfortunately for the historian the "paramount" issue is not always what the platform and the candidates announce it is going to be.

Seldom has this truth been better illustrated than by the campaign of 1900. Unforeseen economic developments had destroyed the effectiveness of the silver issue; but Bryan, whether through principle or through what he regarded as expediency, forced a free silver plank down the throats of a rebellious Democratic convention. This appears to have been a colossal blunder. It completely ruined whatever chances the Commoner may have had of carrying the gold standard East, particularly into the pivotal empire state. As Thomas B. Reed is reported to have drawled with his characteristic amiability, Bryan "had rather be wrong than president."

The silver plank was a godsend to the harassed Republicans. Driven into a defensive position by the embarrassing Philippine insurrection, they promptly and joyously assumed the offensive with the very weapon that Bryan had thrust into their hands. They could scarcely have asked for anything better than an opportunity to fight the campaign of 1896 over again. McKinley straightway took up the challenge and in his letter of acceptance insisted that currency was the "immediate" issue. The cyclonic Roosevelt, the Republican Vice-Presidential candidate, echoed these words in his letter of acceptance, and proceeded to rattle the metallic and horrendous skeleton of free silver with unprecedented ferocity.[3] In other words, each party had its own paramount issue, the validity of which the opposition vehemently denied.

It might be argued that because the McKinley ticket won by a plurality of 861,000 votes the sovereign American people decreed that money and not imperialism was the paramount issue. But such an explanation is far too simple to be satisfying. First of all it is undeniable that in any Presidential campaign a large percentage of the electorate is not concerned with the issues at all. In the year 1900 several million Republicans and several million Democrats were going to vote the straight party ticket whatever (within reason) the candidates or the issues. But it is a time-

[3] *Chicago Record,* September 10, 17, 1900. The Republicans probably would have stressed Bryan's free silver taint in any event, but the silver plank added immeasurably to the force of their counterattack.

honored American custom that parties must have issues. So millions of congenital Democrats worked up what enthusiasm they could over anti-imperialism; and millions of congenital Republicans became alarmed, or attempted to become alarmed, about free silver. The first task is to penetrate this jungle of verbiage and try to determine what issue or issues influenced the votes of those whose minds were open to conviction. In other words, what was the "decisive" issue?

This assignment is by no means a simple one, largely because of the multiplicity and confusion of the issues. Bryan opened the campaign with some heavy blasts about colonialism, imperialism, and militarism; but when he found his audiences singularly unresponsive he swung heavily to trusts, plutocracy, and special privilege. The Republicans emphasized the gold standard, the full dinner pail, continued prosperity, the tariff, patriotism, Bryanistic vagaries, populism, and class hatred. It would not, in fact, be difficult to make up a list of sixty subjects that were discussed during the campaign, ranging all the way from Crockerism to Pettigrewism and from the St. Louis riots to the Boer War. To add to the confusion ten different parties or political groups actively entered the canvass.

The quandary of the conscientious and intelligent voter cannot fail to arouse sympathy. Ex-president Cleveland wrote that he was "pestered to death" with anxious inquiries; and among his papers one may find dozens of letters from correspondents who asked not only for advice as to how to vote but for help in determining the issues.[4] The day before the election the *New York Evening Post* remarked editorially that it had never received such a large number of letters on the issues of a Presidential campaign. One may say in all seriousness that one of the important issues in 1900 was: "What is the paramount issue?"[5]

[4] Cleveland to D. M. Dickinson, October 12, 1900; Cleveland to W. S. Bissell, September 16, 1900, Cleveland MSS. See particularly W. A. Ownby to Cleveland, October 18, 1900, on which appears the penciled annotation, "Dozens like this."

[5] *New York Evening Post,* November 5, 1900. One cartoonist represented the campaign as being the great game of finding the paramount issue. *New York Tribune,* November 2, 1900.

There were many voters who earnestly desired to cast a ballot for both the gold standard and anti-imperialism. But to vote for McKinley and the gold standard was apparently to endorse imperialism; and to vote for Bryan and anti-imperialism was presumably to endorse free silver. Such a militant sound money man as Carl Schurz concluded that imperialism was the more immediate evil, and found himself faced with the "horrible duty" of working for Bryan, or rather against McKinley. On the other hand, ardent anti-imperialists like Andrew Carnegie and Charles Francis Adams regarded economic chaos as the more imminent danger and threw their support to McKinley. It is a significant fact that four of the most effective campaigners for the Republican ticket were leading anti-imperialists: Senators Hoar and Hale, and Representatives Littlefield and McCall.

A large number of Gold Democrats—how many will never be known—heroically voted for McKinley. They concluded that after the United States had first set its own house in order there would be time enough to turn to the Philippine problem.[6] In postelection statements McKinley, Roosevelt, and Hanna freely acknowledged their indebtedness to Democratic support. In fact, so generally recognized was this defection that the press made repeated references to the nonpartisan character of the victory.[7]

A considerable number of those who wished to cast a clear-cut vote against imperialism felt that their only opportunity lay in a third party; but for reasons that need not be discussed here this movement fell through. Others urged Bryan to come out with a ringing pledge not to disturb the gold standard if elected, thus narrowing the paramount issue down to imperialism. But Bryan, foolishly it appears, turned a deaf ear to all such advances.[8] Daniel M. Lord, of the American Anti-Imperialist League, found many

[6] See L. M. Beck to Cleveland, October 31, 1900, Cleveland MSS.; Schurz to E. M. Shepard, October 7, 1900, Schurz MSS.

[7] Philadelphia *Public Ledger,* November 7, 1900; *New York Evening Post,* November 10, 1900; *Indianapolis Journal,* November 7, 8, 1900; *New York World,* November 8, 1900. See also Roosevelt to James Bulloch, November 9, 1900; C. N. Douglas to Roosevelt, November 10, 1900; Roosevelt to Delos McCurdy, November 10, 1900, Roosevelt MSS.

[8] Schurz to Louis Ehrich, October 4, 1900; Schurz to E. B. Smith, October 7, 13, 1900, Schurz MSS.

anti-imperialists who had decided to vote for McKinley because of their greater fear of free silver; and he suggested to Schurz that a protest signed by several hundred thousand such people before the election would convince McKinley that he had not received a mandate to go ahead with expansion. Schurz replied that this plan would be desirable after the election; but if executed earlier it would merely serve to increase the McKinley vote by enabling the anti-imperialists to salve their consciences.[9] The *Springfield Republican* observed that the suggestion of voting for McKinley first and protesting afterwards won many votes for the Republicans, although, as this journal remarked, the cold figures in no way reflected the voters' "mental reservations." [10] So obviously misleading were the election returns that a number of newspapers called upon McKinley not to interpret the results as an endorsement of imperialism. Indeed, there is some scattered evidence to support the thesis, which obviously can neither be proved nor disproved, that if the question had been placed before the electorate solely on its merits the American people would have voted against retaining the Philippines.[11]

In the minds of many voters the problem was one of choosing the lesser of two evils: the platitudinous and presumably malleable McKinley (T. B. Reed's "Emperor of Expediency") or the heretical and rattle-brained Bryan. "Bryanism and McKinleyism!" exclaimed Cleveland, "What a choice for a patriotic American!" In the end thousands of voters cast their ballots for McKinley in spite of his Philippine policy—and hoped for the best. They preferred the known weaknesses of McKinley to the wild theories of Bryan. As a Nebraska editor wrote to Cleveland, "It is a choice between evils,

[9] D. M. Lord to Schurz, October 25, 1900; Schurz to Smith, November 5, 1900; Smith to Schurz, November 7, 1900, Schurz MSS. Lord wrote that almost without exception some fifty Republicans whom he had approached had expressed a willingness to sign such a petition.

[10] *Springfield Republican*, November 7, 1900.

[11] See similar view in A. C. Coolidge, *The United States as a World Power* (New York, 1908), p. 157; also Schurz to Howe, June 22, 1900, Schurz MSS.; *Cleveland Plain Dealer*, November 8, 1900. The *New York Herald* conducted a poll in fifteen of the largest cities in the United States. Of 726 voters interviewed, 324 favored and 333 opposed expansion. Figures cited in San Francisco *Argonaut*, July 23, 1900.

and I am going to shut my eyes, hold my nose, vote, go home and disinfect myself." The New York *Nation* suggested for a McKinley banner: "The Nation's Choice—of Evils." [12]

Although it is obvious that any campaign following the colorful crusade of 1896 would seem a tame affair, one is impressed with the fact that there was a marked falling off of the vote in 1900.[13] The general confusion over the issues, combined with a widespread disgust with both of the candidates, caused a considerable number of voters to stay away from the polls. This appears to have been the case with Grover Cleveland, who, according to one newspaper, planned to register his disgust by going duck shooting.[14]

The obvious lack of interest in the campaign was doubtless due in large measure to the fact that the Philippine issue was now more or less stale. The islands had already been under the stars and stripes for over two years; and the American public, leaping with characteristic avidity from one sensation to another, had apparently already begun to classify them among those things settled and accepted. E. V. Abbot noted the "languid interest" in the question of imperialism and observed that "the Republicans weariedly support the administration and the Democrats weariedly oppose it." [15] Moreover the Republicans were confident of victory; and Hanna, dissatisfied with his early efforts to "shake down" the plutocrats, complained that the big enemy of the party was none other than "General Apathy." Finally, in contrast with 1896, the country

[12] Cleveland to C. S. Hamlin, September 13, 1900, in Allan Nevins, ed., *Letters of Grover Cleveland, 1850–1908* (Boston, 1933), p. 536; J. S. Morton to Cleveland, November 2, 1900, Cleveland MSS.; *The Nation* (New York), CLXXI (1900), 302. See also R. F. Cutting to Herbert Welsh, October 2, 1900; Schurz to Shepard, October 7, 1900; C. W. Eliot to Schurz, October 4, 1900, Schurz MSS. The large protest vote polled by the minor parties is further evidence of disgust with the major party candidates.

[13] That is, relative to the increase in population. Only 64,710 more votes were cast in 1900 than in 1896. For election figures see Edgar E. Robinson, *The Presidential Vote, 1896–1932* (California, 1934), *passim*.

[14] Boston *Evening Transcript*, November 2, 1900. T. B. Reed, W. G. Sumner, and W. S. Bissell all expressed a determination not to vote. See A. W. Thurman to Schurz, October 9, 1900, Schurz MSS.

[15] Abbot to Schurz, October 5, 1900, Schurz MSS. C. F. Adams wrote that he was enjoying "the repose of this presidential election." Adams to Schurz, July 14, 1900, Schurz MSS.

was busy and prosperous, too fat and contented to be aroused to a high pitch of crusading zeal.[16]

It would not, in fact, be too much to say that prosperity was the keynote of the campaign. The closing years of McKinley's term afforded a striking contrast to the widespread distress of Cleveland's second administration. Mark Hanna was not unaware of the potency of stand-pattism and the full dinner pail when he solemnly asserted in an Omaha speech, "There is only one issue in this campaign, my friends, and that is, let well enough alone." [17] The deep-seated fear of Bryan that had been instilled by two extraordinary campaigns of education was abundantly reflected by the stock market, which experienced a tremendous boom immediately after the election. In the contest between the heart and the stomach the "belly vote," as one journal put it, won. The American people were interested primarily in hogs, corn, and wheat; and only secondarily in the Filipinos. Shortly after the election Bryan received a remarkable letter from his campaign manager, Senator James K. Jones of Arkansas, who deplored the heavy falling off of Democratic majorities in his state, and added, "In my own county, men who have voted the Democratic ticket all their lives, voted the Republican this time, openly boasted of it, and gave as the reason, that they did not want any more '5 cent cotton'." [18]

At this point it is possible to answer with some degree of confidence the question as to what was the "decisive" issue in the campaign. Assuming that Bryan had an outside chance to win, the issue that beat him was "Bryanism"—so-called by scores of opposition newspapers. Basically Bryanism was the fear that Bryan would destroy prosperity by overthrowing the gold standard and putting into effect his economic heresies. When the election was over dozens of newspapers insisted that the dread specter of Bryanism had

[16] Herbert Croly, *Marcus Alonzo Hanna* (New York, 1912), p. 328. See also Lodge to Henry White, September 3, 1900, White MSS.; Lodge to Roosevelt, August 30, 1900; H. C. Payne to Roosevelt, August 22, 1900, Roosevelt MSS.; Lodge to Roosevelt, August 18, 1900, Roosevelt to Lodge, August 22, 28, 1900, *Selections from the Correspondence of Theodore Roosevelt and Henry Cabot Lodge, 1884–1918* (New York, 1925), I, 473, 474, 475.

[17] *Public Opinion* (Washington), XXIX (1900), 548.

[18] Jones to Bryan, December 1, 1900, Bryan MSS.

brought about the result. Even the ebullient Roosevelt wrote with unaccustomed modesty that above McKinley, Hanna, and even himself, "it was Bryan . . . who did most" to bring about the result. That Bryan was a burden to the Democratic cause is further attested by the fact that in general he ran behind his ticket. The "great Commoner" himself admitted, after the election, that the prosperity argument was the most effective one used against him by the Republicans.[19]

One final word about imperialism. If it had been the only issue in the campaign, would the re-election of McKinley have been a clear-cut mandate? The answer still is, no. First of all "imperialism" and "anti-imperialism" were but vague catchwords that meant all things to all men, ranging from a permanent occupation of the Philippines to an immediate and cowardly surrender to Aguinaldo. Bryan certainly did not advocate the latter of these alternatives; but this was the interpretation forced upon him by the opposition, notably Roosevelt, who stormed about the country decrying the dastardly attempt to haul down the flag. Thus imperialism became inextricably identified with patriotism; and a number of voters who wished for ultimate withdrawal supported McKinley because they did not wish to uphold the blood-drenched hands of the enemy. After the election, Bryan himself said that although the prosperity argument was the most potent one used against him, the Republican cry, "Stand by the President" won many votes.[20]

Even if imperialism had been clearly defined and had been the only issue, Bryan's record inspired no great confidence in his willingness to withdraw from the Philippines. Whatever may be said in defense of his rather unexpected course in securing the ratification of the treaty with Spain, it is undeniable that he had begun the campaign on the high note of anti-imperialism and then had shifted to trusts. Such chameleonlike conduct was roundly

---

[19] Roosevelt to Lodge, November 9, 1900, *Roosevelt-Lodge Correspondence*, I, 479; *The Nation*, CLXXI (1900), 437; Schurz to Welsh, October 5, 1900, Schurz MSS.; R. F. Pettigrew to Croffut, November 13, 1900, Croffut MSS.; William J. Bryan, "The Election of 1900," *North American Review*, LXXI (1900), 789.

[20] *New York World*, November 9, 1900. In the Roosevelt collection there are several letters from Democrats who deserted Bryan because they felt that he was encouraging the Filipinos to fire on the American uniform.

condemned by the Republicans, including Charles Francis Adams, who remarked in disgust, "I cannot make out whether he is a knave or a fool." [21] And Cleveland wrote, "How do you know what such an acrobat would do on that question [imperialism] if his personal ambition was in the balance?" [22] In other words, many voters concluded, whether correctly or not, that Bryan was just a professional Presidential candidate who was paying lip service to a synthetic issue that might get him into office. The hands were the hands of Esau but the voice was the voice of Bryan.[23]

Even if Bryan had received a clear-cut mandate to withdraw from the Philippines, would his party have permitted him to do so? The recent Spanish conflict, with its fortuitous insular fruits, had in large measure been brought about by Democratic pressure; and although the solid South, for obvious reasons, was going to support Bryan, there was a notoriously strong imperialist sentiment in this section.[24] In addition, the patronage-hungry Democratic party could scarcely have been expected to achieve the self-denial of surrendering these new territories, with their scores of offices for deserving Democrats.[25] Nor did newly developed solicitude of the Democrats for colored peoples ring true to those who knew of conditions in the South. Apparently, as the Republicans taunted their opponents, charity began abroad. Although the Democrats were denouncing imperialism, their platform advocated a protectorate for the Philippines; and was not that imperialism? In fact,

[21] Adams to Schurz, July 14, 1900; Edward Holden to Schurz, November 10, 1900, Schurz MSS.

[22] Cleveland to Judson Harmon, July 17, 1900, Cleveland MSS. Schurz later called Bryan the "evil genius" of the anti-imperialist cause. C. M. Fuess, *Carl Schurz, Reformer* (New York, 1932), p. 366.

[23] See M. E. Curti, "Bryan and World Peace," *Smith College Studies in History* (Northampton, Mass.), XVI (1931), nos. 3–4, pp. 119 ff. for a scholarly yet rather favorable interpretation of Bryan's course at this time.

[24] J. B. Henderson to Croffut, August 23, 1900; Erving Winslow to Croffut, November 8, 1900, Croffut MSS.; Schurz to Winslow, July 22, 1900; Abbot to Schurz, October 5, 1900; Adams to Schurz, October 11, 1900, Schurz MSS; Roosevelt to Bulloch, November 9, 1910, Roosevelt MSS.; *New York Evening Post*, November 5, 7, 1900; Curti, "Bryan and World Peace," pp. 125–126.

[25] Franklin Carter to Welsh, October 2, 1900; W. G. Sumner to Welsh, October 2, 1900; Adams to Schurz, October 11, 1900, Schurz MSS.; Bissell to Cleveland, September 8, 1900, Cleveland MSS.

a number of observers insisted that the difference between the avowed programs of the two parties was so slight as to amount to a discussion of tweedledum and tweedledee. So it was that many voters, regarding the pronouncements of both Bryan and his party as untrustworthy and insincere, cast their ballots for McKinley because they felt that under his leadership the United States would be able to get out of the Philippines sooner than under that of Bryan.[26]

It seems reasonable to conclude, therefore, that the election of 1900 could not have been an endorsement either of McKinley's leadership in general, or of his policy of expansion.[27] One is even tempted to go a step further and add that because of partisan, personal, sectional, and a host of other domestic considerations, Presidential elections have never been and can never be a mandate on any question of foreign policy. Indeed, one wonders if these great quadrennial convulsions can ever be a mandate on anything.

[26] Carter to Welsh, October 2, 1900, Schurz MSS.; F. C. Lowell to Roosevelt, November 7, 1900, Roosevelt MSS. See also Adams to Schurz, July 14, 1900, Schurz MSS.

[27] As compared with 1896 Bryan's popular vote showed large gains in the East, particularly in Massachusetts, the stronghold of the anti-imperialists. But much of this was merely the return of disaffected elements to the party. McKinley gained heavily in the Rocky Mountain and Pacific Coast states, where it was presumed that the lure of oriental trade had created imperialist sentiment. This development, however, was probably due in large measure to Roosevelt's immense popularity, to the death of the silver issue, and to the return of disaffected elements to the party fold. Bryan carried Kentucky, which he had lost in 1896; but here the paramount issue was Goebelism, an outgrowth of factional politics.

WILLARD H. SMITH

✪

Bryan and the Social Gospel

Unlike most religious conservatives, particularly the fundamentalists, Bryan had a great concern for the social implications of his faith.[1] His association with the fundamentalists in his later years, therefore, brought him into contact with many who lacked his social concern, such as Billy Sunday who damned the social gospel, and George M. Price who stated: "When Christ himself was here, though surrounded by crying abuses, oppression, and tyranny, he attempted no civil reforms; nor has he left his church any commission to purify the governments of earth. . . ."[2] Carroll E. Harrington states that the Protestant churches in the 1880's rejected Moodyite revivalism in favor of social reform and adds that in "this rejection the Fundamentalist Movement had its origin." According to Harrington the fundamentalists had by 1912 dissociated themselves from contemporary religious, intellectual, and social affairs of the nation and now "stood at sword's point with the social reformers."[3] Here can be seen the wide gap between

[1] See Norman F. Furniss, *The Fundamentalist Controversy, 1918–1931* (New Haven, 1954), p. 27.

[2] George M. Price, *Back to the Bible or the New Protestantism*, rev. ed. (Washington, 1920), p. 218; Lawrence W. Levine, *Defender of the Faith, William Jennings Bryan: The Last Decade, 1915–1925* (New York, 1965), pp. 275–276.

[3] Carroll E. Harrington, "The Fundamentalist Movement in America,

Reprinted from Willard H. Smith, "William Jennings Bryan and the Social Gospel," *Journal of American History*, LIII (June 1966), pp. 43–60. Reprinted by permission of the Organization of American Historians.

Bryan and the fundamentalists on the need and desirability of social reform in the progressive era.

However, the question should be raised as to what extent the Commoner fits into the pattern of the social gospelers. The more the writer studies Bryan's social and religious thought, the more he feels that though Bryan does have some things in common with the fundamentalists, he also has a number of things in common with the social gospelers. In his *Protestant Churches and Industrial America*, Henry F. May writes about "radical social Christianity," "conservative social Christianity," and "progressive social Christianity." [4] Since these terms refer to political rather than religious radicalism and conservatism, Bryan fits most appropriately into the pattern labeled "progressive social Christianity." In discussing the development of the social gospel in Protestantism during the so-called gilded age, Charles Howard Hopkins points out that part of its heritage stems from evangelicalism.[5] In fact, from John Calvin in Geneva one can trace—through the Puritans, Jonathan Edwards, Charles G. Finney, and on into the gilded age and the progressive era—an evangelical line of leadership that had its Christian social concern. According to H. Richard Niebuhr, Walter Rauschenbusch (one of the greatest advocates of the social gospel) "was also largely dependent upon the evangelical tradition." Hence, even though one thinks of the social gospel as being based on a liberal theology, there was this evangelical side to it. Bryan stood in this tradition.[6] Bryan was not theologically trained, and so far as the record indicates he did not use the term "social gospel." He did, however, use the term "applied Christianity," and it is surprising how similar in this respect his vocabulary was

---

1870–1920" (doctoral dissertation, University of California, Berkeley, 1959), pp. 10, 45, 56.

[4] Henry F. May, *Protestant Churches and Industrial America* (New York, 1949), p. 12.

[5] Charles Howard Hopkins, *The Rise of the Social Gospel in American Protestantism, 1865–1915* (New Haven, 1940), p. 20. Timothy L. Smith also points this out in *Revivalism and Social Reform in Mid-Nineteenth-Century America* (Nashville, 1957), pp. 148–162.

[6] H. Richard Niebuhr, *The Kingdom of God in America* (New York, 1959), pp. 160–162. See also Guy Franklin Hershberger, *The Way of the Cross in Human Relations* (Scottdale, Pa., 1958), p. 77 ff.

to that of Washington Gladden and other well-known advocates of the social gospel. Also, the ideas expressed in Gladden's *Applied Christianity: Moral Aspects of Social Questions* and in his *Recollections* bear a remarkable resemblance to those of Bryan on applied Christianity.[7] To what extent Bryan read Gladden's works is not known. Bryan and Gladden did, however, correspond and were on friendly terms.[8]

The writer's success in locating additional significant amounts of correspondence between Bryan and the advocates of the social gospel has been somewhat limited. There is evidence that Charles M. Sheldon, the well-known Congregationalist minister of Topeka, Kansas, and author of *In His Steps,* was a good friend and correspondent of Bryan.[9] The editor of *The Public,* Louis F. Post, who can probably be classed as a social gospeler of a liberal sort, carried on a considerable correspondence with the Commoner. Post was a single-tax advocate and a supporter of Bryan.[10]

A few brief letters from Bryan to Richard T. Ely indicate that Bryan apparently approved of the work of this liberal economist and advocate of the social gospel. In one letter Bryan thanked Ely for sending him a copy of his *Political Economy* and added that he appreciated the merit of the work. In another, Bryan stated he had ordered Ely's *The Social Aspects of Christianity* and *Socialism* . . . and other books which Ely had recommended on French and German socialism and on monopolies and trusts. "It seems to me,"

---

[7] See, for instance, Washington Gladden, *Applied Christianity: Moral Aspects of Social Questions* (Boston, 1886), pp. 17–18, 34, 176–178; *Recollections* (Boston, 1909), pp. 18–19, 68–70, 101, 309, for his ideas on labor, monopolies, railroads, plutocracy, income tax, and gambling in stocks and produce.

[8] Some of this correspondence is in the Bryan Papers (Manuscript Division, Library of Congress).

[9] See, for instance, Charles M. Sheldon to Bryan, July 7, 1916, *ibid.,* Box 31; Feb. 28, March 12, 1921, Box 33; June 20, 1921, Box 34. In these letters Sheldon commends Bryan for his part in the 1916 Democratic convention, encourages him in his efforts to help strengthen the faith of young people in college, and negotiates with him for an article for the *Christian Herald* of which Sheldon was editor. See also Charles M. Sheldon, *His Life Story* (New York, 1925), pp. 177–178.

[10] These letters by both Bryan and Post are in the Louis F. Post Papers (Manuscript Division, Library of Congress).

wrote the Commoner, "that the practical, every day part of Christ's teachings is overlooked by many who profess to follow Him." Bryan concluded the letter by inviting the economist to come to Lincoln for a visit whenever he could, "and we can have a quiet talk together over the social problems which we have to meet." [11] It appears that Bryan's and Ely's ideas on social reform and applied Christianity were, in most respects, quite similar.[12] The lack of correspondence between Rauschenbusch and Bryan seems strange in view of their having so many common social interests, especially the common concern of keeping the United States out of World War I.[13]

Bryan did not feel it necessary to go as far in the direction of socialism as did such social-gospel advocates as Rauschenbusch, George D. Herron, and William D. P. Bliss. He was, however, sympathetic with the objectives of socialism and was willing to study it, to learn from it, and to accept it in part. He believed in a regulated individualism. "I believe that wherever competition is possible we ought to have competition." But socialism grows, he added, as individualism is abused. "The restoration of competition where competition is possible and the establishment of government ownership where competition is impossible will remove the dangers which are apprehended from socialism." [14] In the light of these principles, although not always urgently pressing all the points, Bryan favored such "socialistic" measures as municipal ownership of utilities, government ownership of railroad, telegraph, and telephone companies, government guarantee of bank deposits, and a system of old age pensions, or annuities as he called it. If there would be opposition to the last because of alleged socialism,

[11] Bryan to Richard T. Ely, Oct. 11, 29, 1901; May 25, 1903, Richard T. Ely Papers (State Historical Society of Wisconsin, Madison).

[12] See Theron F. Schlabach, "An Aristocrat on Trial: The Case of Richard T. Ely," *Wisconsin Magazine of History*, XLVII (Winter 1963–1964), 146–159.

[13] Conference with D. R. Sharpe, Pasadena, Calif., July 26, 1963. Sharpe, the private secretary and biographer of Walter Rauschenbusch, told the author he thought there was such correspondence, but he was unable to locate it.

[14] From an address before the state legislature of Washington, reported in *The Commoner*, March 1, 1907, pp. 1 ff.

he explained, "every cooperative effort of the government is open to that objection," including the post office.[15] The way to stop the spread of socialism and to protect property rights, Bryan often said, was to support reform and social justice.[16]

Many advocates of the social gospel were influenced by Henry George and the single-tax reformers, and in varying degrees the two frequently worked together. Bryan, though not espousing the single-tax doctrine, felt that he and the George group had much in common, and he did have many supporters among George's followers. Bryan wrote to Post that "I count you among the soundest as well as among the most discreet of many political advisors, and it always gratifies me to know that what I do has the stamp of your approval." [17]

Perhaps on no reform were the advocates of applied Christianity more united than on the need to bring about greater justice to labor. Though it is frequently and perhaps too glibly stated that Bryan represented agrarian progressivism rather than its urban counterpart, one nevertheless finds considerable discussion by Bryan of labor problems. Here again his concerns lay more closely to those of the advocates of the social gospel than to those of the fundamentalists. In many cases the discussions are remarkably similar.[18]

Bryan's interest in peace before World War I and his efforts during 1914–1917 to keep the United States out of war elicited a favorable response from several advocates of the social gospel, as well as from others who could not be so classified. Shailer

---

[15] *Ibid.*, Dec. 9, 1904, pp. 2–3.

[16] William Jennings Bryan, "Individualism *versus* Socialism," *Century Magazine*, LXXI (April 1906), 856–859; address by William Jennings Bryan at Cooper Union, April 21, 1908, Bryan Papers (Occidental College Library); *Saturday Evening Post* (n.d.) appearing in *The Commoner*, July 7, 1905, pp. 1–3. See also *ibid.*, Nov. 25, 1910, p. 6; Jan. 1919, pp. 1–2; Oct. 1919, pp. 6 ff.; Jan. 1920, p. 4; June 1920, p. 11.

[17] Bryan to Post, Nov. 12, 1904, Post Papers.

[18] Compare, for instance, Gladden, *Applied Christianity*, pp. 176–178, with the following: Bryan's Cooper Union address; William Jennings Bryan, *The Making of a Man* (New York, 1914), pp. 21–23; *The Commoner*, Jan. 23, 1901, p. 3; Feb. 28, 1902, pp. 1–2; March 7, 1902, p. 4; June 13, 1902, p. 4; Sept. 5, 1902, p. 3; March 20, 1903, p. 2; Sept. 15, 1905, pp. 1–2; Sept. 27, 1907, p. 2; Oct. 1919, p. 2; Aug. 1919, p. 5; June 1922, p. 3.

Mathews, prominent social gospeler of the University of Chicago
and president of the Federal Council of Churches, wrote Bryan
encouraging him to join the Henry Ford peace party in Europe
and do what he could to stop the war.[19] Others, such as Gladden,
George Foster Peabody, Charles Stelzle, Charles S. McFarland,
and the fundamentalist, William E. Biederwolf, likewise encouraged Bryan in his peace position. Like Mathews, the last three had
official positions in the Federal Council of Churches, which had
recently supplemented its earlier strong statement of Christian
social concern with one of concern for peace and a speedy termination of the war.[20]

Bryan's relationship with the Council was cordial, and it continued in this spirit into the postwar period when the lines between
the liberals and fundamentalists became more closely drawn. "It is
a fine thing to have men like yourself friendly to the work of the
Council and loyal to it," wrote Stelzle in 1916.[21] When addressing
the Baltimore Ministerial Union in 1919 Bryan paid this tribute to
the organization: "I am glad to indorse what has just been said in
regard to the activities of the Federal Council of Churches. It is,
in my judgment, the greatest religious organization in our nation.
It gives expression to the conscience of more than seventeen million members of the various Protestant churches; its possibilities
for good are limitless; its responsibilities are commensurate with
its opportunities." [22] In 1922 Robert E. Speer of the Council
thanked the Commoner for his "generous contribution" to the
cause.[23] On a number of occasions Bryan was asked to address
meetings of the Council, the last time being at Atlanta only a few
months before his death.[24]

In addition to the factors previously discussed which con-

[19] Shailer Mathews to Bryan, Oct. 11, 1915, Bryan Papers, Box 30.
[20] See Gladden to Bryan, July 4, 20, 1916, Bryan Papers, Box 31; George
F. Peabody to Bryan, Jan. 15, 1914, Box 29; Charles Stelzle to Bryan, Dec.
26, 1916, Box 31; Charles S. McFarland to Bryan, Dec. 20, 1916; William
E. Biederwolf to Bryan, June 22, 1915, Box 30.
[21] Stelzle to Bryan, Dec. 26, 1916, *ibid.,* Box 31.
[22] *The Commoner,* May 1919, p. 11.
[23] Robert E. Speer to Bryan, July 27, 1922, Bryan Papers, Box 35.
[24] Abstract of address (on "Peace"); McFarland to Bryan, June 10, 1925,
ibid., Box 40.

tributed to the development of the Commoner's Christian social concern, there should be added his admiration for Count Leo Tolstoi. The spirit of this great Russian thinker is frequently manifested in the speeches and writings of Bryan. Having heard so much of this man, Bryan made it a point to visit the Count in his home during a trip to Europe in 1903. The Nebraskan was so deeply impressed that, according to one story, he remained with the Count longer than planned and had to telegraph Czar Nicholas II, postponing a scheduled meeting with him.[25] Not only Tolstoi's pacifism—which apparently had a not unimportant effect on the development of Bryan's own ideas on peace—but the Count's ideas on work, poverty, wealth, social classes, and religion also left their mark on the American visitor and no doubt helped confirm in his mind the applicability of the teachings of Jesus to the everyday affairs of life.[26] Some years later, in reply to a letter from Bryan, Tolstoi wrote that he followed the Commoner's career in the newspapers and added: "I wish with all my heart success in your endeavor to destroy the trusts and to help the working people to enjoy the whole fruits of their soil. . . ." [27] In view of Tolstoi's questionable theological orthodoxy, no strict fundamentalist would have spoken and written so admiringly of the great Russian as Bryan did.

To what extent Bryan's Christian social concern was shaped and developed by his reading cannot be determined precisely. Bryan had a library containing several thousand volumes and there is evidence that he did considerable reading.[28] References in his

[25] Countess Alexandra Tolstoi to author, July 16, 1963; Alexandra Tolstoi, *Tolstoy, A Life of My Father* (New York, 1953), p. 432. There is some evidence that Bryan had seen the Czar before the appointment with Tolstoi, but it is clear that Bryan was impressed and visited Tolstoi much longer than intended. See *The Commoner*, Feb. 5, 19, 1904; Paolo E. Coletta, *William Jennings Bryan. 1: Political Evangelist, 1860–1908* (Lincoln, 1964), pp. 317–318.

[26] William Jennings Bryan, "Tolstoy, The Apostle of Love," *New York Journal* (n.d.), printed in *The Commoner*, Feb. 19, 1904, pp. 3, 6. See also *ibid.*, June 17, 1904, pp. 1–2.

[27] William Jennings Bryan and Mary Baird Bryan, *The Memoirs of William Jennings Bryan* (Philadelphia, 1925), pp. 460–461.

[28] William Jennings Bryan, Jr. to author, Jan. 31, 1964. Mrs. Bryan complained that when her husband was home from his travels he spent his time

speeches and writings to many authors and their works support
this contention although one occasionally gets the impression that
Bryan was so busy writing, traveling, and lecturing that he did
not have sufficient time to read deeply on any given subject. Being
the reformer that he was it is natural to expect, as apparently was
the case, that many of his books were of the reform type. In addition to many references in his speeches and writings to this type of
literature, there are in the Bryan Papers in the Library of Congress
two lists of books from the Bryan library containing more than two
hundred titles dealing with reform and the social gospel. One list is
entitled "Political Reform Books" with the following subdivisions:
"Upon Bimetallism," "Anti-Trust Books," "Socialistic Works,"
"Works of Fiction," "The Land Tax," "Books Upon the Labor
Issue," "Religio-Sociological," "Direct Legislation," "Government
and Municipal Ownership," "Anti-Imperialist Books," "Political
Economy," and "Populistic Books." The second list, simply called
"Book Inventory" and more general in character, also contains
many items on social reform. The two lists include such well-known
works on social reform and the social gospel as Henry D. Lloyd's
Wealth Against Commonwealth; Thomas More's *Utopia*; Edward
Bellamy's *Looking Backward* and *Equality*; Benjamin Kidd's *Social
Evolution*; J. P. Putnam's *The Kingdom of Heaven Is at Hand*;
Christ the Socialist (author not given); George's *Progress and
Poverty* and *The Land Question*; Ely's *Social Aspect of Christianity, Socialism . . .* , and *The Labor Movement in America*;
Herron's *Works*; Sheldon's *In His Steps*; Josiah Strong's *The Twentieth Century City* and *Our Country*; Jacob Riis's *The Children of
the Poor* and *How the Other Half Lives*; Rauschenbusch's *Christianity and the Social Crisis*; Jane Addams' *Democracy and Social
Ethics*; Tolstoi's *Works* (12 volumes); and Post's *Social Service*
and *Ethics of Democracy*. In addition, many books on reform that
influenced the social gospel advocates are listed.[29] These lists, it
would appear, have no little significance for they probably repre-

---

reading and writing. Mary Baird Bryan to Charles W. Bryan, Nov. 24, 1917,
Bryan Papers (Occidental College Library).
[29] These lists are in Boxes 23 and 51.

sent the works from which Bryan got many of his reform ideas, including those on applied Christianity or the social gospel.[30] In discussing such a list one must include the Bible, which of course he always put first as a source and guide for social action.

With these apparent influences in the background one turns naturally to Bryan's ideas on the role of the church in the social order—the central concern of the advocates of the social gospel. From an early date Bryan believed that religion included the whole of life and could not be compartmentalized. The church must not only preach the gospel to save individuals, but it must cry out against the evils of the day and help bring about a better society. And this required the cooperation of all, laity and ministers. Much as he admired the clergy, Bryan felt the work of the layman was just as important in the kingdom of God. When he was a student in college, his pastor's wife tried to interest him in the ministry. His defense for not going into that work was the quotation from Proverbs: "To do justice and judgment is more acceptable to the Lord than sacrifice." [31] Many years later, after Bryan's third defeat as a Presidential candidate, the Reverend French E. Oliver wrote an open letter to him pleading with him to go into the ministry and become an evangelist. "I am firmly convinced that one ambassador of Christ of your calibre is worth more to this nation than ten thousand presidents," wrote Oliver. But the politician could not agree and replied that the work of the reformer was not to be despised, for the Christian in public life had the opportunity to apply the principles of Christianity to contemporary problems. No doubt entered the Commoner's mind as to his duty. "The war is not over," he wrote. "It can not end while there is an abuse to be remedied or a public good to be secured." [32] Once Bryan was asked whether politics could be conducted on Christian principles and whether a politician could be a Christian. He unhesitatingly answered yes, of course, and added that to "love one's neighbor

[30] William Jennings Bryan, Jr. remembered seeing some of these titles in his father's library but of course not all of them. Letter to author, Jan. 31, 1964.

[31] Bryan and Bryan, *Memoirs*, p. 49.

[32] "Mr. Bryan's Work," *The Commoner*, Nov. 27, 1908, p. 2.

as himself is no more a drawback in political life than in a business career.[33]

To Bryan loving one's neighbor as one's self was only half of the Christian formula (the other being to love God with all one's soul, heart, and mind), but it was a very important half. It was the rationale of his Christian social concern and responsibility. Addressing the ministers of Baltimore on "Applied Christianity," Bryan said:

Love of one's neighbor is the only visible proof that can be given of love of God. Praise of God and prayers to God cannot convince, because we hear but one side of the conversation. We are much more interested in knowing God's opinion of a man than we are in knowing the man's opinion of God, and we cannot understand what God's opinion of a man is except as we see him translate his love of God into service to man. Love of neighbor, therefore, is not only a proof, but the only proof that man can furnish to those about him, of his love of God. . . . If a man says he loves God and hates his brother he is a liar. . . . How can a man love God whom he hath not seen if he loves not his brother whom he hath seen? [34]

In an article on "Christian Citizenship" in 1903, in which he discussed the civic duties of the followers of the Nazarene, Bryan said that too many have been so absorbed in contemplating the rewards and punishments beyond that they have ignored the rewards and punishments to be enjoyed or suffered here. Christ, in reviewing the ten commandments, condensed the six which refer to man's duties to his fellowmen into one great commandment, "Thou shalt love thy neighbor as thyself," which, "if fully lived up to, would solve every problem economic, social, political, and religious. Is it not wise," Bryan continued, "to give more emphasis than we have to the manward part of Christ's teachings?" He then quoted approvingly the question put by James Gowdy Clark, "whose songs have been such an inspiration to reformers," when he asked: "How long, O Lord, how long / Shall creeds conceal

[33] Omaha *World-Herald*, June 6, 1897.
[34] *The Commoner*, May 1919, p. 11.

thy human side, / And Christ the God be crowned in song, / While Christ the man is crucified." [35]

This then was the basis of Bryan's strong faith and belief that Christianity had much to say and do with man's life and conduct in the present world. His writings contain innumerable statements to the effect that many Christians have mistaken views on this point. Only a few can be given for illustrative purposes. An editorial, "The Old Pulpit and the New," in the Omaha *World-Herald* which editor Bryan probably wrote, stated that:

Preaching the word must cover a vast field. It is a mistake to suppose that the function of the pulpit is confined within the explanation of the plan of salvation. The Bible does not justify any such conclusion —that is, not for the new pulpit. Only about one-fifth of the writings of the apostles are devoted to the plan of salvation, and all the rest are instructions for man's conduct of life—how he shall live—therefore, whatever touches the ethics of life in the world, directly, is the proper theme for the pulpit of today, and that, too, without reference, except incidentally, to life hereafter. Moreover, it is the duty of the new pulpit to set in motion moral and reformatory forces that shall penetrate to the very center of practical politics or to the center of any other stronghold of political vice and misrule. The new pulpit should be in all sorts of current life, but not of it.[36]

To a "Chinese gentleman" who attacked Christianity because it was too much concerned merely with the contemplation of heaven, Bryan wrote that if the gentleman thought Christ occupied the time of his disciples by discussing the beauties of heaven to the neglect of the present world, he had better reread the Scriptures. "You will discover that the Master seldom referred to the future life but continually emphasized the relations which exist between man and man." [37] In an address entitled "The Larger Life," which Bryan gave on several occasions, he noted that "Sometimes the Christian has placed too much emphasis, relatively, upon

[35] *Ibid.*, Jan. 16, 1903, pp. 1–2.
[36] Omaha *World-Herald*, March 10, 1895.
[37] Grace Dexter Bryan, "William Jennings Bryan," 422, MS., Bryan Papers, Boxes 64, 65.

the future and not enough on the present . . . where Christ spoke once of the world to come, He spoke ten times of man's present relationship to his fellowmen. People used to search the scriptures, and then retire from society and in seclusion seek to prepare themselves for future bliss; now they are coming to understand that to walk in the footsteps of the 'Man of Galilee' they must go about doing good." [38]

In an important article written for *Public Opinion* in 1905, Bryan similarly emphasized that religion, formerly occupied mainly with the contemplation of the unknown future life, was now concerning itself more and more with the present life. "The emphasis is being placed upon the here rather than upon the hereafter." Immortality, he continued, is not to be sought by withdrawal from society, but by actively rendering " 'unto the least of these,' his brethren, the service that the Master was anxious to render unto all." [39]

Since, as Bryan argued, it was the duty of the church to apply Christian principles to the problems of the day, he pleaded over and over that the ministry and laymen must go to work and bring about reforms that would do away with abuses and injustices. "The Church must lead in all moral reforms or forfeit its claims to confidence," he wrote in one of his syndicated Sunday-school lessons. "A heart can be changed in a moment and, therefore, a nation can be born in a day." [40] When one congregation was considering whether to ask its minister to resign because he was too much involved in attacking and trying to remedy the social evils of the community, the Commoner came to his defense, saying: "Surely one must be very blind to the church's obligations if he condemns a minister for interesting himself in the work of social reformation. What is a church for if it is not to stand for morality in all things and everywhere?" [41]

No matter what the nature of the reform was—whether it had to do with taxation, trust regulation, labor, the monetary system, peace and disarmament, temperance, anti-imperialism, woman's

[38] *The Commoner*, June 7, 1912, pp. 2–3.
[39] "The Next Awakening," *Public Opinion*, 38 (May 27, 1905), 805.
[40] *The Commoner*, Dec. 1922, p. 11.
[41] *Ibid.*, Aug. 20, 1909, p. 1. The minister involved was Morton Culver Hartzell, pastor of the South Park Avenue Methodist Church in Chicago.

suffrage, or with the government structure—the church must speak out, wrote Bryan. "These questions are before us. They cannot be avoided; they must be settled, and church members must take their part in the settlement; ministers also must have a voice in this work." [42] On profiteering, for example, of which there was too much at all times and especially during World War I, Bryan felt so strongly that he laid the matter before the Presbyterian General Assembly in its 1920 session. He suggested the churches ought to take the lead in arousing public opinion against the crime of profiteering. He pointed out that the profiteers would be going to the penitentiary someday, and he thought it would be embarrassing "to have a sheriff enter a prominent church and take a prominent member from a prominent pew and show that he has been stealing from all the rest of the congregation." Bryan argued that all profiteers should be driven out of the Presbyterian Church so that "when they go to the penitentiary, they will not go as Presbyterians. There should be no Presbyterian ward in the profiteer prison." [43] And in 1919 in an open letter to the churches of the United States Bryan wrote: "Do you not see the growing antagonism between Capital and Labor? . . . Can the churches be indifferent to such a result? . . . Capital and Labor *must be brought together.* . . . Can you neglect this great opportunity—aye, this great duty?" [44]

Bryan made it clear that the teachings of Christ applied also to the structure and administration of government as well as to the life and conduct of the individual.[45] He was explicit that the means to be used to bring about the better social order were political as well as religious. "Christian men *must* take an interest in politics," he wrote to an inquiring friend. They are responsible for the wrong they permit as well as for what they actually advocate.[46] It is not only the Christian's duty to vote, "but it is his duty to vote right." Voting right means that he must be careful not to support parties and candidates that stand for policies which would result in the

[42] Christian Citizenship," *ibid.*, Jan. 16, 1903, pp. 1–2; *ibid.*, May 1921, p. 1; Oct. 1919, p. 2; May 1919, p. 11.

[43] *Ibid.*, Sept. 1920, p. 8.

[44] *Ibid.*, Oct. 1919, p. 2.

[45] *Ibid.*, May 1919, p. 12.

[46] Bryan to Bryan N. Railsback, Dec. 29, 1920, *ibid.*, Jan. 1921, p. 2.

few living in luxury and the many struggling for a bare existence. "Whenever God is as faithfully served at the ballot box as He is in the church," Bryan optimistically concluded, "it may be depended upon that the era of trusts, of imperialism, of spoliation and of corruption will be at an end, and the probability of evils in our public life will be reduced to the minimum." [47]

The opposition of the Commoner to trusts and monopoly is, of course, well known. In few if any areas were his moral thunder and criticism hurled with greater force than in these. Here too the church was to take its unequivocal stand. The greatest task, he said, was to protect "God-made man from the man-made giant. . . . Can we, as Christians, be indifferent if this man-made giant tramples upon the rights of the God-made man?" [48] And what about these man-made giants and the men connected with them, many of whom call themselves Christians? More particularly what about gifts from these questionable sources to such worthy institutions as churches and colleges? The Commoner took a dim view of such gifts and of the donors. Many blasts of criticism against plutocrats and financial racketeers are to be found in his speeches and writings. Noting the lack of ethics in high finance, he remarked: "The thimbleriggers at a street fair are engaged in more honorable business for they cheat openly, but these thimbleriggers of high finance rob the helpless and the dependents under the guise of doing an honest business." [49]

No business received more barbed shafts from Bryan than did the Standard Oil Company and those connected with it, especially John D. Rockefeller. This company, according to Bryan, was guilty of all the crimes in the calendar and the men connected with it acted upon the same principles as the burglar and highwayman. Standard Oil money was tainted, he added, and no church or college should soil its hands with it.[50] Urging people to read Lloyd's *Wealth Against Commonwealth,* Bryan remarked: "If but a few of the facts set forth in [this book] are correct, no criminal

[47] *Ibid.,* Nov. 2, 1906, p. 9.
[48] *Ibid.,* May 1919, p. 12.
[49] *Ibid.,* July 14, 1905, p. 1.
[50] *Ibid.,* March 31, 1905, p. 3.

now incarcerated in the penitentiary for larceny has shown more indifference to human rights and property rights than this same Rockefeller." [51] Bryan was opposed to receiving such money not only because he felt it came from tainted sources but also because it might have the effect of silencing criticism of trust methods. The Morgans, the Rockefellers, and the Schwabs, he said, attempt to coerce the church and "have silenced many a tongue that ought to be thundering in high places and against larceny on a grand scale." The sanctimonious sinners who robbed their neighbors all week could not cover up their sins by piously contributing a part of their plunder to the church.[52] Similarly, Bryan did not think it was possible for the sinners to cover up their sins by religious preachments and prayers. Rockefeller, said Bryan, made pious remarks about religion and then raised the price of oil! Noting that the Standard Oil leader had addressed a Sunday school in Cleveland, the Commoner remarked: "Many people will wonder how Rockefeller summons courage to preach so much religion while he practices so much sin.[53]

In 1905 when Gladden led a group of Congregational clergymen in opposing a gift of one hundred thousand dollars offered by Rockefeller to the Congregational Board of Foreign Missions, Bryan leaped to Gladden's defense and wrote additional articles against accepting tainted money.[54] Rockefeller's record, Bryan contended, "shows extraordinary moral obliquity. He had so long accustomed himself to putting money-making above ethical considerations that he can bankrupt a competitor through the rebate system, bribe a college with a donation or evade a court summons with equal complacency.[55] Bryan's opposition to educational institutions accepting tainted money involved him in conflict with his alma mater, Illinois College, and the University of Nebraska. Bryan

---

[51] "Monopoly and the Church," *ibid.*, Nov. 29, 1901, p. 2; "Gifts From Monopolists," *ibid.*, June 5, 1903, p. 3.

[52] *Ibid.*, April 15, 1904, p. 2.

[53] *Ibid.*, Dec. 4, 1903, p. 1; Aug. 24, 1906, p. 4.

[54] *Homiletic Review*, XLIX (May 1905), 345–347; "The Next Awakening," *Public Opinion*, 38 (May 27, 1905), 807; *The Commoner*, April 7, 1905, pp. 6–7; April 14, 1905, pp. 1, 2, 15.

[55] *The Commoner*, Sept. 22, 1905, pp. 1–2.

had been asked to become a member of the board of trustees of his alma mater but refused to do so until the college terminated an affiliation arrangement with the University of Chicago. Bryan had no love for this "institution which Rockefeller is backing." He feared that the affiliation arrangement gave the University of Chicago "a partial supervision over the studies taught at the college," and he believed that his alma mater ought to be "independent of the Rockefeller influence and free to teach economic truth without fear or favor." In order to get Bryan on the board, Illinois College authorities terminated the agreement with the University of Chicago. Through the columns of *The Commoner* Bryan praised Illinois College for its courage, and he advised parents who had boys to educate that they could send them to this institution with the assurance that their minds "will not be biased in favor of organized wealth by teachers who receive their daily bread from the hands of the beneficiaries of the trusts." [56] Later, however, the same problem arose again when President Charles Henry Rammelkamp wanted to apply for Rockefeller and Carnegie grants. Bryan refused to listen to any plan for aid from either source and resigned from the board.[57] Similarly, Bryan opposed the acceptance of a Carnegie or Rockefeller grant by the University of Nebraska. "This Carnegie fund is the most insidious poison that now threatens our nation. It will do more harm to us than all the efforts of the millionaires." [58]

Another point on which Bryan was much closer to the social gospelers than to the fundamentalists was that of his ideas of progress. May has pointed out that the fundamentalists in the progressive era, thinking that the reform approach was all wrong, felt themselves surrounded by enemies of a bewildering variety and were very pessimistic about the chances of saving their contemporaries. Since many of them were premillennialists they were of the opinion that trying to bring about a better social order was wasted effort. Only Christ's second coming would usher in the

[56] *Ibid.*, Jan. 27, 1905, p. 2.
[57] Charles Henry Rammelkamp, *Illinois College: A Centennial History, 1829–1929* (New Haven, 1928), pp. 464–465.
[58] *The Commoner*, Feb. 5, 1909, pp. 4–5; Feb. 26, 1909, p. 1.

thousand-year reign of peace. May then remarks, with exaggeration: "The righteous minority would then be given the chance, from Heaven, to watch the revilers and backsliders suffer. This was the only prospect that put Fundamentalists, in the Progressive era, in a relatively cheerful frame of mind." [59] For Bryan this pessimistic mood was completely out of character. He seemed as naively optimistic about continued world improvement and progress as any of the advocates of the social gospel. For Bryan this progress would come through spiritual or Christian means, but not through apocalyptic millennialism. For one thing he was not a stickler for millennialism, and certainly not for premillennialism. Bryan is reported to have told Clarence True Wilson on one occasion that "there are so many people who do not believe in the first coming of Christ that we ought not to worry them about the second coming until we can get them to accept the first." Wilson thought this statement was worth its weight in gold and hoped the Commoner would not give his support to the extremists who were dividing into pre- and postmillennial camps, the "worst misinterpretation of the Scripture that curses our generation." [60]

Bryan's optimism and faith in progress were founded on a Bible-based morality and Christianity back of which stood an eternal God. He was fond of quoting the Scripture which says: "One with God shall chase a thousand and two shall put ten thousand to flight." [61] Bryan felt that he, or any Christian reformer, was that one with God. An abundance of evidence of Bryan's optimistic faith in progress is available in his speeches and writings. Only a few examples can be given.

In his address to the Ministerial Union in Baltimore in 1919 he asked whether those who believed in the power of God and had taken their oaths at His altar had "any doubt that every righteous cause will triumph, and that God's arm is strong enough to bring victory to his side?" [62] The Commoner talked and wrote a great deal about conscience and moral sentiment. In one of his

[59] Henry F. May, *The End of American Innocence: A Study of the First Years of Our Time, 1912–1917* (New York, 1959), pp. 128–129.

[60] Clarence True Wilson to Bryan, Nov. 3, 1923, Bryan Papers, Box 38.

[61] *The Commoner*, May 1919, p. 12.

[62] *Ibid.*, pp. 11–12.

Chautauqua lectures in 1920 he said: "Law is but the crystallization of conscience; moral sentiment must be created before it
can express itself in the form of a statute." And everyone who
helps quicken the conscience of others helps the community.[63]
Years earlier he wrote that as the conscience of an individual can
be aroused and change him from a fiend into a ministering angel
so the conscience of a community, state, or nation "contains
dynamic force sufficient to destroy any threatened evil and to
propagate any needed truth." [64] In an article written for the *Saturday Evening Post* in 1907 he stressed the point that there was
a moral awakening in the world, and its effects were especially
noticeable in this country "in the growth of altruism, in the increase in church activity, in the larger consideration given to soci-
ological subjects and in the demand for a nearer approach to justice
in government." [65]

Bryan's trip around the world in 1905–1906 seems to have confirmed his optimism and faith in progress. Speaking before the
American Society in London on the return journey he declared
there was never so much altruism in the world and never so much
of a feeling of brotherhood. "I have felt more pride in my own
countrymen than ever before as I have visited the circuit of schools,
hospitals and churches which American money has built around
the world. The example of the Christian nations, though but feebly
reflecting the light of the Master, is gradually reforming society." [66]
In a great address at the Edinburgh World's Missionary Conference
in 1910 Bryan expressed his optimism on the progress of Christianity in solving the world's problems and in promoting world
brotherhood. Reporting on the conference for *Outlook,* he wrote:
"The old faiths are crumbling and Christianity is destined to take
their place." [67] The optimism exuded by Bryan in a Jefferson birth-

[63] William Jennings Bryan, "But Where Are the Nine?" *ibid.,* Sept. 1920,
p. 8.
[64] "The Next Awakening," *Public Opinion,* 38 (May 27, 1905), 805; "A
Conscience Campaign," *The Commoner,* Jan. 22, 1904, p. 2.
[65] William Jennings Bryan, "The Moral Awakening," *Saturday Evening
Post,* 179 (Dec. 15, 1906), pp. 3–4.
[66] *The Commoner,* July 6, 1906, p. 2.
[67] *Ibid.,* Aug. 19, 1910, pp. 1 ff.; *The Outlook,* XCV (Aug. 13, 1910), 824.

day speech in 1911 indicated that the millennium was at hand: intelligence and intellectual capacity were increasing; educational standards were rising; moral standards were improving; people were studying ethics as never before; the spirit of brotherhood was abroad in the land; there was more altruism than ever before; the tide was running in favor of democracy; the peace movement was spreading; reason was asserting itself; and moral forces were taking control. "The morning light is breaking. Day is at hand." [68] At Boise, Idaho, in March, 1912 he spoke in similar vein: "The era of the brotherhood of man is not coming. It is here now." [69]

Bryan, like many other progressives and advocates of the social gospel, was deeply shocked and disturbed by the outbreak of World War I. A strong opponent of war for many years, he was, as Secretary of State, in the midst of his efforts to negotiate his peace treaties when the war came. He became even more troubled as it appeared increasingly probable that the United States would enter the conflict. He was opposed to our entry into the war because he thought war was wrong and un-Christian, and also because he thought it would halt the march toward progress.[70] Disappointed as he was, his faith and optimism were too deeply ingrained to be long suppressed. In September, 1917 he was saying that democracy was growing stronger and monarchy weaker. "Some day, democracy will prevail everywhere—hail the day!" [71] The Democratic defeat of 1920 did not discourage him: "Let no Democrat despair. Today clouds conceal the shining sun," but there have never been so "many people yearning for reform as there are today." [72] In an interview given the press on his sixty-first birthday in 1921 he expressed gratification and satisfaction with the enactment of so many of the reforms for which he had battled. "God is on His throne," he said, "and the teachings of the prince of peace exert

---

[68] *The Commoner*, April 21, 1911, pp. 1 ff. This address, prepared by Bryan for the Jefferson birthday banquet April 13 in Indianapolis, was read by someone else since the Commoner had to attend the funeral of his friend, Tom Johnson. See also the article, William Jennings Bryan, "The Passing of Plutocracy," in *ibid.*, April 14, 1911, p. 1, for similar statements.

[69] Boise *Capital* (n.d.), printed in *ibid.*, March 8, 1912, p. 3.

[70] Levine, *Bryan*, pp. 59–60.

[71] *The Commoner*, Sept. 1917, p. 3.

[72] *Ibid.*, Nov. 1920, p. 2.

an increasing influence on the hearts of mankind." [73] The Democratic gains made in the election of 1922 encouraged the Commoner, and he reported that progressive sentiment was growing.[74]

Even Bryan's fight against modernism and evolution, as Levine
has well pointed out, is to be interpreted partly in the light of his
fear of the influence these theories might have had in slowing up
the march toward social reform and progressivism.[75] This was not
a new fear on the part of Bryan although it is true that he began
to act on it in the 1920's more than formerly. As early as 1905
he saw the possible detrimental effect of social Darwinism on reform and progressivism. In that year, Edward A. Ross, then teaching at the University of Nebraska, found Bryan reading *The Descent of Man*. Bryan told him that such teachings would "weaken
the cause of democracy and strengthen class pride and the power
of wealth." [76] This conviction of Bryan was confirmed when after
World War I he read Vernon Kellogg's *Headquarters Nights*, a
book which purported to show that the philosophy of the Germans
was "a crude Darwinism ruthlessly applied to the affairs of nations." [77]

In giving more attention to religious subjects in the 1920's
Bryan did not admit that he was giving up politics and political
means to attain the good society. He simply was using both approaches. A cartoon published in the Chicago *Daily News* in
1922 portrayed Bryan as abandoning the elephant hunt to pursue
the monkey, Darwinism, into the jungle. When the cartoon came
to the attention of Bryan, he wrote the cartoonist a friendly letter
saying that exaggeration is legitimate but "if you would be entirely
accurate you should represent me as using a double-barreled shot-
gun, firing one barrel at the elephant as he tries to enter the
treasury and another at Darwinism—the monkey—as he tries to

[73] New Haven *Union* (n.d.), printed in *ibid.*, April 1921, p. 13.
[74] *The Commoner*, Dec. 1922, p. 1.
[75] Levine, *Bryan*, pp. 254, 268–270.
[76] Edward Alsworth Ross, *Seventy Years of It: An Autobiography* (New
York, 1936), p. 88.
[77] Richard Hofstadter, *Social Darwinism in American Thought, 1860–1915*
(Philadelphia, 1945), p. 173.

enter the schoolroom." [78] "I am as deeply interested in politics as I ever was," stated Bryan in 1923 when announcing his candidacy for delegate to the Democratic national convention in 1924.[79] He joined the antievolutionists not to retreat from politics but to "combat a force which he held responsible for sapping American politics of its idealism and progressive spirit." [80]

In conclusion, as one looks at the entire life of Bryan, it can be said that he did stress religion and orthodoxy more in his later years, but he also retained a progressive spirit and a lively concern in the application of Christian social teachings to the world order.[81] Viewing evolution rather narrowly in terms of Herbert Spencer and William Graham Sumner, Bryan was repelled by the type of struggle and competition implied in the term "survival of the fittest." This, he felt, could not be reconciled with his ideas of reform, social justice, and applied Christianity.[82] The picture which a number of writers have left to the effect that Bryan started out as a liberal and ended his life as an ultraconservative and a reactionary is hardly correct.[83] An ultraconservative in the 1920's, while denouncing evolution, would hardly have advocated, as did Bryan, progressive labor legislation; liberal tax laws; government aid to the farmers; public ownership of railroads, telegraph, and telephones; federal development of water resources; government guarantee of bank deposits; two additional federal departments of education and of health; a federal law preventing profiteering; and, under certain circumstances, state-owned and operated gasoline filling stations.[84] Nor would an ultraconservative

[78] Bryan to Mr. Brown, March 31, 1922, contained in editorial in Chicago *Daily News*, April 14, 1922.

[79] Miami *News-Metropolis*, Nov. 1, 1923.

[80] Levine, *Bryan*, p. 270.

[81] *Ibid.*, p. 251.

[82] See William Jennings Bryan, *In His Image* (New York, 1922), Chap. 4, esp. pp. 107–110, 123–126, 130, 133–134.

[83] See, for example, Paxton Hibben, *The Peerless Leader: William Jennings Bryan* (New York, 1929), p. 369. The present writer also heard the social historian, Timothy L. Smith, make a similar statement in an address at Goshen College, Nov. 19, 1964. See also Timothy L. Smith to author, Nov. 24, 1964.

[84] Bryan to Gov. John W. Martin (Florida), Feb. 10, 1925, Bryan Papers,

likely have written as follows about the Supreme Court decision in 1922 which struck down the federal law attempting to prohibit child labor: "It has been hailed as a victory for state rights but it is no such thing; it is a victory for capitalism whose greed coins the blood of little children into larger dividends." [85]

It can also be said that Bryan was religiously orthodox throughout his life, but he did not emphasize his orthodoxy as much before World War I as he did afterward. Finally, taking his life as a whole, it can be said that his sensitive social concern and great reform activity aligned him more closely with the advocates of the social gospel than with the fundamentalists. Since his fundamentalist activity was associated primarily with the last few years of his life, and partly misunderstood at that, so many people remember this and forget the other.

Box 40; Levine, *Bryan,* p. 364; "A Few Needed Reforms," statement in Bryan Papers, Box 50. This statement is unsigned and undated but the handwriting is clearly that of Bryan, and the context indicates it was written in the 1920's. There are numerous articles by Bryan in *The Commoner* in the postwar period on his plan for government ownership and operation of the railroads. See, for examples, *The Commoner,* Dec. 1918; Jan., May, Oct. 1919.

[85] *The Commoner,* June 1922, p. 3.

Bryan and the Progressives

The years between the turn of the century and 1917 have come
to be known in American history as the progressive era. This was
a period when the nation seemed to awaken from slumber as a new
dawn chased away shadows of venality and selfishness from political and economic life. He who does what is true, reasoned Americans, comes to the light, and they were ready to believe that the
rosy tints sweeping over the landscape emanated from the light
that shone more and more unto the perfect day. The dawn symbolized progress, for progress was as pervading and as inevitable
as the dawn. Progressivism was not peculiar to any single element
of American society. It was a mass movement encompassing populistic agrarianism and urban humanitarianism, rural radicalism
and respectable middle-class reform. Its philosophy could not be
expressed in neat, consistent, logical formulae; it was without
dogmatic structure, if not without dogma.

Admittedly the progressive impulse was so complex as to defy
generalization. For purposes of analysis, however, the classification
proposed by Richard Hofstadter is helpful. There were, he suggests, two broad influences in progressive thought, one formed out

Reprinted from Paul W. Glad, *The Trumpet Soundeth, William Jennings
Bryan and His Democracy, 1896–1912* (University of Nebraska Press,
1960), pp. 110–117, 120–128, 133–139. This chapter is an expanded and
modified treatment of a paper read at the May 1957 meeting of the Mississippi Valley Historical Association. The paper, "Bryan and the Urban
Progressives," appeared in *Mid-America*, XXXIX (1957), pp. 169–179.

of the agrarian tradition, and the other shaped by what were primarily urban developments.[1] Never really becoming identical, the two influences often overlapped and appeared to merge. To contrast the disciples of Bryan with the apostles of Roosevelt is to contrast one type of progressivism with the other, and one of the supreme ironies of the Commoner's political career is that he found himself in opposition to men whose feelings at many points matched his.

The identification of urban with rural progressive thought was made easier by the agrarian bias of most reformers and their tendency to shape programs with a view toward the West. T.R. wooed and won the heart of middle-class America, both in the cities and on the farms. That a newspaper editor from Emporia, Kansas, should give articulate expression to Roosevelt's opinions is a monument to the universality of their appeal. Yet in spite of similarities between the two strands of progressive thought, differences did exist, and Bryan labored to make them apparent to his compatriots. He was not entirely successful in his opposition to the Roosevelt administration, but his efforts aided the reform movement which was his primary concern.

The Commoner was perceptive in detecting the apparently unimportant differences in stress and emphasis which were evidence of a significant difference in mentality between the urban progressives and the rural wing of the movement for which he was the spokesman. That he sensed the difference in mentality also seems likely, but he never spelled it out in specific terms. He neither probed deeply into the philosophical assumptions of his opponents, nor felt compelled objectively to ask why they held the views they did. He was not searching for understanding of American urban development; he was far more concerned with meeting arguments than with finding reasons for their existence. He was, furthermore, only remotely connected with the problems of urban life. He had been reared in a rural environment, he established his permanent residence in a state with economic interests that were overwhelmingly agricultural, and the moralism of the Middle Border had profoundly

[1] Richard Hofstadter, *The Age of Reform: From Bryan to F.D.R.* (New York, 1955), p. 133.

influenced his thought. Although he had great sympathy for the industrial laborer and shaped his platforms to appeal to workers, this sympathy was not the result of firsthand experience, careful observation, or thorough investigation.

Bryan's attitudes were grounded in his emotions rather than in reason. When he followed the dictates of his heart rather than his mind, Bryan was romantic, and his ready acceptance of the farmer's cause in the populist period indicates a romantic temperament. He did not offer proof that the "gold ring" or the "money power" had deliberately set out to bilk the farmer of his just rewards. He only saw that the stout-hearted pioneer men and women who had braved the elements in establishing homesteads on the plains were suffering, and relying on his intuition, he concluded that much of their suffering was the result of heartless and callous exploitation. The Commoner was sensitive to social wrongs, just as revivalists have been sensitive to sin. The parallel can be extended. The revivalistic solution for evil is conversion, and Bryan sought to convert Americans, particularly those living in the metropolitan centers of the East where Satan was most active.

On the afternoon of August 8, 1896, Bryan boarded the train to begin a journey that would take him to Madison Square Garden for official notification of his nomination. It was a dramatic moment: the Boy Orator brought to mind the youthful David going out to slay Goliath. In response to calls for a speech, he said:

In ordinary times I would have desired to have the notification take place at my home. But this is not an ordinary campaign, and, feeling that the principles in which we are interested should rise above any personal preferences which we may have, I expressed the desire to be notified in New York, in order that our cause might be presented first in the heart of what now seems to be the enemy's country, but which we hope to be our country before this campaign is over.[2]

Not only would the giants of Wall Street be slain, but conversion would occur on a grand scale. The devil would be defeated, the enemy's country would be won, and the people would be saved. The incident illustrates Bryan's approach to social and economic

[2] William Jennings Bryan, *The First Battle* (Chicago, 1896), p. 300.

problems: what the nation needed was not analysis of the causes of injustice but conversion to reforms that would restrain evil.

Progressive leaders of urban mentality were also concerned with placing limitations on wrongdoing; they too spoke in moral terms. Yet their method of dealing with wickedness tended to be realistic rather than romantic or revivalistic. Well-educated and moderate, they encouraged painstaking investigation and fact-finding; unlike Bryan and his agrarian followers, they distrusted emotion and placed their faith in reason. In the preface to his little book *Sin and Society,* which had great appeal for the urban progressive, Edward Alsworth Ross wrote:

This book deals with sin, but it does not entreat the sinner to mend his ways. It seeks to influence no one in his conduct. It does seek to influence men *in their attitude toward the conduct of others.* Its exhortation is not *Be good,* but *Be rational.* To modify conduct one touches the heart. To modify the judgements on conduct one speaks to the intellect. The latter is the method of this book. Its aim is to enlighten rather than to move.[3]

The Commoner preached a message of love and taught that America would progress to the fulfillment of her mission when conversion permitted love for man to rule in every heart. The urban progressives espoused a scientific humanism. "Your pious leanings are not in accord with the progressive reform and regenerative movement of the age," wrote one of Bryan's correspondents.[4] Such men believed that progress would come through the exercise of man's rational faculties, that if social evils were to be eliminated it would be as the result of scientific investigation.

Bryan and the urban progressives therefore developed differing conceptions of reality. When the latter undertook the investigation of slum conditions, the frauds perpetrated by political machines, the manipulations of financiers, and the widespread vice that flourished in rapidly growing cities, they came to the conclusion that evil-doing was universal. Every class, every interest group, every section was directly or indirectly responsible for failure to realize

[3] Edward Alsworth Ross, *Sin and Society* (New York, 1907), p. vii.
[4] H. G. Day to Bryan, January 24, 1901, Bryan Papers (Manuscript Division, Library of Congress).

in full the promise of American life. The urban progressives saw dangers in powerful labor unions as well as in powerful trusts; they condemned passivity to corruption as well as corruption itself. Bryan, with his invincible faith in the common man, believed that wrongdoing was the work of a vicious few. Reality for him included the dignity of those who earned their bread by the sweat of their brow as well as the utter depravity of a few conspirators of great wealth and power who had selfishly appropriated what rightfully belonged to the sons of toil. Repeatedly Bryan drew upon this view of reality, as he did when dashing off his comment on "Frenzied Finance," Thomas Lawson's widely read muckraking series dealing with operations of the stock market:

Mr. Lawson's phrase, "Frenzied Finance," is too mild. Conscienceless finance is a more accurate description of what goes on in Wall street. "Frenzied" would imply an excitement so intense as to temporarily suspend the operation of the reason, but some of the Wall street transactions are *deliberately contrived schemes* for deception and pillage.[5]

The rapid industrialization of the United States after the Civil War brought a train of abuses deplored by both urban and rural progressives and figuring prominently in their respective conceptions of reality. Just as these views on reality differed, so also did urban and rural reactions to postwar economic developments differ. The nationalizing of business was accompanied by a status revolution in which the old gentry of long-established wealth and social position saw itself being replaced by the new captain of industry as a controlling power in American life. According to Professor Hofstadter, this displacement was the motivating force behind the political activities of urban progressives.[6] What evidence supports his contention? Statistical studies by George Mowry and Alfred D. Chandler, Jr. reveal that with few exceptions progressives belonged to the middle class, that most were college graduates, that they held positions of responsibility in the professions and in business, that many of them came from old and respected families, that the ma-

---

[5] *The Commoner*, January 20, 1905. Italics mine. See Thomas Lawson, "Frenzied Finance; The Story of Amalgamated," *Everybody's*, XII, XIII, XIV (January 1905–February 1906).

[6] Hofstadter, *The Age of Reform*, pp. 135–138.

jority belonged to Protestant churches with a New England background, and that a great many opposed Bryan in 1896.[7]

No doubt such substantial and respectable men felt threatened by the parvenu who had acquired great power in industry, and no doubt they were attracted to a movement that promised to control him.[8] At this point the interests of urban and rural progressives coincided; both wished to curb the malefactor of great wealth, albeit for slightly different reasons. The yeoman farmer of the Jeffersonian tradition had disappeared; at least the most powerful and influential population groups were no longer agrarian. The populist effort was after all an attempt to regain what farmers thought had been lost as a result of the machinations of the money power. If the urban progressives felt the pressure of a status revolution, the rural progressives believed they had already experienced one. While one group appealed to those who had something to lose, the other felt that something had already been lost. This sense of loss—or impending loss—made both wings of the progressive movement susceptible to the virus of nativism.[9]

Immigrants poured into the United States in unprecedented numbers between the turn of the century and the outbreak of World War I, but it was not size alone that distinguished this human tidal wave. It came at a time when Western farmers still nursed some of the xenophobia left over from populism, and when the urban gentry exhibited concern over loss of status. Unlike earlier migrations, this one for the most part was made up of peoples from southern

---

[7] George Mowry, *The California Progressives* (Berkeley, 1951), pp. 87–88; George Mowry, *The Era of Theodore Roosevelt* (New York, 1958), pp. 86–87; Alfred D. Chandler, Jr., "The Origins of Progressive Leadership," *The Letters of Theodore Roosevelt*, 8 vols. Elting Morison and John M. Blum, eds. (Cambridge, Mass., 1951–1954) VIII, 1462–1465.

[8] A penetrating contemporary comment on the middle-class protest of the early nineteenth century may be found in Walter Weyl, *The New Democracy* (New York, 1914), pp. 242–249. See also Hofstadter, *The Age of Reform*, pp. 146–148; Mowry, *The Era of Theodore Roosevelt*, pp. 95–96.

[9] John Higham, *Strangers in the Land, Patterns of American Nativism, 1860–1925* (New Brunswick, N.J., 1955), pp. 4–11. Higham here defines nativism as "intense opposition to an internal minority on the ground of its foreign (i.e., 'un-American') conditions." This opposition, he points out, was directed against supposed revolutionaries, Catholics, and certain racial groups.

and eastern Europe; by 1907 about 80 per cent came from Italy, Austria-Hungary, Poland, and Russia.[10] Although the wave struck the American coast with prodigious force, it did not have the momentum to carry a majority of these people beyond Eastern cities and out to farmlands of the Middle Border. The shock of its impact was felt throughout the country, however, and it seemed all the more severe because in religion most of the immigrants were either Roman Catholic or Jewish.

Religion for the newcomer was a way of life providing continuity with the past. For this reason churches of the "Little Italys" and "Little Polands" and synagogues of the ghettos tended toward conservatism; permanence of form offered security in a world of uncertainty.[11] The rural progressives were so far removed from metropolitan slums that they were not much concerned with the psychological or spiritual needs of those who lived there. They probably could not have seen religion through immigrant eyes anyway, for their own churches were Protestant, their denominational affiliations were tenuous, and theirs was the optimistic and moralistic faith of the Middle West. The nativism that sometimes characterized rural progressive thought was therefore in large measure a reaction to immigrant religion. Like many of the populists who believed Jewish bankers were a part of the Lombard Street–Wall Street conspiracy against them, rural progressives could be anti-Semitic. They were, however, more likely to be alarmed by what they regarded as the Catholic menace, which was usually in some way or other associated with the money power; nativism among the followers of Bryan was most commonly directed against Rome.[12]

Urban progressives were also troubled by the immigrant, his outlook, and his institutions. They were, of course, much closer to problems resulting from the congestion of various ethnic groups in some of the least desirable sections of large cities. Huddled there in

[10] Roy L. Garis, *Immigration Restriction, A Study of the Opposition to and Regulation of Immigration into the United States* (New York, 1927), pp. 204–208; Carl Wittke, *We Who Built America* (New York, 1945), pp. 406–407.

[11] Oscar Handlin, *The Uprooted* (Boston, 1952), pp. 124–129; Marcus Hansen, *The Immigrant in American History* (Cambridge, Mass., 1942), pp. 90–91.

[12] Higham, *Strangers in the Land*, pp. 178–182.

squalor and poverty, immigrants were easy prey for machine politicians. Progressives of the cities, with their yearning for good government, were deeply disturbed, and they enlisted in the effort to facilitate Americanization of newcomers. But the great gulf fixed between immigrants and reform groups in metropolitan areas was difficult to bridge. The immigrant regarded political relationships as fundamentally personal, and he remained indifferent to the abstract appeals of urban progressives. Efficiency, system, order, balanced budgets, improved administration, and lower taxes were rejected by the slum-dweller. He wanted humanity, not balanced budgets; sympathy and assistance, not efficiency and order; mercy without justice, not justice without mercy.[13] And for all the graft and corruption associated with city machines, this much can be said for them: they did understand the immigrant mind and they did provide help when help was needed. "I stick to my friends high and low, do them a good turn whenever I get a chance, and hunt up all the jobs going for my constituents," said George Washington Plunkitt of Tammany Hall.[14] Here was an approach the immigrant could comprehend, and when reformers attacked the boss, they served only to clothe him in the Lincoln green of Sherwood Forest and surround him with the prestige of a Robin Hood.

Disappointed in the results of their efforts, some of the urban progressives accepted nativist myths. Others, with a devotion to duty that commands respect, continued to labor in the slums and in settlement houses. In spite of racism and nonsense in both its branches, the trend of the progressive movement was in the direction of at least a theoretical acceptance of the immigrant. Lincoln Steffens and Frederick Howe pointed out that not all the shame of the cities was attributable to the newcomer. Bryan often meliorated the extreme nativist views of his supporters. . . .[15]

[13] Handlin, *The Uprooted*, pp. 218–221; Hofstadter, *The Age of Reform*, pp. 180–184; *The Public*, I (May 7, 1898), p. 3.

[14] William L. Riordan, *Plunkitt of Tammany Hall*, Roy V. Peel, ed. (New York, 1948), p. 63. See also Lincoln Steffens, *The Shame of the Cities* (New York, 1957), pp. 205–206.

[15] E. A. Ross, who was closely associated with both urban and rural progressives, is perhaps the most conspicuous for his racist views. See Ross, "The Causes of Race Superiority," *Annals of the American Academy of Political and Social Science*, XVIII (1901), 67–89; Ross, *Social Control*

Although nativism could be found in both progressive types, the xenophobia of the Midwest was religious in emphasis, while in the cities it had other—often racist—characteristics. This phenomenon helps to explain the divergence between the urban and rural mentality. Racism can have a pseudoscientific rationale, and most of the racist arguments rested on what purported to be scientific foundations. The religious opposition to immigrants, on the other hand, resulted in part from the cluster of romantic and sentimental ideas that made up the faith of the Middle Border.[16] The differences between urban and rural progressive leaders who did not succumb to nativism are even more important as well as more suggestive of the same dichotomy. Seeking rational solutions to immigration problems, urban reformers stressed the duties of citizenship, demanded that newcomers meet their responsibilities, engaged in slum clearance, and provided settlement houses for the underprivileged. The rural progressives who followed Bryan would use even nativists in the war against sin; they fought conspiracy, not environment.

Much of Bryan's opposition to Theodore Roosevelt can be traced to the contrast between rural and urban attitudes toward reform. Although a member of that class threatened by status revolution, Roosevelt was, to be sure, an imperfect symbol of the urban progressive impulse. He was certainly not one to view public issues with calm, scientific detachment. Muckrakers such as Ray Stannard Baker, John S. Phillips, and Charles Edward Russell, who prided themselves on their objectivity, thought him too partisan

---

(New York, 1916), pp. 28–35; Ross, *The Old World in the New* (New York, 1914), *passim;* Ross, *Seventy Years of It,* pp. 223–229. For comments on the nativist elements in the progressive movement, see Mowry, *The Era of Theodore Roosevelt,* pp. 92–94; Eric Goldman, *Rendezvous with Destiny* (New York, 1952), pp. 77–79.

[16] The best-known racists such as Madison Grant and Henry Cabot Lodge were conservative. Further, racism was not as widespread in the urban East as it was in the South or on the Pacific Coast. Yet Theodore Roosevelt, E. A. Ross, and other progressives often pointed to Anglo-Saxon or Teutonic superiority over other races. Higham, *Strangers in the Land,* pp. 131 ff., 175–182; Oscar Handlin, *Race and Nationality in American Life* (New York, 1957), pp. 57 ff.

and ambitious to further significantly the cause of reform.[17] To many reformers he seemed no less equivocal than most politicians. "Mr. Roosevelt's reconstructive policy does not go very far in purpose or achievement," admitted Herbert Croly in 1909. But at the same time he added that "limited as it is, it does tend to give the agitation for reform the benefit of a much more positive significance and a much more dignified task." [18]

In this strange combination of positive force with moderation and dignity Roosevelt typified an important segment of progressive thought. His violence was usually expressed in words, not deeds, but it was not without influence. It served to provide Americans with a kind of moral purgative. To the urban progressive mind the psychic function of reform became increasingly important as the movement gained momentum. William Allen White thought that Roosevelt was "a force for righteousness" because his power was a spiritual one.[19] While they did not think in terms of conversion, progressives of metropolitan mentality, like agrarian reformers, sought an awakened conscience for America.

Legislative or material results, desirable though they always seemed, were not the sole object of urban progressive endeavor. In 1900 *The Public* printed a fable:

Once upon a time some Reformers, looking very ferocious, came upon some Ordinary Persons. All this in a certain large and populous town.

"Can you show us any tiger's tracks?" asked the Reformers.

"We can show you a tiger," replied the Ordinary Persons.

"All we want is tracks!" protested the Reformers, and went their way with much noise and were presently elected to fat offices, it being possible to fool enough of the people enough of the time.[20]

Urban progressives sought tracks and they found them; yet they often did not take the lead in suggesting means of preventing tigers

[17] C. C. Regier, *The Era of the Muckrakers* (Chapel Hill, N.C., 1932), p. 198.

[18] Herbert Croly, *The Promise of American Life* (New York, 1909), p. 167.

[19] W. A. White, "Roosevelt: A Force for Righteousness," *McClure's Magazine*, XXVIII (January 1907), 393; Hofstadter, *The Age of Reform*, pp. 210–212.

[20] *The Public*, III (May 26, 1900), 107.

from running about. Their programs were moderate, for they trusted tigers to behave once their tracks had been exposed to public scrutiny. Meanwhile, Bryan believed that he had treed a tiger. Having done so, he could not see much point in tracking its spoor; it should be killed or caged, he thought, and he called on "the people" to aid him in disposing of the beast. Roosevelt with his forceful language and moderate policies was a representative product of urban progressivism. Bryan, leading agrarian progressives, helped to bring about action by constantly demanding it.

T.R.'s debt to the Commoner has often been noted.[21] And the points at issue between the two were, in William Allen White's view, "so entirely technical, so nice in their adjustment, that it will strain democracy to its utmost to furnish public wisdom to see the truth and keep the demagogue's foot off the scales." [22] Yet while differences between the programs advocated by Bryan and Roosevelt may have been subtle, they should not be obscured by similarities. Apart from the obvious fact that the support which each man received came from different sources, there was sufficient conflict on public questions to encourage debate and criticism.

The most fundamental disagreement concerned foreign policy, where Bryan's desire for world peace ran counter to the bellicose imperialism of the Rough Rider. Perhaps Henry Blake Fuller was unfair when he suggested that T.R. delighted in "the spatter of brains upon the plains—and the gore that is mushy and thick." [23] Nevertheless, it was the combative side of Roosevelt's character that drew some of Bryan's sharpest criticism. The Commoner thought the strenuous life, as defined by T.R., was a reversion to a barbaric conception of virtue, for it placed "physical courage above mental greatness and moral worth." He was scandalized

[21] Hofstadter, *The Age of Reform*, pp. 132–133; Paxton Hibben, *The Peerless Leader: William Jennings Bryan* (New York, 1929), p. 260; Henry F. Pringle, *Theodore Roosevelt* (New York, 1931), pp. 368–370; George E. Mowry, *Theodore Roosevelt and the Progressive Movement* (Madison, Wis., 1946), p. 33; Arthur W. Dunn, *Gridiron Nights* (New York, 1915), pp. 154–156. These are only a few of the many works that make this point.
[22] White to Roosevelt, October 16, 1908, William Allen White Papers (Manuscript Division, Library of Congress).
[23] Quoted in F. H. Harrington, "Literary Aspects of Anti-Imperialism," *New England Quarterly*, X (1937), 655.

when Roosevelt told the cadets at West Point, "A good soldier
must not only be willing to fight; he must be anxious to fight." This
"fit of animal enthusiasm," thought Bryan, "revealed a moral de-
formity which must shock such of his friends as are not wholly
carried away with the bloody and brutal gospel of imperialism." [24]

The evidences of brutality in Roosevelt's character are less significant than the relationship between imperialism and the progressive movement. Many of the progressives were, in fact, carried
away by the "bloody and brutal gospel." [25] Herbert Croly, who
was highly influential in shaping urban progressive opinion, believed that "the irresponsible attitude of Americans in respect to
their national domestic problems may in part be traced to freedom
from equally grave international responsibilities." The United
States was manifestly justified in assuming responsibilities in Cuba
and Puerto Rico. The Philippines constituted a more expensive obligation and their possession seemed to result in no obvious benefits
to the United States. But Croly argued that they did have a peculiar
value: they helped "American public opinion to realize more
quickly than it otherwise would the complications and responsibilities created by Chinese political development and by Japanese
ambition." Croly did not urge war for its own sake, nor did he
plead for American intervention where the interests of the United
States were not involved. He did contend that if the nation wanted
peace, "it must be spiritually and physically prepared to fight for
it." His argument—one that many progressives found attractive—
was that "peace will prevail in international relations, just as order
prevails within a nation, because of the righteous use of superior
force." [26]

In the first decade of the twentieth century not many reformers
associated, as did Bryan, the fight against imperialism abroad with
the fight for progressivism at home. On the contrary, most of them
found a certain harmony between the ideological content of im-

[24] *The Commoner*, August 8, 1902.
[25] William E. Leuchtenburg, "Progressivism and Imperialism; The Progressive Movement and American Foreign Policy, 1898–1916," *Mississippi Valley
Historical Review*, XXXIX (1952), 483. See also *Public Opinion*, XXXV
(October 1, 1903), 421.
[26] Croly, *The Promise of American Life,* pp. 308–312.

perialism and that of progressivism. Roosevelt refused to consider American withdrawal from the Philippines because the Filipino would "wallow back into savagery." He believed that in working for the Panama Canal despite objections from Colombia he was "certainly justified in morals, and therefore justified in law." In his famous "Corollary" to the Monroe Doctrine, he said that the American desire "to see all neighboring countries stable, orderly, and prosperous" might require intervention in their affairs.[27] Brandishing his "Big Stick," the President leaped onto the horns of a dilemma: it was sometimes impossible to combine humanitarian ideals with imperialistic or nationalistic aspirations. And when urban progressives were faced with a choice between the two, they usually chose imperialism or nationalism. Herbert Croly, for example, was highly critical of Tolstoi. The saintly Russian had "merely given a fresh and exalted version of the old doctrine of nonresistance, which, as it was proclaimed by Jesus, referred in the most literal way to another world. In this world faith cannot dispense with power and organization." [28]

On the home front the struggle between Bryan and the urban progressives centered around the problem of organization. This conflict demanded consideration of two basic questions: how far big business should be permitted to expand, and how far the national government should be permitted to go in controlling the activities of business. Both Bryan and the urban progressives condemned the abuses of big business. The Commoner was never more critical of captains of industry than Roosevelt was during the

[27] Roosevelt to E. E. Hale, December 17, 1901, Roosevelt to M. A. Hanna, October 5, 1903, Roosevelt to Elihu Root, May 20, 1904, Roosevelt Papers (Manuscript Division, Library of Congress); *The New York Times,* May 21, 1904. See also Howard K. Beale, *Theodore Roosevelt and the Rise of America to World Power* (Baltimore, 1956), pp. 23 ff.

[28] Croly, *The Promise of American Life,* p. 282; Leuchtenburg, "Progressivism and Imperialism," pp. 485, 503. There were, of course, progressives of considerable stature who did not agree with Croly's analysis, and who rejected its international implications as well as its Hamiltonian emphasis in domestic affairs. Robert La Follette was a prototype for such men, and in these matters he stood closer to Bryan than to Croly. For a commentary on the differences between Croly and progressives of the Middle West, see Russel B. Nye, *Midwestern Progressive Politics* (East Lansing, Mich., 1951), pp. 274–278.

anthracite strike of 1902. While negotiations were taking place, T.R. commented upon the "gross blindness" of the mine operators. He thought they had failed "absolutely" to recognize that they had duties with respect to the public.[29] When they said that they would die of cold before yielding to arbitration, Roosevelt pointed out that "*they* were not in danger of dying of cold," for they would pay higher prices and suffer no discomfort. What they were really saying was "that they would rather somebody else should die of cold than that they should yield." This, thought the President, was an impossible position. "May heaven preserve me," he wrote, "from ever again dealing with so wooden headed a set, when I wish to preserve their interests." [30]

In spite of his invective Roosevelt was ambivalent toward big business. He did, after all, wish to protect business from socialism and "anarchic disorder." William Howard Taft, writing to the President from Manila during the furor of 1902, gave clear expression to the Rooseveltian and urban progressive point of view. "The blindness and greed of the so-called captains of industry would pass my comprehension," he confessed, "if I had not been made acquainted with the unconscious arrogance of conscious wealth and financial success. By your course you are saving these gentlemen from a cataclysm that they do not seem to understand the danger of." Taft thought that as a result of the anthracite settlement Roosevelt was in a position "to guide the feeling against trusts and the abuses of accumulated capital, in such a way as to remedy its evils without a destruction of those principles of private property and freedom of contract that are at the base of all material and therefore of spiritual and intellectual progress." [31] Unlike Bryan, Roosevelt and Taft did not fear bigness in business; their concern, and the concern of most urban progressives, was that trusts be controlled to prevent abuses. "What we believe in, if I understand it," wrote Taft somewhat uncertainly during the campaign of 1908,

[29] Roosevelt to J. B. Bishop, October 13, 1902, Roosevelt Papers.
[30] Roosevelt to Mrs. W. S. Cowles, October 16, 1902, Roosevelt Papers.
[31] Taft to Roosevelt, November 9, 1902, William Howard Taft Papers (Manuscript Division, Library of Congress).

"is the regulation of the business of the trusts as distinguished from its destruction." [32]

The urban progressive was willing to concede that the formation of trusts was not only inevitable, but in many respects beneficial. Herbert Croly believed that huge corporations, even though sometimes guilty of abuses, had contributed to American "economic efficiency." They had brought order out of industrial and commercial chaos by substituting cooperative for competitive methods. And where the small businessman was not able to hold his own, Croly saw "no public interest promoted by any expensive attempt to save his life." Legislation designed to maintain competition was not only expensive; it was discriminatory. The Sherman Anti-Trust Act, for example, encouraged small business at the expense of big business, and it therefore discriminated for small business against the general good. Corporations should not be hampered in their natural growth, Croly thought, for this growth resulted in efficiency. On the other hand, in order to prevent abuses, large business organizations should be limited by broad powers exercised in the national interest.[33] Because powers so extensive could only be lodged in the national government, Croly and the urban progressives demanded centralization.

Bryan and the rural progressives did not accept either the logic or the conclusion of this argument, and the struggle over organization thus developed into a conflict involving principles of federalism. In 1907 Bryan observed that there were two forces at work within the nation, "one force tending to bring the government nearer to the people and the other tending to carry the government away from the people." He thought that "opposition to the rule of the people usually takes the form of the advocacy of legislation which removes authority from a point near to the people to some point more remote from them." [34] Senator Beveridge suggested

[32] Taft to Roosevelt, July 12, 1908, Taft Papers. See also Hofstadter, *The Age of Reform*, pp. 213 ff.; Louis Filler, *Crusaders for American Liberalism* (New York, 1950), pp. 51–53; Walter Johnson, *William Allen White's America* (New York, 1947), pp. 145–146.

[33] Croly, *The Promise of American Life*, pp. 358–362.

[34] *The Commoner*, September 20, 1907.

that Bryan need have no fear of centralization of power in the
national government, for the national government was nothing
more than the people of the forty-six states acting in the mass.
Bryan replied that "when the people of a state act together on a
local matter they are nearer to the subject under discussion, and,
therefore, can act more intelligently." [35] The Commoner remained
firm in the belief that "every attempt to take authority away from
the community and vest it in some power outside of the community
contains a certain amount of infidelity to the democratic theory of
government." The true Jeffersonian democrat would not take from
the national government any power necessary to the performance of
its responsibilities, Bryan admitted, but he would regard the con-
solidation of all political power in Washington as "a menace to
the safety of the nation." [36] National legislation dealing with the
trusts should be supplemented to statutes already in existence in
the states.

In 1910 when Roosevelt enunciated his New Nationalism—the
very phrase suggests his debt to Herbert Croly—at Osawatomie,
Kansas, Bryan was highly critical. T.R. was traveling a perilous
road at breakneck speed. Indeed Bryan thought the Rough Rider
had already galloped past a number of milestones: he had wished
to put "the national need before sectional or personal advantage";
he had insisted that "every man holds his property subject to the
general right of the community to regulate its use to whatever degree the public welfare may require it"; he had declared that
"combinations in industry are the result of an imperative economic
law which cannot be repealed by political legislation" and that
the only solution to problems resulting from such combinations was
to control them completely "in the interest of the public welfare";
he had confessed his impatience with "the impotence which springs
from overdivision of governmental powers" and he had hailed the
executive as "the steward of the public welfare." [37] Although this

[35] *The Commoner*, April 19, 1907. Bryan at this time was conducting a
debate with Senator Beveridge in the pages of the *Reader Magazine*. Much
of the debate was reprinted in *The Commoner*. See also Claude Bowers,
Beveridge and the Progressive Era (New York, 1932), pp. 259–261.

[36] *The Commoner*, September 20, 1907.

[37] Hermann Hagedorn, ed., *Works of Theodore Roosevelt*, 20 vols. (New
York, 1923–1926), XIX, 16–27.

might have been acceptable urban progressive dogma, Bryan thought that Roosevelt had here raised issues which must in time separate him from Republican insurgents and alienate those Democrats who had been in sympathy with policies T.R. had stolen from Democratic platforms.

The Commoner had no doubt that the Hamiltonian doctrines of the New Nationalism were dead, yet he felt compelled to whistle in the graveyard. Even the Rough Rider, Bryan assured himself, could not popularize such a program, for "the trend is toward democracy and away from the aristocratic ideas of Alexander Hamilton." The New Nationalism was not really new; it was merely the latest indication of that "restiveness" which Roosevelt had always displayed when confronted by constitutional limitations. And what of this doctrine of executive stewardship? Did Roosevelt mean that "the executive department is to exercise a fatherly interest and act independently of the wishes of the people?" If so, thought the Commoner, he was advancing a doctrine as dangerous as it was strange to Americans: "the doctrine of monarchies, not the doctrine of republics. . . ." [38]

Few periods in American history have been characterized by a livelier popular interest in issues than the progressive era. In a period before radio and television the media through which these issues could be discussed were limited. The speaker's rostrum was widely used, but its limitations were many. Chautauqua companies marshaled speakers and did much to eliminate difficulties in getting those speakers before audiences. Even so, only a small percentage of the American people was reached, and much time was consumed in reaching those few. The written word, therefore, proved a more effective medium for the discussion of issues, and the journalistic outpourings of the progressive period constitute one of its salient features. Although Bryan's fame rested in large part upon his oratory, his weekly newspaper *The Commoner* was as important an organ as his matchless voice in the expression of his views. And

[38] *The Commoner,* September 16, October 14, 1910. See also Fremont Older to Upton Sinclair, August 3, 1910, Upton Sinclair Papers (Special Collections, Indiana University Library, Bloomington).

newspapers and magazines—particularly the latter—were even more vital for the urban wing of the progressive movement. The literature of exposure, which is as old as the bawdy planet, took on a new intensity when packaged in magazines of national circulation. The titans of progressive journalism were the muckrakers, and a more zealous body of fact-finders would be difficult to imagine. They were not purveyors of a romantic sensationalism; their readers were sophisticated and respectable. The muckrakers were, in other words, representative of the urban progressive impulse. . . .

Although Bryan himself did not engage in muckraking, he was in some measure both responsible for it and dependent upon it. Ray Stannard Baker thought the writing of the muckrakers captured American readers because the country had for years been berated by agitators with their charges of corruption and privilege "which everyone believed or suspected had some basis of truth, but which were largely unsubstantiated." This agitation was the result of a deep-seated unrest, and Bryan's campaigns seemed to Baker "vigorous, if blind, expressions of the same unrest." [39] After years of dissatisfaction, then, during which the search for a bête noire led to confusion through the multiplication of unproved assertions, the muckrakers arrived with their accurate and objective articles of exposure. Perhaps they would have appeared had there been no unrest, no Populist party, no silver crusade, and no reform pressure, but this seems doubtful. Certainly Baker's thesis that readers were more receptive to the muckrakers for having experienced late nineteenth-century agitation has much to recommend it. Insofar as Bryan had some share in this agitation, he helped to make muckraking possible.

The Commoner's association with the muckrakers goes further, however, for he used their findings to support his arguments. Again and again he was able to point to their articles as proof of what he had been saying since his entry into public life. In 1905 after citing a series of investigations before the courts, together with the work of Thomas Lawson, Ida M. Tarbell, and Charles Edward Russell, Bryan made an observation similar to the one S. S. Mc-

[39] Ray Stannard Baker, *American Chronicle* (New York, 1945), pp. 183–184.

Clure had made two years before: "Here we have bankers, railroad magnates, promoters, manufacturers and speculators all vieing with each other in the use of methods which offend against both statute and moral law." But McClure had suggested that existing evils were attributable to society as a whole and that reform must come from "all of us." Bryan, uncompromising, never gave up the idea that the "money trust" was responsible for the sins of society. "The thimbleriggers at a street fair," he wrote, "are engaged in more honorable business for they cheat those who are foolish enough to risk their money on a game known to be dishonest, but these thimbleriggers of high finance rob the helpless and the dependents under the guise of doing an honest business." [40] Working from this assumption, it was easy for Bryan to suggest a program for the reform of abuses; it is always easier to pass laws preventing the misdeeds of a few than to legislate for a whole people.

The interaction between Bryan and the muckrakers in the journalistic sphere parallels the interaction between the rural and urban wings of the progressive movement in the realm of political action. The urban progressives, feeling the pressures of a status revolution, demanded reform and through the muckrakers provided concrete evidence of evils in American society. Yet the urban progressives were reluctant to suggest specific policies for making reform effective. The rural progressives started with a program they had inherited from the populists, and this program, modified, seemed to meet the problems which troubled the urban wing of the movement. Thus it would not be too much to say that the two wings of progressivism were complementary; the urban group demonstrated the need for a change, while the rural group led by Bryan produced a program which became the basis for change.

Roosevelt's adoption of plank after plank from the Bryan platform becomes intelligible when it is seen as the result of this dialectic at work within the progressive movement. T.R.'s support of rural planks of course drew considerable comment from political observers and indeed from Bryan himself. Such comment began to appear in quantity shortly after the election of 1904. Bryan then

[40] *The Commoner*, July 14, 1905.

took occasion to point out that in the advocacy of freight regulation for railroads, Roosevelt was on Democratic territory. The President was receiving support from Democrats everywhere, he said, "not because he has discovered a new reform, not because democrats have abandoned their principles or that republican doctrines have become acceptable to them, but rather because Mr. Roosevelt has taken up a reform which was long ago and repeatedly suggested by the democratic party." [41]

T.R., however, appropriated more than rate regulation. In 1906 the *New York World* printed a remarkable editorial entitled "The Roosevelt-Bryan Merger." Using Bryan's recent Madison Square Garden speech and the President's annual message as a basis for comparison, the editorial discussed the basic agreement between the two men on the income tax, publicity for campaign contributions, enforcement of the Sherman Act, licensing corporations, government by injunction, the eight-hour day, arbitration of labor disputes, free trade for the Philippines, and the inspection of meat. After examining the points on which there was a difference of opinion, the editorial concluded that

if Mr. Roosevelt would advocate tariff revision and Mr. Bryan would stop advocating government ownership of railroads they would be substantially in accord. . . . Accepting Mr. Roosevelt and Mr. Bryan as the leaders of their respective parties we defy anybody to say where the dividing line is beyond which a voter has ceased to be a Roosevelt republican and becomes a Bryan democrat. There has been no such obliteration of party lines in American politics for three-quarters of a century. The Roosevelt-Bryan merger is one of the most extraordinary events in American history, especially in view of the fact that Mr. Bryan claims to be "more radical than ever," while Mr. Roosevelt persists in regarding himself as a rational conservative battling manfully "against the demagogue and the agitator." [42]

[41] *The Commoner*, February 17, 1905. Later in the year Bryan wrote: "President Roosevelt endorses the democratic doctrine of railroad rate legislation; Governor La Follette endorses rate legislation and also the democratic doctrine of primary elections; Governor Cummins endorses the democratic doctrine of tariff revision; editor [Victor] Rosewater endorses the democratic doctrine of election of senators by popular vote—next?" *The Commoner*, September 8, 1905.

[42] *New York World*, December 5, 1905.

Bryan was soon speaking to this point with increasing frequency, for both parties were preparing for the Presidential campaign ahead. In May 1907 at Newark, New Jersey, he addressed the People's Lobby, a nonpartisan organization. "I have so many opportunities to be partisan that I welcome an opportunity to be non-partisan," he began. Then with tongue in cheek he confessed that "I find it very difficult to be partisan now even when I want to be, for if I make a straight-out democratic speech, the first thing I know the president makes one of the same kind and then the subject immediately becomes non-partisan." [43] During the campaign of 1908, after the nominations were made, the Nebraskan frequently asserted that he, and not Taft, was Roosevelt's legitimate political heir. In a typical utterance, Bryan said:

There are certain things that come naturally by descent, and reforms come by descent. You can not convey a reform by will. The President has tried to bequeath certain reforms to the Republican candidate, but I am the next of blood in the reform business, and they come to me. In fact, I think I could make it stronger than that. If a man dies and leaves no children the property goes back to his parents, and so far as reforms are concerned the Republican party has died without heirs, and the reforms go back to the one from whom the Republican party got the reforms. So I think I have a right to expect a good many Republican votes this year. [44]

The victory of Taft in November did not ring down the curtain on this line of argument. When T.R. began to expound his New Nationalism, Bryan repeated many of his old allegations. In 1911 he encouraged his followers to rejoice that Roosevelt had "AT LAST thrown his influence on the side of the popular election of

[43] *The Commoner*, May 24, 1907.

[44] *The Literary Digest*, XXXVIII (September 12, 1908), 335. Bryan also charged that Taft, as Roosevelt's nominee, had taken over many Democratic planks. "This does not injure me in the slightest, I think," wrote Taft to Roosevelt, "but indicates a testiness on his part, being deprived of some of the arguments which he might have made." Taft to Roosevelt, July 31, 1908, Taft Papers. *The New York Times* posed the question: "Will the American people have the Roosevelt policies continued and administered by Mr. Taft or by Mr. Bryan?" It then went on to compare the two, leaving no doubt that it considered Taft the better man. *The New York Times*, July 10, 1908.

senators and the initiative and referendum." The former President had become a convert on several propositions, however, and so far as he had supplemented his original commentary on the New Nationalism, "it is simply democracy under another name, and the new name does not fit it as well as the old name." [45]

While Bryan's influence on the urban progressives has received much emphasis, little attention has been paid the urban progressive influence on Bryan. To say with Vachel Lindsay that T.R. aped Bryan is to voice a partial truth; equally accurate would be the observation that Bryan aped T.R. Roosevelt at heart was conservative, and were it not for his desire to thwart radicalism by correcting some of the evils of the status quo, he might never have become a progressive at all. Even as a progressive he made a habit of balancing good and evil: the good trust as opposed to the bad trust, for example. In politics he dealt with machines, but he did so to buy votes for good legislation. "T.R. saw the machine; he did not see the system," thought Lincoln Steffens. "He saw the party organizations of the politicians; he saw some 'bad' trusts back of the bad politics, but he did not see the good trusts back of the bad trusts that were back of the bad machines." [46] Roosevelt represented the powerful but neutral state, or thought he did. And in the eyes of his followers he doubtless appeared to be standing righteously above partisan strife and acting in the interests of the public welfare. His position as a neutral resulted in equivocation— bristling equivocation, for Roosevelt was by nature a violent man and his nervous energy required an outlet. It resulted also in a modification of what had originally seemed a radical platform; in his hands the Bryan planks were cut and planed and used to construct a moderate program. [47]

It took no keen perception to see that Roosevelt was immensely popular with voters, and before long Bryan was taking pains to

[45] *The Commoner*, March 3, 1911.

[46] Lincoln Steffens, *Autobiography*, 2 vols. (New York, 1931), p. 505. For an evaluation of Roosevelt as a "broker of the possible," see Mowry, *The Era of Theodore Roosevelt*, pp. 110–115.

[47] Hofstadter, *The Age of Reform*, pp. 232–234, 236–238. A typical example of Roosevelt's balancing of good and evil may be found in Baker, *American Chronicle*, p. 203.

point out that he too was fundamentally conservative. "Not only is the reformer the real defender of property rights, but he is the best friend of the very persons who abuse him," he wrote in 1905. "Just as that physician is the best one who points out to his patient the dangers of the disease from which he suffers and proposes the best remedy, no matter how severe, so those are the best friends of the rich who attempt to restrain excesses and to correct abuses." [48]

The new moderation of the Commoner created a stir in the press during the campaign of 1908. The *New York Evening Post* observed that twelve years earlier Bryan had been regarded as a kind of "bogey man," an agitator and innovator, a "stirrer-up" of class hatred. "But today," commented the editorial writer, "Bryan has changed all that." Eastern newspapers which had been overwhelmingly opposed to the Nebraskan in his earlier campaigns were impressed with the Democratic platform of 1908. *The New York Times, Press,* and *Herald* all agreed that it was a platform on which Roosevelt could stand as comfortably as Bryan, and the *World* was pleased that it avoided the disastrous blunders of the past.[49] The *World* also thought that Bryan was an entirely new personality. "The old-time impulsiveness has utterly vanished and exaggerated caution has taken its place." [50] In his speeches the Commoner substantiated this impression. "The Democratic party seeks not revolution, but reformation," he said in accepting his nomination. "I have such confidence in the intelligence as well as the patriotism of the people, that I cannot doubt their readiness to accept the reasonable reforms which our party proposes, rather than permit the continued growth of existing abuses to hurry the country on to remedies more radical and more drastic." [51]

Just before the election one of the few prominent Bryan Demo-

[48] *The Commoner,* July 7, 1905.
[49] *Literary Digest,* XXXVI (May 30, 1908), 778; *ibid.,* XXXVII (July 18, 1908), 72.
[50] *New York World,* July 5, 1908.
[51] *Campaign Textbook of the Democratic Party, 1908,* p. 243; *The Commoner,* August 28, 1908; *Literary Digest,* XXXVII (August 22, 1908), 233–235. For comments on Bryan's apparent conservatism see *The Public,* IX (April 7, 1906), 4; Chicago *Record Herald,* August 7, 24, 1908; Des Moines *Register and Leader,* August 22, 1908; Springfield *Illinois State Register,* November 3, 1908.

crats in New York, William J. Gaynor, sent a message of good will
to the Commoner. "You will *probably* bring your party into power
now; certainly four years hence," he wrote. "The day of raillery
and tirade against you is gone by even in New York newspapers.
I suppose you are aware of their changed tone of respect and good
will toward you. Those of us who were with you from the first are
now respectable citizens again." After Taft's election Gaynor
wrote again, this time in the spirit of *ave atque vale:* "You will
have a larger place in the history of the country than most of our
Presidents. . . . The opposition in a constitutional government
often does more good and achieves a greater reputation than those
in actual control of the government." [52]

These two letters are suggestive of the paradoxical relationship
between Bryan and the urban progressives. After his defeat, Bryan
continued to urge the efficacy of a two-party system, a system
which had, for all its shortcomings, led to progress. And he continued to argue against the formation of a third party by Republican and Democratic reformers because he thought the two historic
parties provided the best means for securing reform legislation:

Let the democratic reformers fight for the control of their party, and
let the republican reformers fight for the control of the republican
party. If the democratic reformers control the democratic party, and
the republican reformers fail to control the republican party, then let
democrats appeal to republican reformers to cross the party line and
put reforms above party. The appeal will be heeded by a multitude
of republicans. If, on the contrary, the republican reformers secure
control of their party and the democratic reformers lose control of
theirs, there is no doubt that the republicans could count on the support of many democrats.[53]

The one possibility that Bryan omitted here—that both parties
should become parties of reform—was the one that did, in fact,
occur when T.R. occupied the White House.

As a critic Bryan found much to discuss during these years;
although he failed to win election to the Presidency, he did see the
enactment and adoption of many reforms he had proposed. Gaynor

[52] Gaynor to Bryan, October 19, November 13, 1908, Bryan Papers.
[53] *The Commoner*, July 16, 1909.

was certainly justified in crediting Bryan's opposition with some share in bringing about the positive results of the progressive era. At the same time the very success of a modified Bryan program tended to make the Commoner himself more moderate and respectable, and, toward the end of Roosevelt's administration, less effective as a leader of political opposition. The conservatism of Taft soon aroused Bryan's antipathy, and once again the issues which separated the Nebraskan from the party in power seemed more clearly defined. But temporarily at least, success in failure had been accompanied by failure in success.

NORBERT R. MAHNKEN

✪

Bryan Country

One phase of the life and career of William Jennings Bryan has been almost entirely ignored by his biographers and critics. That phase relates to Bryan's influence on state and local alignments of his day. Bryan the Congressman, Bryan the Boy Orator, Bryan the Presidential candidate, Bryan the cabinet official—these appear in dozens of word portraits. However, the area in which the Great Commoner made his most significant impress on his life and time, namely in helping to shape for a generation the local pattern of the Democratic party, has hardly been mentioned. To get a complete picture of Bryan one must, therefore, examine in some detail his relation to state political currents.

Oklahoma is uniquely suited for a study of this phase of Bryan's career. Perhaps no other territory or state was as close to Bryan as was Oklahoma. In few other areas did political leaders and the general public so enthusiastically follow the footsteps of the Peerless Leader. In no other state were so many of Bryan's theories put into practice as in Oklahoma. The story of the famed Nebraskan's association with Oklahoma reveals his influence on reform movements at the local rather than national level, and leads to the conclusion that at that level of politics he was a giant among his political fellow-men. Bryan in Oklahoma found a situation far different from that in the nation at large, for among the residents

Reprinted from Norbert R. Mahnken, "William Jennings Bryan in Oklahoma," *Nebraska History*, 31 (December 1950), pp. 247–274.

of that area he moved in an environment that was friendly and receptive to his suggestions. Above all else, an examination of Bryan's activities in Oklahoma seems to demonstrate that biographers, seeking to fasten a label on Bryan, have so far failed to discover the most apt and descriptive one of them all, namely Bryan, the "Voice of Rural America."

The parallelism in the political philosophy of William Jennings Bryan and that of the mass of Oklahomans was not accidental. Both Bryan and Oklahoma had entered the national scene at the same time and under much the same conditions. The Unassigned Lands in Oklahoma had been opened for settlement by the great "run" of April 22, 1889; a year later Oklahoma Territory was organized and launched on its turbulent political career by the Organic Act of May 2, 1890.

The early settlers of Oklahoma, many of whom had fallen victim to land mortgage companies and the declining price level for farm commodities, brought their traditional party loyalties with them. But with their loyalty to party these early Oklahomans also brought—or soon developed—new and strange political and social ideas, based on their experience, and on their contact with the Farmers Alliance and the populist movements. Demands for tax and tariff reform, currency management and expansion, regulation of corporations, and increased direct participation in government were almost universally approved in the new territory. The impact of populism on all Oklahomans, regardless of their political faith, was greater than they realized.

Bryan, too, was the product of agrarian discontent. His first election to Congress in 1890 came in a year in which Nebraskans were showing at the ballot box their dissatisfaction with the depressed state of agriculture on the Great Plains. Bryan; Omer M. Kem, a Populist; and W. A. McKeighan, a Democratic-Populist fusion candidate were sent to the House of Representatives as a completely new Congressional delegation. The explanation for their victory lay in the popular discontent which the Farmers Alliance and the Populist party had sensed and exploited. Bryan from the beginning of his political career was probably more influenced by populism than he realized.

The early Congressional career of Bryan did not bring him strikingly to the attention of Oklahomans. Local Democratic editors noted with only passing interest Bryan's great tariff speech of 1892 which first brought him national acclaim. His later Congressional appearances, while opposing the repeal of the Sherman Silver Purchase Act in 1893, and while defending the income tax law in 1894 merely brought routine comments in the Oklahoma press, such as that "Mr. Bryan made the speech of the day in favor of silver," [1] that "Congressman Bryan thinks he has solved the income tax problem, and will offer a bill for that purpose in the House." [2]

It was not until Bryan and other Western Democrats aggressively began to criticize and challenge the conservative program of the Cleveland administration that he became a personality in whom Oklahomans were actively interested. The increasingly conservative tenor of the Cleveland administration ran counter to the prevalent pattern of thinking on the Great Plains. Presidential policies, such as his demand that the Sherman Silver Purchase Act be repealed, his sale of government bonds to a New York banking syndicate to restore the treasury's gold supply, his smashing of the Pullman strike, all were viewed by Western Democrats as evidence of Cleveland's growing conservatism and the crystallization of his thought processes in the field of economic and social reform. Many Western Democrats were convinced that only through a complete alteration of the character, program, and leadership of the party could the Democratic party develop any future in the West. The result was an intraparty struggle which was to grow in intensity between 1894 and 1896.

Oklahomans witnessed at first hand the struggle within the Democratic party between Cleveland conservatives and agrarian reformers. The majority of Oklahoma Democrats by 1894 were unquestionably sympathetic to free silver, the income tax, effective corporation and monopoly control, and the other items in the reform program of that day. At the same time, however, many local leaders of the Democratic party in Oklahoma Territory were conservative. Some were conservative by choice, being southern

[1] El Reno *Democrat*, August 25, 1893.
[2] *Beaver County Democrat*, October 20, 1893.

Bourbon Democrats whose pattern of thinking was still conditioned by Reconstruction days and who had little sympathy for the
reformist groups. Others were conservative of necessity. Since Oklahoma was still in territorial status all the executive and judicial
positions were appointive in character. Governor, secretary, the
minor administrative positions, judges, marshall, land office officials—all were selected by President Cleveland and his subordinates. Oklahoma editors and party wheelhorses seeking appointive
posts soon learned that reformers need not apply. Bitter factional
strife was inevitable.[3]

During 1895, while the administration was gradually losing control of the local party machinery in Oklahoma, Bryan made his
first visit to the territory. His appearance was a part of that extensive speaking tour which carried the gospel of free silver throughout
the South and West. During the last week of June, 1895, Bryan
delivered major addresses at Enid, Guthrie, and Oklahoma City,
and at Purcell in the Chickasaw Nation of Indian Territory. The
Oklahoma City meeting of June 25, 1895, was typical of them all.
Local Democrats took the leadership in arranging the details of
Bryan's visit, but they were aided by Populist co-workers, and
even by Republicans interested in the silver movement.[4] Bryan
made two appearances, the first of them in the afternoon at an out-
door meeting in Smith's Grove on the east edge of Oklahoma City.
It was the usual type of political meeting so dear to the heart of
Oklahomans raised on the heady diet of Populist campaigning.
From the speaker's platform, gaily decorated with bunting, plac-
ards and flags, a brass band entertained the audience until the
speaker arrived. Around the edge of the gathering were clustered

[3] Typical of the attitude of the proadministration group was the comment on Bryan by C. J. Nesbitt, the pro-Cleveland editor of the Kingfisher
Times (issue of March 12, 1894): "Rarely since the formation of the
government and the division among the people of political parties has a
more striking example of the fallacy of insubordination within the pale of
a party been more forcibly illustrated than in the case of Mr. Bryan of
Nebraska (for opposing the repeal of the silver purchase clause). There are
other apostates both in the Senate and House, and they will go with Bryan.
The sooner the better."

[4] In fact, C. G. Jones, chairman of the Oklahoma County Republican
Central Committee, presided at one of the meetings.

the usual refreshment stands, the hawkers of "16 to 1" hats and other souvenirs, the catch-penny games, and the pre-Fourth of July fireworks stands. In spite of the sweltering heat over 1,500 people came to listen to Bryan's 150-minute speech.[5] They proved a highly receptive and enthusiastic audience.

After Bryan's evening oration at the Opera House before an audience that included leading figures from all three parties a Territorial Free Silver League was organized with tremendous enthusiasm. Sidney Clarke, former Congressman from Kansas, who had been an active Boomer, and who was now busily fishing in the muddy waters of Oklahoma politics, was elected president of the league; M. L. Bixler, prominent Norman editor, was chosen vice-president; and Leo Vincent, territorial organizer and publicist for the Populist party, was named secretary. After adopting ringing resolutions favoring free silver and thanking Bryan for his appearances, the meeting adjourned in the early hours of the morning.[6] The meetings at Enid, Guthrie, and Purcell were equally successful and enthusiastic.

Bryan completely captivated his audiences during his first tour of Oklahoma Territory, and won the undying loyalty of many of his hearers. The avid interest aroused by his visit is shown both by the lengthy discussion of his appearances in the press, and by the sudden revival of the organized free silver sentiment in the territory. Local editors went to great lengths to picture this rising star on the political horizon to their readers. Numerous pen sketches, some of them hardly recognizable, were printed. Detailed descriptions of Bryan's appearance, mannerisms, speaking techniques, and line of argument on the silver question appeared everywhere. The comments found in the Guthrie *Daily Leader,* a leading Democratic journal, were typical:

Mr. Bryan is a portly, handsome man, with firm, determined features. His hair is dark, his mouth is large, and his voice clear and silvery as a bell. The resemblance between the Nebraska silverite and the late Sam Randall is striking indeed [how that comment must have pained both

[5] Oklahoma City *Daily Times Journal,* June 26, 1895. This was the conservative estimate of a generally unfriendly newspaper.
[6] Edmond *Sun-Democrat,* June 28, 1895.

Bryan and the soul of the late Pennsylvania arch conservative!]. He held the closest attention of his audiences, and made a most profound impression on his hearers. His arguments were backed up by statistics, his logic was forceful and convincing, and his speech sparkled with wit and wisdom. Congressman Bryan is, to use the street vernacular, a "hot thing." . . . It is not unlikely that Mr. Bryan will shine as a presidential possibility next year. . . .[7]

During the next months Bryan's popularity mounted steadily. He was the "young knight of bimetallism," the "noble champion of the common man," and the "idol of the West"—phrases which appear over and over again in the writings of that period. That Bryan was Presidential timber, and deserved the support of Western Democrats, was a generally accepted feeling—as one editor stated it when summing up Bryan's first visit, "To Hon. Wm. J. Bryan: Dear Bill: You are all right. You can put your clothes in Oklahoma's trunk." [8]

The territorial convention of the Democratic party, held at Oklahoma City on May 25, 1896, was a bitter and turbulent one. Cleveland supporters from among the ranks of appointive officials in the territory sought to get a resolution adopted which would endorse the Cleveland administration. The convention emphatically voted it down. Another attempt to weaken the convention's declaration in favor of free silver also collapsed. The victory for the reformers was complete. There was much sentiment at the convention for Bryan as Presidential nominee, but eventually the convention instructed its six delegates to the Democratic national convention to vote for Richard P. Bland of Missouri, the long-time leader of the Congressional silver bloc.[9]

In the Indian Territory section of the future state of Oklahoma much the same thing was happening. The Democratic Indian territorial convention was described as "the largest and stormiest gathering ever held in the territory." [10] A series of progressive resolutions was finally adopted. The delegates to the national con-

[7] Guthrie *Daily Leader*, June 27, 1895.
[8] *Ibid.*, June 28, 1895.
[9] Norman *State Democrat*, May 28, 1896.
[10] Claremore *Progress*, June 13, 1896.

vention were instructed to support Bland "as long as there is in
their judgment any possibility of his nomination," and thereafter
were authorized to cast their votes "for any candidate in harmony
with our silver platform." [11] Robert L. Owen, later Senator from
Oklahoma, and Joe M. LaHay, a talented and aggressive Cherokee
Indian, were the acknowledged leaders of the delegation, and both
were sympathetic to the candidacy of Bryan. Several of the delegates from Indian Territory, led by Owen, deserted Bland for
Bryan on the second ballot, and all six had drifted into Bryan
camp by the time that the last roll call was taken.[12]

Oklahoma Democrats were well pleased with the outcome of
the Chicago convention. The repudiation of Cleveland, the adoption of a progressive platform, and the nomination of their hero—
what more could they ask? Oklahomans felt that they had played
a vital part in the nomination of Bryan, both because of the early
and active support given Bryan by the delegates from Indian Territory, and also because the timely shifting of the six votes of Oklahoma Territory gave Bryan the required two-thirds majority and
set off the mad demonstration in his behalf. Oklahoma had insured
the nomination of Bryan!

Interest in the 1896 elections was intense. The future of silver,
the qualifications of Bryan, the question of whether the Democratic
party could shake off the handicap of Clevelandism and the blame
for the Depression of 1893 were heatedly debated throughout the
territory. When the election returns revealed a victory for McKinley
and the national Republican ticket, the veil of gloom became thick
and heavy throughout most of Oklahoma. Many, however, were
inclined to be philosophical rather than bitter about the defeat of
Bryan. Typical comments on the Republican victory were: "It was
a victory for the trusts" [13] or, "We were crucified on a cross of
gold." [14] Most penetrating of the postmortem pronouncements of
Democratic editors, and certainly the most accurate from the his-

---

[11] South McAlester *Capital*, June 11, 1896.

[12] Bryan reported that he "had the promised support of half of the delegation on the second ballot."—William J. and Mary Baird Bryan, *The Memoirs of William Jennings Bryan* (Chicago, 1925), p. 106.

[13] South McAlester *Capital*, November 12, 1896.

[14] Guthrie *Daily Leader*, November 5, 1896.

torian's point of view was the verdict of M. L. Bixler, that "Bryan rescued the party from the paralysis into which the depression and Mr. Cleveland placed it." [15]

Oklahoma voters, because of their territorial status, were only observers as far as the Presidential race was concerned. They could, however, express their convictions in local elections for members of the territorial legislature, and for county officials. In these contests Oklahoma voters dramatically indicated their sympathy for the type of program Bryan advocated. Democrats and Populists put fusion candidates in the field, and won all thirteen seats in the territorial council. Only three Republican members out of a total of twenty-six were returned to the lower house, a very sharp break from the previous legislature, in which the Republicans had controlled both houses with sizeable majorities. Bryanism, free silver, the income tax had proven popular with the voters.[16]

Bryan's second visit to Oklahoma, a very brief one, came in 1897. While on the first of his many paid lecture tours, the Nebraska orator stopped at several Oklahoma points. Traveling along the Santa Fe's main line to Texas, Bryan made numerous rear-platform appearances, shaking the hands of the faithful, and making a few remarks to the eager crowds that gathered at stations along the way—Newkirk, Ponca City, Perry, Mulhall, and Orlando. Bryan's major address was delivered at Guthrie, the territorial capital. In spite of the cold and sloppy December day, the gathering at Guthrie was a "red letter event." Inevitably, the First Regimental Band was there "in full force" to lead the parade from the depot through the business section. At the Opera House Bryan, after a flowery introduction by Roy V. Hoffman, Assistant U. S. Attorney for the territory, delivered his usual vigorous and moving silver speech. He did, however, couple with it support for a free homes bill, and immediate statehood for Oklahoma—both of which were currently popular in the territory.[17]

Following Bryan's appearance at the Opera House, a reception

[15] Norman *State Democrat*, November 12, 1896.
[16] Guthrie *Daily Leader,* February 6, 1897. To demonstrate their appreciation, the newly elected members of the legislature invited Bryan to address them, but he was unable to accept their invitation.
[17] Guthrie *Daily Leader*, December 5, 1897.

in his honor was held at the home of H. H. Hagan, prominent Guthrie citizen. The list of guests included all the leading figures of the territory—Governor Cassius Barnes, the Supreme Court justices, leaders of the legislature, and outstanding editors. The mellowing effects of the evening's gathering were noticeable, and even Frank Greer, editor of the arch-Republican *Oklahoma State Capital* and possessor of the most vitriolic pen in the territory, commented rather graciously that, "Mr. Bryan is a magnetic orator, it is a pleasure to hear him, whether you agree with him or not." There was some complaint from among Bryan's followers that they should be required to pay fifty cents to hear their champion,[18] but generally it was agreed that his visit was a huge success, and that it was a real honor and pleasure for the people of the territory to have an opportunity to see and hear the "next President."

This 1897 visit of Bryan is mentioned only because it is typical of the half-dozen visits of Bryan during the next decade. On his various lecture tours Bryan could always be assured of large audiences in Oklahoma. In 1902 and 1903 he spoke on "A Conquering Nation" before at least twelve different audiences.[19] In 1906 and 1907 he made numerous platform appearances while discussing "Non-Partisan Politics" or "The Old World and Her Ways." Always there were with the paid speeches these smaller gatherings of friends and supporters, at which contacts were renewed, party plans and policies discussed, and political fences mended all around. There is no point in discussing in detail the subsequent appearances of Bryan before Chautauqua groups, for they all followed the same pattern.

[18] This attitude was expressed in typical, if not too literate fashion, by the editor of the Orlando *Weekly Herald* (December 10, 1897): "The majority of people do not care to pay an admission price to hear a political speech by the young free silver apostal [*sic*]. Many a good honest vote that was Mr. Bryan's in 1896, and possibly would of been his in 1900 stood on the streets, either not having or not choosing to pay the half dollar required to hear their idol expound his famous theories."

[19] These were at Blackwell, Perry, Kingfisher, Enid, Medford, Guthrie, Norman, Chandler, Shawnee, Oklahoma City, Hobart, and Lawton, under varied auspices—e.g., a Baptist College, an Epworth League, an Elks Club, a committee to raise funds for a school piano, and at Shawnee the Six O'clock After Dinner Business Men's Club.

Interest in political affairs fell off sharply in Oklahoma between 1897 and 1900. The Democratic-Populist legislature of 1897, checked by an unfriendly governor and Congress, failed to usher in the political millennium. The rains again fell and barns and granaries bulged in hitherto improvident Oklahoma. New gold discoveries and their corresponding increases in circulating medium coupled with the impact of the Spanish-American War raised the prices of farm commodities. The result was, as one ardent partisan sadly pointed out, that "the starch has gone out of politics, even in Oklahoma." [20] Not only that, but the war produced a new rival for the affections of Oklahomans in the ebullient Theodore Roosevelt. A sizeable group of Roosevelt's "Rough Riders" were recruited in Oklahoma, 80 of them in Oklahoma Territory, and 125 from Indian Territory. Local interest in their accomplishments was understandably high.

Under these circumstances Bryan was moved from the center of the local stage. Occasional paragraphs dutifully reported his organization of Nebraska volunteers, and his tribulations with an administration that seemed to find no opportunities for military glory for the famed Nebraskan. These accounts, however, made drab reading when compared with the glorious tales of Roosevelt's exploits, Rough Rider victories, and the valorous deeds of home-town heroes.

The territorial party conventions of 1900 were uneventful. It was generally agreed that Bryan would be the candidate, and that the 1896 platform and imperialism would be the issue as far as the Democrats were concerned. Both Indian Territory and Oklahoma Territory, after routine local meetings, sent delegations to the national convention pledged to Bryan. When the national convention, meeting at Kansas City, gave the nomination to the Nebraskan, few Oklahomans evidenced much interest in its activities. Oklahoma City was witnessing a more exciting event—the annual reunion of the Rough Riders, complete with Teddy Roosevelt himself. It was estimated that 15,000 Oklahomans descended on Oklahoma City to enjoy the bands, parades, speeches, and all the colorful nonsense

[20] Guthrie *Daily Leader*, April 13, 1898.

that made a Rough Rider reunion something for the city fathers to anticipate with mixed feelings of joy and trepidation.

Bryan's defeat in 1900 did nothing to weaken his position among Oklahoma Democrats. By now the party in Oklahoma had assumed a pattern of beliefs and traits which it was not to abandon for many years. Shaped by the yearnings and feelings the Great Commoner so well expressed during these years, and strengthened numerically by accessions from Populist ranks, the Democratic party in Oklahoma was a typically agrarian progressive force—"dangerous Western radicals" to Eastern observers. To its members Bryan was in the best party tradition of Jefferson and Jackson. There was no criticizing or challenging his leadership. One of the interesting manifestations of this sentiment was the attempt to induce Bryan to move to Oklahoma. Thomas H. Doyle and other leading Democratic advocates of immediate statehood in 1902 attempted to persuade Bryan to move to Oklahoma, head the drive for immediate statehood, and incidentally strengthen still further the party's position in the territory. In return Bryan was promised that as soon as statehood had been won, he would be sent to Washington as Senator, so that he could rebuild his political fortunes by way of a Senatorial career. Bryan graciously declined the offer, pointing out that he could not easily remove his journal, *The Commoner,* and his other interests to the politically more favorable climate of Oklahoma.[21]

Theodore Roosevelt's record as a reform President posed a serious problem for the Democratic party. For two successive elections the party had offered itself to the voting public as the party of reform as opposed to Republican "stand-pattism." Now, after 1901, it found itself faced by a Republican President who proclaimed himself in favor of a "square deal" for labor, and a program of trust busting. While Teddy's actions might not always be as bold and daring as his verbal blasts, they were effective enough to convince many people that progressivism was no longer the trait of a single political party. This change in the character of the Republican administration resulted in a revival of the old conservative

---

[21] The details of this incident were related by Doyle himself several years later. See Guthrie *Daily Leader*, December 27, 1907.

forces in the Democratic party. The result in 1904 was the rejection by the Democratic convention of Bryan's leadership, the resurgence of the Cleveland type of Democracy, the formulation of an uninspiring platform, the selection of the drab and unimaginative Alton B. Parker of New York as the candidate, and finally, the most decisive defeat the Democratic party had ever suffered since the Civil War. Bryan and his Western associates had fought vainly to prevent the party from drifting off into such a hopeless position, and when the returns finally indicated how disastrous the defeat had been, they were inclined to agree with the Oklahoma observer who remarked:

> We are frank to confess that we did not endorse all that Judge Parker stood for. We are of the breed of Democracy represented by Thomas Jefferson in its foundation, and represented by William Jennings Bryan today, if you please.[22]

Bryan's greatest service to the Democratic party was undoubtedly rendered in the years between 1905 and 1908. His campaign —at first waged almost single-handedly—to revive the spirit of liberalism within the party bolstered the hope and courage of those who wished to make the organization once more the symbol of reform. That Bryan by 1907 had again restored himself to the position of leadership in the party, and that no one seriously challenged his right to a third nomination in 1908 is evidence enough of the startling success of his efforts. His defeat in 1908 in the final analysis was perhaps not as important as the fact that the party again had been committed to the liberal tradition, and this time more firmly. The election of Woodrow Wilson in 1912 was the real victory of Bryanism. For Wilson reaped the harvest of the seed that Bryan had sown. He rode into the White House on the shoulders of Bryan and his friends just as he had previously ridden into lesser positions in New Jersey on the shoulders of other friends.

Bryan's greatest service to Oklahoma also came during these same years, specifically during 1906 and 1907. These were years which brought the final struggle and victory to the movement for Oklahoma statehood. After 1900 the question of statehood for

[22] Guthrie *Daily Leader*, November 14, 1904.

Oklahoma had been the chief topic of interest to the people of that area, all of whom felt that they were now politically mature and entitled to admission. Various factors delayed statehood—the question of single or double statehood, that is, should Indian Territory be organized as a separate state or included with Oklahoma Territory; the widely varying economic and political pattern of the two areas; the future status of the Five Civilized Tribes and their institutions. Even more important had been the attitude of national party leaders. Democrats and Republicans alike had approached the question of statehood from the point of view of what it might do to their party's strength as a whole. Many Republican leaders, fearing that Oklahomans would elect Democratic officials, had procrastinated, using every sort of delaying tactic. Occasionally they openly had stated that they wanted no Senators and Representatives coming to Washington from this unstable region, if those Senators were to be Democratic, and even worse, Democrats who for many years had been riders on, or even drivers on the Bryan bandwagon.

By 1905, however, it was apparent that statehood could not with good grace be further delayed. The Dawes Commission had virtually completed its work of allotting in severalty the lands of the Five Civilized Tribes; nine out of ten settlers agreed on single statehood as the desirable plan as of that date; there were almost 1,500,000 people in the two territories, a number so large that their claims of statehood hardly could be denied. After lengthy debate, Congress finally passed and the President signed on June 16, 1906, the enabling act which outlined the path to statehood for Oklahoma. Indian Territory and Oklahoma were to be combined and admitted as one state. The important election of delegates to a constitutional convention to formulate the basic law of the state was to be held November 6, 1906.

With statehood assured, everyone immediately became interested in the question of the personnel of the constitutional convention, and the type of document they would write. During the long years of territorial status and "carpetbag rule" Oklahomans had acquired definite ideas as to what they wanted in their basic law. Pressure groups such as the Farmers Union, the United Mine Workers, the prohibitionists, the women's suffrage advocates, the Sequoyah delegates,[23] and railroad and other corporate interests all had evolved demands which they wished to see incorporated in the constitution. The result quite naturally was widespread interest, both locally and on a national scale, in the trend of events in Oklahoma.

No one displayed greater interest in these events than William Jennings Bryan. Four times during the next sixteen months he appeared in the state to add finishing touches to Democratic campaigns or plans. His active interest was further displayed by the many news stories and editorials which kept readers of *The Commoner* aware of controversies and trends in the newly formed commonwealth. The Nebraskan was to make significant contributions to the Democratic victories in Oklahoma, and at the same time the active participation of Bryan in Oklahoma in turn played a vital role in restoring him to his position of leadership in the party on a national scale.

As November 6, 1906, approached, it was apparent that the contest for positions as delegates to the constitutional convention were to be unusually bitter. The Republican party, finding itself on the defensive and losing influence in both Oklahoma Territory and Indian Territory, made an extraordinary effort to elect a large portion of the delegates. Likewise, the Democratic party, sensing victory in the fall election, conducted a vigorous campaign. The result was an electoral contest characterized by much mud slinging and vicious political infighting. Democratic orators, noting that several of the Republican aspirants for convention seats had served as legal advisors to railroad corporations, immediately charged that all Republican candidates were "tools of the corporations." Republicans in turn denounced the Democrats on the one hand as being the representatives of Southern reactionary bourbonism and, on the other hand, as being dangerously radical. These verbal barrages produced hard feelings, damaged reputations, and an occasional libel suit.

Both major parties invited leading national figures to support

[23] This was the name given to those delegates from Indian Territory who in 1905 had drawn up a constitution for a separate state, the state of Sequoyah.

their party candidates. Vice-President Fairbanks came from Washington and filled several speaking engagements in both territories in support of the Republican candidates. Kansas Republican leaders also appeared on numerous platforms. Not to be outdone, the Democrats also imported widely known orators, among them, "Pitchfork Ben" Tillman of South Carolina and Governor Jeff Davis of Arkansas. Democratic leaders had kept a watchful eye on the journeyings of William Jennings Bryan. The Great Commoner had just returned from his triumphal world tour on August 30, 1906. Among the various delegations waiting to speak to Bryan on his arrival in New York City was a group of Oklahoma Democrats headed by Thomas H. Doyle, W. L. Eagleton, George Whitehurst, T. F. McMechan, and Roy Stafford of the Oklahoma City *Daily Oklahoman*. They asked Bryan to visit Oklahoma and speak in support of the Democratic candidates for the constitutional convention. He agreed, and promised that he would take several days during the latter part of September to make a tour of the Twin Territories.[24] This news made headlines in every Oklahoma newspaper as the editors reminded their readers that they would be presented with another opportunity to see "a President of the United States—the next one." [25]

Bryan entered the heated campaign on September 26th. He came to Indian Territory from Arkansas, where he had just delivered a major address at Little Rock. His tour through the territories called for a speaking itinerary that must have taxed even the powerful Bryan vocal cords. From the time that he entered Indian Territory and made his first address at Wilburton until he left Oklahoma Territory two days later, Bryan made sixteen speeches, ranging from one-half hour to an hour in length, in addition to several short talks at whistle stops along the way. The tour was a gigantic success, such as is usually reserved for the conquering hero. Con-

[24] Guthrie *Daily Leader,* September 1, 1906.
[25] *Wilburton News,* September 28, 1906. The places at which Bryan spoke, together with the local estimate as to size of crowd (highly unreliable) follow: Wilburton, 3,000; South McAlester, 5,000; Eufala, 2,000; Muskogee, 2,000; Vinita, 10,000; Tulsa, 12,000; Pawnee, 8,000; El Reno, 4,000; Clinton, 5,000; Geary, 6,000; Alva, 6,000; Enid, 15,000; Blackwell, no estimate.

temporary accounts reported audiences of several thousand at
every stop, with the largest gatherings at Enid and Oklahoma City,
where some 18,000 were estimated to have heard the silver-
tongued orator. The size of the audiences was a notable tribute to
the leader who had so completely won the loyalty of the southwestern frontier.

The details of the tour had been carefully worked out by the
territorial chairman, Jesse Dunn. At each of the appearances in
Indian Territory, Bryan was introduced by one of the chiefs of the
Five Civilized Tribes, all of whom rode on the special train through
the territory. There were few formal receptions, and to save time
the local committees were instructed to arrange for a meeting place
as near to the railroad station as possible. Time might be at a
premium but under these circumstances it was still possible to
arrange for the parades so dear to the politicians of this period.
Thus, at McAlester, coal miners in their work clothes with their
miners' lamps alight and followed by bands and the usual torch-
light parade, marched in a colorful procession. At Vinita the parade
was headed by Major J. B. Turner's "horsemen" who thundered up
and down the streets as many a "round-up club" was to do at a
later date. Schools were dismissed, shops closed, and entire rural
communities emptied until the Bryan entourage had passed.

Bryan's speeches followed a set pattern. In each of them he appealed to his hearers to vote for Democratic delegates to the convention as representatives "whose sympathies are with the people
and who are not representative of such interests as may prove antagonistic to your wishes." [26] Such delegates would write into the
constitution provisions for the initiative and referendum, the control of corporations, and the protection of labor. With the usual
peroration praising the Democratic party, Bryan would retire amid
the cheers and shouts of his audience.

The local committees had received one interesting set of instructions from Party Chairman Dunn:

There will be no handshaking. There is a limit to human endurance,
and Mr. Bryan will closely approach it if he keeps these speaking en-

[26] Tulsa *Democrat,* September 28, 1906.

gagements, without being racked and torn by the glad hand. On account
of the many meetings he is holding, his hands and arms are now
swollen so it is impossible for him to shake hands.[27]

The arm and hand might be weak, but the voice still had its
old-time fire. Bryan's physical stamina was truly amazing. On September 27, when he spoke at Vinita, Tulsa, Pawnee, Perry, Guthrie, Oklahoma City, and El Reno, he delivered his first address at
8:30 A.M. and his last beginning at 11:30 P.M. In spite of this
strenuous program, Bryan was ready to speak early the next
morning before a throng of 5,000 at Clinton. After appearing at
five widely scattered points in western Oklahoma, Bryan did not
finish his schedule for that day until 2 A.M. the next morning. After
considering how taxing such a tour must have been, one wonders
at the correctness of a contemporary observer who noted that
Bryan "is older than he was and looks it, and his voice is hardly
as strong as it was in 1896." [28] Among those who heard him on
this tour, there was probably general agreement with the same
editor's further comment that Bryan "has lost none of his mag-
netism nor his directness—he is the greatest living American."

The extent of the Democratic victory in the November election
was a surprise to everyone. Democratic leaders had predicted that
they might have a majority of thirty in the constitutional convention, yet the body was finally made up of 99 Democrats, 1 Independent, and 12 Republicans—the twelve apostles, as the press at
once labeled them. It is not difficult to explain the collapse of Republican strength. The long delay in statehood for which the
Republicans were held responsible, the many "carpetbag" officials,
the fact that many strong Republicans as federal officeholders
were disqualified from seeking convention seats, the supposed sympathy of some Republicans for Negro equality, and the identification of other Republicans with corporate interests—these proved
insurmountable handicaps in the campaign. The Democratic suc-
cesses, however, were due not only to these negative factors, but
also to the positive appeal of the liberal program advocated by

[27] Guthrie *Oklahoma State Capital,* September 26, 1906.
[28] Vinita *Leader,* October 4, 1906.

Bryan, by local Democratic leaders, and by pressure groups such as organized labor and the Farmers Union.

The members of the constitutional convention assembled at Guthrie November 20, 1906. The convention was organized and moved ahead under the leadership of William H. Murray, Charles N. Haskell, and the other members who had participated in the unsuccessful movement to create Sequoyah as a separate state. Although these men had no doubts as to their ability to formulate an adequate basic law without outside interference, they did send letters to several important politicians asking them to present their views as to what should be incorporated in the constitution. Bryan was also invited to appear before the convention. Although pre-arranged speaking engagements made it impossible for him to do so, he sent a lengthy letter in which he discussed in considerable detail the items and clauses which he believed should be included in the constitution.[29] Examining the letter is tremendously interest-ing, not only because it shows how the lines of thinking of the Great Commoner and the Oklahoma agrarians were completely parallel, but also because virtually every item suggested by Bryan was eventually incorporated into the constitution.

The major portion of the letter dealt with corporations and the powers of a proposed corporation commission. The commission should be empowered to prohibit the issuance of watered stock, to limit intercorporate stock holdings, to check interlocking direc-torates, to require publicity for specified types of corporate opera-tions, and to impose a wide range of related restrictions. Other sections expressed his support of the initiative, referendum, recall, direct primary, and clauses authorizing municipal ownership of utilities. For labor he suggested clauses guaranteeing trial by jury in contempt cases, and sections authorizing the legislature to fix wages and hours standards and to establish a board of arbitration in labor disputes. The letter is carefully written, shows much thought, and is a rather effective answer to those hostile critics of Bryan who insisted that he never was able to think through carefully any specific problem. The effect of the letter on members of the consti-

[29] The letter is found in the *Journal of the Constitution Convention of Oklahoma*, pp. 389–396.

tutional convention cannot be evaluated, of course, though it certainly strengthened the convictions of those members whose thinking ran along the same lines.

When the Oklahoma constitution was completed and put before the public, it was at once obvious that it was a unique document in many ways. It was lengthy—the longest state constitution of its day. It was detailed—with the powers of various state officials carefully defined and limited. It had an unusually long list of elective officials—probably a natural reaction to the many years under appointive territorial officials. It was progressive—progressive to the point where it appeared dangerously radical to many people. The constitution authorized the direct primary and the widest possible use of the initiative and referendum; it included numerous protective clauses for the benefit of labor and provided that "the right of the state to engage in any occupation or business for public purposes shall not be denied or prohibited." [30] The section on corporation control was very detailed, almost equal in length to the entire federal constitution. There was considerable national interest shown in the constitution since it was so typical of the thinking of the Western agrarian groups.

After considerable bickering over submitting the constitution to popular vote, Governor Frank Frantz and the members of the constitutional convention finally agreed that on September 17, 1907, Oklahomans should vote on ratifying the constitution, and at the same time elect a ticket of state officials. The Democrats hurriedly arranged a party primary (financed by party funds since no appropriation was available) and selected a slate of candidates headed by Charles N. Haskell, who sought the gubernatorial chair, and Robert Owen and T. P. Gore, who were the party's designees for the two Senatorial positions. The Republican convention chose Frantz as the party's nominee, and decided to follow the path of opposing the constitution while at the same time urging the selection of Republican officials.

The contest over ratification of the constitution saw Oklahoma inundated by another wave of oratory. Members of the constitutional convention enthusiastically defended their handiwork. Point-

[30] Article II, Section 31.

ing out that the convention had been guided by the slogan "Let the People Rule," Democratic leaders supported the document as the most progressive and democratic of its day, ideally suited to local conditions and needs. Republicans, on the other hand, attacked the constitution for its great detail, its "radical" character, and the fact that it would handicap the state's development by discouraging capital from entering the state.

As the contest over ratification became more heated, and became almost a national issue, "visiting statesmen" in large number were brought in once again. The Republicans induced Senator Chester Long of Kansas, and Secretary of the Interior James R. Garfield to appear at several places and condemn the constitution. The major blast on the Republican side, however, was delivered by Secretary of War William Howard Taft, who spoke in Oklahoma City on August 24, 1907. Since Taft was already being mentioned as a Presidential possibility for 1908, and because he was assumed to be the "political phonograph of the Roosevelt administration" [31] and representative of administration opinion, a large crowd gathered at Oklahoma City to see and hear the administration stalwart. Taft left no doubt as to his convictions. To his point of view the constitution had no merit. He denounced its length and detail by terming it a "code of by-laws"; he criticized the form of the clauses authorizing the initiative and referendum; he described it as dangerous to business interests. He urged his audience to reject the constitution, wait until the next session of Congress should pass another enabling act, and then rewrite the constitution under more balanced leadership.

Sponsors of the statehood movement were much disturbed by this statement of policy, not so much because of its possible impact locally, but because Taft's views might represent administration hostility, and might produce an unfavorable reaction throughout the nation. Their answer was to import the outstanding figures they could obtain to appear and defend the constitution. In steady streams Congressmen from Arkansas, Iowa, and Missouri traveled through the territory. Champ Clark, Congressman from Missouri who was later to serve as a popular speaker of the House of Repre-

[31] Oklahoma City *Daily Oklahoman,* August 27, 1907.

sentatives, was a tremendous success in his appearances at Oklahoma City and elsewhere. The star performer, however, was William Jennings Bryan. Bryan had been given the honor of keynoting the Democratic campaign. While on a Chautauqua tour through the territory, Bryan stopped at Oklahoma City, June 18, 1907, and spoke to the Democratic state convention which had been called to work out details of the coming campaign. His stirring speech left no doubts as to his enthusiasm for the Oklahoma constitution:

I tell you that you have the best constitution of any state in this union, and a better constitution than the constitution of the U. S. This constitution is written from the standpoint of the people. . . . Do not be afraid to trust the people. . . . Our government must either be dominated by the few or the many, and I prefer to risk the many. . . . You have made a constitution your people can control.[32]

During the first week in September Bryan was called back to make another series of appearances throughout the state. At this time he was brought back specifically to reply to Taft's speech, and to try and counteract the possible national effect of that speech. Seven scheduled appearances were arranged—at Vinita, Tulsa, Sapulpa, Chandler, Oklahoma City, Woodward, and Alva. It was the usual triumphal Bryan tour. Crowds numbering 3,000–5,000 appeared at each of the smaller towns, while at Oklahoma City some 6,500 people crowded into Convention Hall. Here Bryan in particular directed his attack against Taft's comments. The sections and characteristics of the constitution with which the Secretary of War had found fault were defended in detail, by argument, by pointing out that Republican states had incorporated similar clauses, and by appealing to local pride and prejudice. Taking a sly poke at Taft's suggestion that Oklahomans reject the constitution, and wait for a new enabling act and a new convention, Bryan remarked that such a suggestion could naturally be expected from one who was inclined to postpone everything. "The Great Postponer" was Taft's label for many years in Oklahoma. Chairman J. D. Jennings, of the Oklahoma County Democratic committee, summed up what he considered the likely effect of Bryan's latest appearance: "The banner of victory was already nailed to the flag-

[32] *Ibid.*, June 19, 1907.

staff of the Oklahoma democracy, but Bryan clinched the nails last night." [33]

The election returns of September 27 showed an overwhelming victory for the forces that had drawn up the constitution. The document was approved by a vote of 180,333 to 73,059. The entire slate of Democratic candidates for the executive offices was elected. The legislature, which was to meet in its initial session December 2, 1907, was made up of 93 Democrats and 16 Republicans in the lower house, while of the 44 members of the Senate 39 represented the victorious party. Here was a victory which must have pleased Bryan greatly, one of the few he was to enjoy. *The Commoner* reflects the enthusiasm of Bryan and the staff. Not only did its columns report the travels and speeches of its editor while in Oklahoma, but news accounts, cartoons, and editorials all gave support to the victorious group. When the votes on ratification were tabulated and the extent of the victory apparent, Will M. Maupin, traveling correspondent for *The Commoner,* and a versifier of some ability, dashed off lines which had some of the exuberance of the title song of a later-day Rodgers and Hammerstein musical:

Got some word from Oklahoma on the Wednesday morning wire
Just some facts about th'election and they filled us full of fire,
Just some good election figures, and we just leaned back and laughed
At the way young Oklahoma handed limes to William Taft.
. . . .
Got some word from Oklahoma, and we've swept the platter clean
Licked the grasping corporation and the carpetbag machine.
Three times three for Oklahoma, Forty thousand, Hully gee!
Please excuse us if we holler, for our souls are filled with glee.
. . . .
There's a new star on the banner and it's shining mighty bright
And she's safely democratic—Oklahoma, you're all right! [34]

When the first Oklahoma legislature met, one of its earliest resolutions was to invite Bryan to appear before it. He agreed and December 21, 1907, was designated as the date for his appearance. The occasion was to serve two purposes—first, to thank Bryan for

[33] *Ibid.*, September 7, 1907.
[34] *The Commoner,* September 27, 1907.

his energetic services in behalf of statehood, and second, to pledge formally the support of the Democratic party of the new state to Bryan's candidacy for the President in 1908. It was a great day for all concerned. The legislature met at 2 P.M. in joint session at Guthrie's Brooks Theatre. Standing room was at a premium as everyone sought to witness the gala occasion. Even the chaplain of the House of Representatives fell in with the spirit of the occasion. The local paper's account of his part in the brief morning session of the legislature is a gem. The chaplain, after a lengthy prayer on Bryan's behalf, concluded:

"Lord . . . if it is according to Thy will, let him be the next President of the United States."

There was a unanimous "Amen" from the Democratic side at the conclusion of the prayer, and Speaker Murray said, "All in favor of that make it known by saying "Aye!"

Shouts of "aye" came quickly, followed by a loud applause.[35]

Overwhelmed by the answer his petition had received (from the members of the House—not the Divinity) the chaplain repeated it at the afternoon joint session. Lieutenant Governor Bellamy presided, and Speaker Murray introduced Bryan, and presented him with an elaborate scroll, signed by all the leading officials of the state, listing and expressing appreciation for the many contributions of Bryan to Oklahoma statehood, and to the victory of 1907.

The ceremony was, for all of its somewhat flamboyant character, a genuine and sincere expression of the local feeling that Bryan had made a real and important contribution to statehood, and the formulation of the state's basic law.

At an evening "dollar dinner" prepared for some 400 loyal Democratic workers, the party formally pledged Bryan its support in 1908. After a series of short speeches acknowledging the state's debt to the Nebraskan, Robert L. Williams, chief justice of the state supreme court, announced, "We want no novice for our standard bearer in 1908. We want a man whom we know and can trust." [36]

[35] Guthrie *Daily Leader,* December 21, 1907.
[36] *Ibid.,* December 22, 1907.

Bryan's visit also called attention to another instance of the close identification of interests and action between himself and Oklahoma's political leaders. One of the outstanding bits of legislation of the Haskell administration had been the bank guarantee law. This measure, passed in an attempt to prevent a repetition of the many bank failures that had accompanied the Panic of 1907, was the pioneer law of its kind in the nation. Bryan enthusiastically applauded the measure, and on the occasion of this visit to Oklahoma reminded his hearers that he introduced such a law in Congress some fifteen years earlier,[37] and that he still considered it an ideal law to be applied on a national scale. It became a major issue in the 1908 Presidential campaign.

Oklahoma Democrats played a very active part in the 1908 contest. Governor Haskell was the featured speaker at the Lincoln meeting on January 15 which launched the Democratic state campaign in Nebraska, and which was interpreted as formally starting the Bryan bandwagon.[38] Haskell also sought, and finally obtained, the position as chairman of the national convention's resolutions committee. As the date of the convention approached, the "Big Four" of Oklahoma's political machine, Haskell, Murray, Robert Williams, and J. B. Thompson, journeyed to Lincoln, and discussed with Bryan the details of the planks to be included in the platform.[39] Oklahoma's two Senators were featured speakers at the convention, Senator Gore producing a rousing rally for Bryan, and Senator Owen discussing in detail the operation of Oklahoma's bank guarantee law. The inclusion in the party platform of the national bank guarantee clause was largely the work of Owen and Haskell.

Shortly after the convention adjourned Haskell was appointed to the position of treasurer of the national committee. In that position he proved something of an embarrassment to Bryan. For Haskell rather than Bryan for a time threatened to become the chief issue in the campaign. The opposition accused Haskell of

[37] The bill was H. R. 3378, *Congressional Record,* Vol. 25. Editorials in *The Commoner* had immediately revived the proposal after the panic of October 1907, and aggressively advocated it in every issue.

[38] *The Commoner,* January 24, 1908.

[39] Guthrie *Oklahoma State Capital,* July 2, 1908.

being unduly friendly to the Prairie Oil and Gas Company, a
Standard Oil affiliate, and also charged him with fraudulent deal-
ings in Indian land titles. The charges proved so embarrassing that
Haskell was asked to resign.[40]

Collaboration between Bryan and Oklahomans reached its highest point in 1907 and 1908. Throughout succeeding years much
the same pattern applied. Everyone is familiar with the manner in
which Bryan on the one hand and Oklahoma Democratic forces on
the other shifted the national convention of 1912 away from
Champ Clark and over to Woodrow Wilson.[41] Many of the later
social movements in which Bryan became interested were sympathetically treated in Oklahoma—his interest in world peace and
neutrality, his support of fundamentalism in religion, his advocacy
of the temperance movement. If anything, Bryan's popularity grew
in Oklahoma during later years. As he turned away from the political field and confined his activities to the nonpolitical realm of
Chautauqua addresses, many who had formerly been hostile for
political reasons now came to admire him. At the time of Bryan's
death in July, 1925, many Oklahomans felt that they had suffered
a personal loss.

Bryan indeed had influenced Oklahoma history as has perhaps
no other national political figure. The character of the Democratic
party in Oklahoma, its program for an entire generation, local
laws such as the bank guarantee law, and the Oklahoma constitution itself were guided in varying degrees by the hand of the Great
Commoner.

Oklahomans in turn regarded Bryan as highly as they have ever
respected any politician from outside the state. That regard was
demonstrated in countless ways—by the action of the first legislature; by the active support given to Bryan's political campaigns,
especially in 1908; by the contest in the constitutional convention

[40] Details of this incident are best recorded in Josephus Daniels, *Editor in
Politics* (Chapel Hill, 1941), pp. 543–545.

[41] The author is aware of attempts by recent writers to minimize the influence of Bryan and his supporters. Careful study and discussion with
several of the participants, including "Alfalfa Bill" Murray, seems to bear
out the fact, however, that the traditional historical interpretation is far
more accurate.

to determine which county should have the honor of being named "Bryan County." Most of all, though, it is demonstrated by the fond memories of Oklahomans today. Virtually every resident of the state who lived through those years has his own memories of Bryan, his own anecdote to tell. In those tales and anecdotes one can sense the high regard for Bryan's sincerity, for his never losing the "common touch," for his ability to laugh, even at himself, and for his conviction that rural America was the only basis on which a sound and stable nation could be built. Bryan was indeed the Voice of Rural America. Therein lay his greatness, and his weakness as well.

Perhaps it would be well to let the parties involved speak for themselves. In 1908, while on their way to a national convention at Denver, a group of Oklahoma admirers stopped in Lincoln to pay tribute to Bryan. Still celebrating their recent victory of statehood, the group presented Bryan with a new flag with 46 stars, and a specially inscribed, leather-bound copy of the Oklahoma constitution.[42] To this group of admirers Bryan made one of his shortest and most sincere speeches:

Politically, I suppose I am nearer kin to Oklahoma than to any other state in the union, and I can say that without hurting the feelings of anybody in Nebraska. Nebraska Democrats will tell you, and the Republicans will not deny that I am nearer Oklahoma Democrats and politics than I am to those of Nebraska.[43]

And what of the Oklahomans of that day? Their collective attitude was probably best expressed by an editor who penned a few lines in a cluttered print shop out on the high plains of Oklahoma's southwestern frontier. He was P. Y. Brinton, editor of the Hobart *Weekly Chief,* who wrote after Bryan's visit to Hobart in 1903:

Bryan has come and gone. . . . He will go down in history as one of the truly great, whether he is chosen President of the United States or not, without a blemish or stain upon his character, leaving as a legacy new and advanced ideas and theories of government.[44]

[42] This well-worn document is to be found in the library of the Nebraska State Historical Society.
[43] Guthrie *Oklahoma State Capital,* July 5, 1908.
[44] Hobart *Weekly Chief,* January 21, 1903.

✪

Secretary of State

The passage of time has been unkind to the reputation of William Jennings Bryan. Few can call to mind the image of the young crusader who voiced the protest of the prairie farmer and who thrilled huge audiences with his impassioned demands for social justice; instead, there has emerged the picture of a stubborn, often obtuse defender of outmoded ideas, a man who failed to keep abreast of his times and who, characteristically, passed from the American scene while trying to prevent the teaching of the principles of evolution. Indeed, even at the time he was serving in the Cabinet of Woodrow Wilson, Bryan represented, not the wave of the Wilsonian future, but the legacy of the populist past; he was a man to whom many Democrats owed deep political obligations but for whom the more sophisticated progressives already had an abiding distrust. And, in midcentury America, even the values of the agrarian tradition which Bryan represented have become suspect; the contemporary historian often interprets Bryan as the foremost exponent of an unfortunate "agrarian myth" which no longer has a place in an urbanized, industrialized society.

Bryan's record in the Department of State produced little admiring comment from either contemporaries or later historians. His appointment as Secretary of State was the signal for all but a few

Reprinted from Richard Challener, "William Jennings Bryan," in Norman A. Graebner, ed., *An Uncertain Tradition* (McGraw-Hill, 1961), pp. 79–100. Copyright © 1961 by McGraw-Hill, Inc. Used by permission of McGraw-Hill Book Company.

loyal Democratic newspapers to launch scathing criticisms and to continue the barrage as long as he remained in office—whether the subject was his aversion to alcohol, his handling of appointments in the diplomatic service, or his reaction to the German submarine. His resignation in 1915, an act which Bryan hoped would rally the country to the cause of peace, merely added to the tumult and provoked at least one influential daily to write of his "unspeakable treachery." There was, to be sure, a brief period in the 1930's when Bryan was held in higher regard. In a decade when Americans rejected all world responsibility and regarded their participation in World War I as the greatest aberration in the nation's history, writers were at least willing to credit Bryan with good intentions. He, after all, had realized that money was the greatest of all contrabands and that defense of the right of Americans to travel on belligerent passenger vessels would lead to conflict with Germany. But even in revisionist historiography Bryan does not emerge as a compelling figure. If his pacifistic instincts were sound, he could not develop a policy which would halt the drift toward war. If he did forsee the future with clairvoyance, he was still powerless to win Woodrow Wilson to his point of view. For, as many have pointed out, Wilson was his own Secretary of State whenever the great issues were under debate, and Bryan was necessarily cast in the role of subordinate whenever the President chose to tap out messages to foreign governments on his famous portable typewriter.

Indeed, whether one examines the contemporary or the historical record, it is almost ridiculously easy to file a long bill of particulars against the "Great Commoner." There is virtual unanimity of opinion about Bryan's attitude toward appointments in the American Foreign Service. He stands condemned as a spoilsman, one of the last out-and-out defenders of the idea that any American—in particular, any American who has contributed to his political party—is qualified to represent his country abroad. Virtually everyone who has written about Bryan has quoted with appropriate relish the notorious letter to James Sullivan in which the Secretary of State blandly wrote about the need to find jobs for "deserving Democrats."

More significant is the criticism which grows out of contemporary re-examinations of the intellectual tradition of American diplomacy. The prevailing interpretation, one which mirrors the current involvements of the United States in a world of power, severely condemns the national effort in foreign policy for having been excessively concerned with what are described as moralistic pronouncements and legalistic solutions. The realists look almost in vain for Secretaries of State who understood the operations of the balance of power, thought in terms of the national interest, or recognized the necessity of balancing commitments with a willingness to utilize the instruments of coercion if need arose. Bryan, it is scarcely necessary to say, abjectly fails to meet the realist criteria. With his rejection of power politics, his penchant for moralizing, his addiction to platitudinous speeches, and his reliance upon the tenets of Christian pacifism, Bryan seems to be the symbol of virtually every error that is condemned by contemporary critics of the American diplomatic tradition. Indeed, as one recent writer has observed, since Woodrow Wilson shared many of Bryan's mistaken assumptions, it was disastrous for his administration to have as Secretary of State a man who did not bring a different point of view to discussions of diplomatic policy and who "harbored the very attitudes that at once inspired and handicapped his chief."

There was, to be sure, one area of the world—Latin America—in which Bryan did practice a form of "realism," but, ironically, he receives no credit for this. Bryan's special brand of Latin-American intervention, which, like the policy of his predecessor, ultimately rested upon the sanction of marines and New York bankers, has long since been repudiated by the United States. Over three decades ago this approach was found to be no longer viable in the face of increasing nationalism in Latin America.

Yet Bryan may have some claims to a more respectable place in American diplomatic history. Certainly he cannot be dismissed as a mere cipher who was always bypassed and disregarded by the President. The most careful student of Woodrow Wilson has recently taken great pains to point out that Bryan and Wilson consulted with each other upon innumerable subjects and that, for both men, the collaboration was often close and rewarding. Wilson obviously had many initial reservations about the man whom he appointed to oversee American foreign policy, but, as time passed, he did develop a high respect for Bryan. It was with regret, as the correspondence over the *Lusitania* notes clearly demonstrates, that the President overruled his Secretary of State, for Wilson realized that Bryan almost instinctively reflected the attitudes and opinions of the great democracy which he represented. Moreover, within the administration Bryan was an indispensable link between the old and the new, the one Democrat who made it possible for populists and progressives to create a working majority and thereby write the New Freedom into American law. The passage of the Federal Reserve Act, to mention but one piece of legislation, would never have been possible if Bryan had not played this useful role. It must also be said that, whatever the merits or demerits of his attitude toward the problem of war, Bryan had the courage of his convictions. When differences of opinion became irreconcilable, he did what few American politicians have ever brought themselves to do: he resigned from the Cabinet and attempted to take his case to the country. And even within the walls of the supposedly cynical Department of State, this act of self-denial moved great numbers of government employees, some with tears in their eyes, to come to say a word of farewell to a man willing to give up the second highest position in the United States government on a matter of principle.

II

Even in an age when the qualifications for the post of Secretary of State were something less than demanding, William Jennings Bryan brought dubious credentials to that office. His principal claim was that of the elder statesman, the three-time loser as standard-bearer of his party who, over the years, had won for himself a personal following that numbered in the millions and was composed "of friends who were all but worshippers." Equally relevant was the fact that at the dramatic Baltimore convention of 1912 Bryan had played a decisive role in swinging delegates to the cause of Woodrow Wilson. It was clear that no one really wanted to appoint Bryan to the highest position in the Cabinet, but it was equally clear that

no one wanted to run the risk of not including him in the new
administration. Bryan, in short, was appointed as a reward for
years of faithful service to the Democratic party as well as from
fear that, if he were not included in the new administration, he
might produce incalculable harm.

His intellectual qualifications for the Secretaryship were no more
impressive than his political claims. A man of fixed ideas, Bryan
had a decided tendency to oversimplify complex issues, to look
upon tangled diplomatic problems as relatively simple matters of
right and wrong, and to believe that controversy could be eliminated by the application of a few homely truths. Typically, Bryan's
very first set of instructions, which he sent to American officials in
revolution-torn Mexico, noted that "as disagreements generally
arise from misunderstandings or from conflicts of interest, it is wise
to remove misunderstandings by conference and to reconcile conflicting interests by mutual concessions. . . ." It was the responsibility of Americans to work for cooperation between the various
conflicting factions in Mexico "upon a basis of justice to all at home
and abroad."

Bryan's general outlook on the world was that of an unsophisti-
cated opponent of anything that could be called imperialism. Indeed, much that Bryan attempted to do can be explained by pointing out that, in his political lexicon, imperialism was a cardinal sin.
As a matter of strict principle, he opposed virtually everything that
Philander C. Knox and the advocates of "dollar diplomacy" held
dear, and he wrote fondly of his desire to replace their policies with
"a system more in harmony with our nation's traditions and ideals."
Dollar diplomacy, indeed, appeared to Bryan as merely the foreign
policy of the same wicked business interests whose domestic policies he had long fought and opposed. At one of the first Cabinet
discussions of the Mexican Revolution, the Secretary endorsed
fully the proposition "that the chief cause of this whole situation,"
as Josephus Daniels, himself a Bryanite, phrased it, "was a contest
between English and American oil companies to see which would
control." When Bryan was approached about continued American
participation in a Chinese loan consortium, he rejected any such
action on the grounds that the consortium granted monopolistic

privileges to a restricted group of American financiers. His record of continuous opposition to imperialism was clear. Although he had supported the great crusade to free Cuba in 1898 and had, for mistaken reasons, advocated ratification of the treaty which added the Philippines to the American domain, he never again wavered in his opposition to what he regarded as the naked imperialism of the Republican administrations of McKinley, Roosevelt, and Taft.

A no less significant aspect of Bryan's outlook was his pronounced moralism and his belief that the United States, as the foremost democracy in the world, had a duty to set an example for the other, less fortunate nations which had not yet scaled the heights of American achievement. When he opposed American intervention in Mexico in 1913, he rested his case in large part upon the argument that "our nation claims to stand in the forefront of the world's civilization and aspires to be the greatest moral influence in the world. We cannot hope to realize our ambition or to support our claim if we are willing to engage in war with a neighboring people merely to protect property which has been acquired with a full knowledge of the risks attendant upon it." This was not a new attitude for Bryan. In a speech delivered long before he became Secretary of State, he had envisioned a future in which the rest of the world would look upon the United States as "the supreme moral factor in the world's progress and the accepted arbiter of the world's disputes." This moral perspective affected not only Bryan's general outlook but also his daily conduct of the business of the Department of State. He was opposed, for example, to recognizing the Huerta regime in Mexico, even though this step was recommended as a matter of practical necessity. He was, as he put it, "so unaccustomed to the consideration of public questions separated from both morals and the principle of popular government that I was not able to endorse the position of those who favored the recognition of Huerta."

Bryan, of course, had had no formal experience with the business of diplomacy. He had traveled abroad, but there is no evidence that his visits to Latin America, Europe, and the Far East had provided him with insights into the state of affairs in those regions. It seems, rather, that Bryan saw what he wanted to see and that his travels only confirmed what he had suspected beforehand. Certainly his Latin-American trip merely produced speeches in which he told his Latin-American audiences that they were the victims of imperialism, and his conversations with Tolstoi in Europe simply reinforced his pacifistic convictions. His reaction to the proposed appointment of Charles Eliot, the former president of Harvard, as American Minister to the new republic of China, clearly indicated his lack of knowledge about actual conditions in foreign countries. To appoint a Unitarian to this position, Bryan immediately protested, would be an insult to China; the Chinese revolution, he insisted, was a Christian movement conducted by men who had imbibed deeply the Christian faith.

Bryan had one principal aim: to further the work of the peace movement by negotiating a series of treaties which would make it virtually impossible for the United States to go to war with any nation. Believing that the principles of Christian pacifism were viable to meet the conflicts of nations, he had consistently preached peace on the Chautauqua circuit. There had indeed been no more fervent worker in that garden. Since 1904 he had favored a series of agreements—ultimately dubbed the "cooling-off treaties"—whereby no nation would go to war until there had been a twelve-month period of grace during which the basic facts underlying the dispute would be investigated. The plan was not original with Bryan, for he was by no means an original thinker, but it did reveal his abiding faith in the goodness and rationality of man. It was inconceivable to Bryan that any people, once the issues had been clarified and publicized, would deliberately choose the course of war and reject the possibility of compromise. Even after the European war had broken out, Bryan wrote to Lloyd George reaffirming his belief in international arbitration: "There is no dispute that must necessarily be settled by force. All international disputes are capable of adjustment by peaceful means. Every guarantee that can possibly be secured by war can be stated as a condition precedent to peace."

In March, 1913, the future Secretary's qualifications and objectives appeared sufficient to both Bryan and Wilson. Indeed, when the two men discussed Bryan's pending appointment, they considered only two matters—Bryan's desire to avoid serving alcoholic beverages at official functions and Wilson's attitude toward the projected cooling-off treaties. The new administration was primarily concerned with domestic problems and with creating the conditions for the New Freedom at home. So little were the two men aware of international difficulties that the President could remark—and it was *not* in the spirit of prophecy—that it would be ironic if his administration had to pay great attention to foreign affairs.

Certainly Bryan assumed office without any sense of deep concern for the nation's diplomatic future. He would simply reverse the imperialism of his predecessor and re-establish American foreign policy upon moral foundations. He would negotiate his long-sought peace treaties. In addition, he would reward loyal Democrats who had long labored in the political wilderness. These were modest goals which, in other times and circumstances, might have been possible to achieve. But, unfortunately for Bryan and his reputation, the future was to involve the United States in problems for which neither he nor the President was intellectually prepared.

III

Bryan was no less controversial during his Secretarial years than he had been in the days when he advocated the panacea of free silver. At the outset there was the expected quota of unflattering comment about what the newspapers called "grapejuice diplomacy" —dinners and receptions without benefit of alcohol. His penchant for leaving Washington for periodic speaking engagements on the Chautauqua circuit drew the fire of critics who charged that the Secretary lacked interest in his job and that it was improper for him to accept payment for public lectures. These tours, however, were a virtual necessity for Bryan's peace of mind. Since he took seriously his title as the Great Commoner and regarded himself as the representative of the people in the councils of government, he felt an inner obligation to speak in public of his work for peace and justice. Moreover, since his natural means of communication was the emotional address rather than the written report or the reasoned memorandum, he could not long have remained content if the opportunity to perform as an orator had been denied him.

The greatest criticism of Bryan was directed against his unabashed devotion to the tenets of the spoils system, for although the American Foreign Service was as yet essentially unreformed, there were already many who believed that diplomatic appointments should bear some relationship to merit and professional qualifications. Historians have recounted the lugubrious details of how Bryan replaced experienced diplomats with an unappetizing collection of political war horses, and there is no reason to repeat these stories here. But it should be emphasized that there was nothing malicious in this practice. Bryan, with his Jacksonian faith in the common man, honestly believed that, just as he himself was qualified to conduct the affairs of state, any average American could carry on the relatively simple task of representing his country abroad. It is also true that he and Wilson distrusted many of the officials appointed by previous administrations and believed that they represented a point of view antithetical to the ideals of the New Freedom. Even so, the work of replacement was essentially that of an American politician doing what politicians in this country have always done—finding suitable rewards for those who have served their party. At an early Cabinet meeting, Bryan reported that he was having great difficulty finding a suitable place for the brother of the chairman of the Democratic National Committee. Even Bryan admitted that the candidate, although admirably suited for government employment, was not particularly qualified for a position in the Consular Service. He therefore proposed a trade. "I will give a man a position at $4,000," he told his colleagues, "if you will give me a $4,000 job in another Department." The Attorney General rose to the bait. "All right," he answered, "I will give him a place if you will let me name the minister to Persia." Bryan just as promptly accepted. "All right, send over your man," he said.

The new Secretary of State was held in low esteem both by foreign officials and by many of his associates in the administration. Some diplomats, such as the British Minister, Cecil Spring-Rice, came close to being openly contemptuous; and the general

European opinion of Bryan was summed up in a remark that Colonel Edward M. House recorded in his diary: "Mr. Asquith cast the usual slur upon Mr. Bryan." Indeed, on countless occasions House admonished Wilson not to rely upon Bryan in his dealings with European governments. "Please let me suggest that you do not let Mr. Bryan make any overtures to any of the Powers involved," the Colonel wrote in the summer of 1914. "They look upon him as absolutely visionary, and it would lessen the weight on your influence if you desire to use it later yourself." Walter Hines Page, the American Ambassador to Great Britain, regarded Bryan as little more than an untutored frontiersman with no understanding of the great issues of Anglo-American relations. Page incessantly complained that Bryan mishandled official correspondence to such a degree that it was impossible for him to learn what was going on in Washington and pointless for him to try to keep the Secretary of State informed about events in London. Likewise, a number of Bryan's associates in the administration left behind memoirs in which they recorded their doubts about his administrative ability and his general fitness for office.

Much of this criticism can be at least partially discounted. Colonel House, cherishing his own position as the unofficial adviser behind the Wilsonian throne, had never truly respected Bryan and was always more than willing to assume diplomatic assignments which properly belonged to the Secretary of State. Although he had learned to respect Bryan's good intentions, he also clearly believed that his own outlook in world affairs was broader and wiser than that of the Great Commoner. Within the Democratic party, too, there were leaders who represented a more sophisticated point of view; to them Bryan's rural enthusiasms would be suspect automatically. European governments, eager to obtain American support for the policies which they pursued after the outbreak of war in 1914, could scarcely be expected to view with much favor a man devoted to strict neutrality and pacifism. Their ministers and ambassadors, trained in a tradition in which the forms of diplomacy were often as important as the content, naturally looked upon Bryan with disfavor. Thus, one should be properly skeptical about much of the criticism of Bryan which is to be found in the diaries, memoirs, and autobiographies of the Wilson era. But not entirely. The virtually unanimous disapproval of Bryan indicates that he lacked the qualities which alone permit an American Secretary of State to deal effectively with foreign governments and thereby to advance the interests of his country.

Bryan faced certain obstacles on the Washington scene which added to his troubles as Secretary of State. There was Colonel House, who had already established his own personal influence with the President. And the Texas colonel, whatever his faults and limitations, was no isolationist who wished merely to shelter America from European storms. He proposed imaginative schemes to avert world conflict through an Anglo-German-American agreement, he outlined a far-reaching project for Pan-American union, and he suggested many plans whereby the United States could play an effective role in the European conflict. It was therefore not surprising that Wilson, whose mind could also encompass the vision of aiding humanity in the whole, was not only attracted by the grandiose schemes of House but also tempted—to the disadvantage of Bryan—to give important diplomatic assignments to his unofficial adviser. Moreover, within the Department of State there was a highly competent international lawyer, Robert Lansing, whose stature with the President steadily increased and whose reasoned documents on the issues of the European war carried ever-increasing weight at the White House. As luck would have it, Bryan was absent from his post during the autumn of 1914 and concerned with the November elections at the time when the principal business of the Department of State was to establish the American attitude toward the British blockade of the Central Powers. Thus it was Lansing who handled the American response to all the issues related to the blockade and who thereby established a position for himself in the policy-making process that made him virtually coequal with Bryan.

In the last analysis, however, the crucial fact is that Bryan was Secretary of State to a Chief Executive who, despite his lack of experience in diplomacy, firmly believed that he had both the right and the duty to direct all phases of foreign policy. Wilson's energy and direction did not reduce Bryan to the status of a mere sub-

ordinate without the power of initiative or an adviser who was
never consulted. The record is quite the contrary. On many issues,
such as the negotiation of the cooling-off treaties or the daily
conduct of Latin-American affairs, Wilson was quite content to
leave the development of policy in the hands of his Secretary.
Moreover, whatever the subject, there was an extensive interchange
of notes and memoranda between the two men; the sheer bulk of
the Wilson-Bryan correspondence indicates that Bryan was never
bypassed to the extent that Cordell Hull was during World War II.
Wilson and Bryan, as Ray Stannard Baker has attested, were
united by many common beliefs and had "a common devotion to
a body of ideas and ideals as deep and as old as the foundations
of the nation." The record again bears reliable witness to the fact
that the President came to have abiding respect for his Secretary
of State—"my elder son" was the epithet which Wilson used in
conversations within his own family.

On such fundamental issues as the handling of the *Lusitania*
notes, Bryan could not develop arguments sufficient to convince
his chief to treat the Germans with leniency. But it is also clear
that, even on this bedrock issue, the President felt it necessary to
weigh carefully the arguments presented by his Secretary of State.
On more than one occasion Bryan's advice compelled Wilson
to pause, to reconsider his own ideas in the light of his Secretary's
criticism, and only then to move ahead. Yet when the issues were
sufficiently crucial or when the President's own emotions and
intellect were involved, Wilson was clearly his own Secretary of
State. Of this there can be no doubt. Bryan might be consulted, his
views might be given proper consideration, but final decisions were
made in the White House. Thus, the administration's policy toward
Mexico, the stand taken on the Panama Canal tolls, and the handling of the German submarine problem were all the work of
Wilson; Bryan was, at best, the informed subordinate. This, however, was not necessarily a reflection upon Bryan's abilities or an
indication that the President did not respect his Secretary. Robert
Lansing, a far more knowledgeable and able man than Bryan,
received the same treatment when he succeeded Bryan as Secretary of State. If both men were subordinates, the reason lies in

the character and temperament of the President—in his conviction that ultimate responsibility was his and in his confidence in his own mission.

Another characteristic of Wilson's handling of foreign affairs which adversely affected Bryan's position was the President's predilection for using special agents or personal favorites to carry on the work of American diplomacy. The already muddy waters of Mexican-American relations were further dirtied by a steady procession of Presidential agents given special assignments to report their observations to the White House. Colonel House was sent on various missions to Europe about which Bryan was not fully informed and over which he certainly had little control. That this confused the conduct of foreign policy is unquestionable. It is quite clear that on more than one occasion the British assumed that House spoke for the American government and, as a result, not only regarded some of his statements more seriously than was wise but also tended to disregard the words of Bryan. Similarly, though Page complained that Bryan did not keep him informed about developments in Washington, at least part of the reason for this situation was that Bryan was aware of the elaborate House-Page-Wilson correspondence which was conducted through unofficial channels; Bryan could assume, with more than a little justice, that he had no responsibility to tell Page about things which the Ambassador was already learning from other sources. Thus, some of the confusion attendant upon American diplomacy in these years resulted not from Bryan's lack of administrative ability but from Wilson's tendency to rely upon personal agents and to bypass normal channels of communication. But this situation lasted long after Bryan had resigned, and Robert Lansing—as any study of the Peace Conference of 1919 will reveal—labored under the same handicaps.

IV

But, whether or not Bryan was master in his own house, he can be appraised only in terms of the policies which he recommended or sanctioned during his slightly more than two years in office.

What did he hope to accomplish in the Far East or in Latin America? Were his objectives in the national interest? And how, above all, did he react to the European war, for the raging conflict in Europe confronted Bryan with the gravest dilemmas that any American Secretary of State had encountered since the time of William H. Seward.

In the spring of 1913, Far Eastern problems seemed ridiculously easy to handle. It was the American purpose to aid the Chinese revolution and to halt the meddling of American imperialists. Thus it was decided to accord diplomatic recognition to the new Chinese republic and to withdraw governmental support from the bankers' consortium. These decisions were based not upon prolonged study of the power relationships in the Orient but upon the essentially moralistic logic that monopolistic grants of financial rights were contrary to American principle and that recognition would demonstrate American approval for China's presumed evolution toward democratic institutions of government. Nor, of course, was there any apparent reason to consult the few holdover experts in the State Department; their opinions, conditioned by the years of dollar diplomacy, could be presumed irrelevant. Both Bryan and Wilson, in short, labored under the early-twentieth-century version of the "China myth"; theirs was the delusion, as Arthur Walworth has succinctly written, "that the millions of China . . . were groping toward a Christian democracy patterned upon the Republic of the United States, and that it was the manifest duty of good Americans to aid them."

Far Eastern skies, however, soon became threatening and caused far more difficulty than either Bryan or Wilson had anticipated. Japan was angered by proposals before the California legislature to deny Japanese the right to own land. As the dispute, at first underestimated by Wilson and his Cabinet, became more serious, Bryan became deeply involved. His role, from first to last, was conciliatory. He made fruitless efforts to persuade the Californians to modify their pending legislation; he and Daniels were the Cabinet members most strongly opposed to suggestions from the army and the navy that the United States begin taking advance military precautions by changing the disposition of fleet units in the Far

East; and he continually tried to convince Baron Chinda, the Japanese Ambassador in Washington, that the United States wanted to preserve friendly relations with his country. Typical of Bryan's attitude during the controversy was his often-quoted remark— made to Chinda when that diplomat apparently thought that the United States had made its "final" offer—that "nothing is final between friends."

The crisis of May, 1913, vanished almost as rapidly as it had appeared. But when World War I broke out, the Japanese, who had long been thwarted in their expansionist moves, realized that the disruption of the balance of power in the world provided them with a splendid opportunity to resume their course of empire. When Japan began to press her claims upon China, Bryan naturally sided with the Chinese and became involved in the familiar American diplomatic game of note writing. One of his last major acts in the Department of State was to reassert, in the face of Japan's Twenty-one Demands, the traditional American insistence upon recognition by all nations of the territorial and administrative integrity of China.

It would be difficult to discover any immediately harmful consequences of Bryan's Far Eastern diplomacy. The settlement of Japan's expansionist claims was not worked out until after the European war was concluded, and the touchy issue of alien-land legislation, which, like that of Oriental immigration, had started in the era of Theodore Roosevelt, was to drag on, with only partial alleviation, until long after Bryan had departed the national scene. In the short run, Bryan's conciliatory tactics in 1913 were certainly beneficial; the President's military advisers were unduly alarmed, and their military plans, if executed, might have fanned embers into flames. Yet in point of fact Bryan did very little except offer soothing words; he was, for example, far less severe with the recalcitrant Californians than Roosevelt and Root had been at the time of the first Japanese-American crisis. The quick passage of the incident owed less to Bryan's diplomacy than to Japanese reluctance to turn it into a major issue. On the other hand, the uncritical way in which Bryan allied himself with the Chinese added one more important link to the chain of events whereby Americans came to think of themselves as the chosen friends and protectors of China. Moreover, the series of notes in which Bryan indicated American opposition to the Twenty-one Demands led to unnecessary complications in later negotiations, for they were so imprecisely stated that they could be given different interpretations in Washington and in Tokyo.

Bryan's record in Latin-American affairs is a far more perplexing one; it is, indeed, a record which must forever confound the historian who desires to fit his subject into any neat pattern of consistency. Bryan began, as in the Far East, with the desire to undo the imperialistic wrongs of the past, but, as his critics have noted gleefully, he ended by sponsoring as many interventions as had his predecessor. This inconsistency between intent and deed resulted in part from Bryan's inexperience. Since he knew almost nothing about actual conditions in Latin America, he was compelled, in spite of himself, to listen to the advice of officials in the Latin-American Division who had long since become convinced that only the techniques of intervention would work effectively in the countries to the south. Then, too, although Bryan was essentially a pacifist, he was not deficient in patriotism (he had, after all, volunteered in 1898), and he was fully aware of the need to protect the routes to and from the Panama Canal. He found no conflict between his anti-imperialistic philosophy and the presumed need of the United States Navy to acquire bases protecting the Windward Passage. Indeed, as early as June, 1913, Bryan was hard at work trying to obtain from Haiti a coaling station long prized by American admirals. When the effort failed, he was no less eager than Knox to get the Haitians to promise that the potential naval base would never be leased to any other foreign country.

Bryan's interventions in Latin America can also be explained in part by the sheer lack of alternatives. Once he had decided that it was necessary to stabilize conditions in a particular country, it was obviously necessary to find the money for the task. But when Wilson would not approve some of Bryan's unorthodox financial remedies and when Congress proved reluctant to move with any celerity, Bryan found himself obliged to turn to the same banking houses which had been patronized by Knox. Finally, and more regrettably, Bryan's interventions were the result of his naïveté. His plan for the reformation of Nicaragua included provisions, comparable to the terms of the Platt amendment, whereby American military intervention would be entirely legal in the event of revolution or disorder. When Bryan argued in behalf of these provisions, he stressed repeatedly that the Nicaraguan government itself wanted to give such rights of intervention to the United States. But Bryan never asked himself why the Latin-American officials were so willing; he never considered that in Nicaragua, where revolution was then the national pastime, an unpopular, discredited regime might desire the privilege of calling on the United States marines, seeing in their intervention the only means of remaining in office.

Yet these reasons alone could never have led Bryan to drink at the well of imperialism. There was also—indeed, there had to be—the firm belief that America was performing a service by bringing the benefits of its own successful national experience to the aid of less privileged peoples. For, as Arthur Link has persuasively argued, both Bryan and Wilson were motivated by a missionary zeal to render disinterested service. Thus, although their interventions may have been similar in kind to those of Knox and Taft, there was a marked difference in motive. Furthermore, there were more than a few scattered occasions when Bryan issued statements designed to protect Latin Americans not only from American financial interests but also from their own susceptibility to exploitation. One note, for example, declared that the Department of State had a responsibility to prevent citizens of the United States from obtaining excessive financial privileges in Latin America. It would, indeed, be difficult to imagine such a memorandum emanating from the desk of Knox or his assistant, Huntington Wilson.

The Secretary of State was unquestionably bothered by the implications of his "imperialism." He tried to develop new approaches or different rationales which would make what he was doing acceptable to his conscience. His solutions were both inventive and ingenious; even if incapable of fulfillment, they indi-

cated that Bryan was a man who did not live entirely by plati-
tudes and who put much time and thought into his work at the
Department of State. One remedy which he suggested was a re-
working of the Monroe Doctrine to bring it into line with the
contemporary situation. The real danger to Latin America, Bryan
argued, came not from European political or military threats but
from the impact of foreign financial interests. Local rulers in Latin
America, in their eternal search for funds, turned to Europe for
financial assistance and, with this foreign help, were able to maintain themselves in power. At times the foreign bankers themselves
obtained a stranglehold upon the economy of the country. But in
either case, Bryan was careful to point out, "the people are as
helpless as if a foreign army had landed on their shore." On
another occasion he argued that American bankers pointed to the
disordered political conditions in Latin America as an excuse for
demanding exorbitant rates of interest or as justification for calling
upon the United States Navy to send gunboats to protect their
investments. The solution for these varied problems, Bryan contended, was for the United States government itself to provide the
necessary loans, to peg them at low rates of interest, and to establish provisions whereby a part of the interest could be set aside for
the eventual repayment of principal. It was Wilson who found
this proposal too unorthodox and who never expressed more than
polite interest in it. Yet, although Bryan's project was obviously
related to his naïve tendency to place excessive blame upon "the
interests," it did anticipate methods of international financing
which in more recent years have become commonplace—the substitution of intergovernmental loans for private business arrangements.

The problem of Mexico was second only to the European war
as a cause of diplomatic difficulties for the Wilson administration.
Mexico, to be sure, was the private preserve of the President, and
American policy toward Victoriano Huerta and Venustiano Car-
ranza was determined by Wilson himself. But the views of Secretary and President on the Mexican problem were marked by only
minor points of disagreement; Bryan, for example, was unhappy
about the landing at Vera Cruz and more than a little relieved

when the intervention of the ABC powers (Argentina, Brazil, and Chile) offered Wilson a way out of his difficulties. On balance, however, the coincidence of viewpoints was more striking than the dissimilarities. Indeed, when Bryan curtly rejected one of Huerta's notes during the controversy that followed the arrest of two American sailors at Tampico, Wilson scribbled the marginal comment, "Your reply . . . is exactly what I would have wished it to be." Bryan certainly did not attempt to rock the Wilsonian boat over Mexico. It was typical of his attitude that, when the American admiral at Tampico first reported the arrest of his sailors and his demand for a public apology, the Secretary of State merely passed the message on to the President without analysis and with the uncritical comment that he could see no way that the officer could have acted otherwise. When questions were raised about the right of American sailors to land at Tampico, Bryan was quite content to accept the arguments put forth by the General Board of the Navy (which naturally put the onus upon the Mexicans) and to transmit these to Mexico City as representing the opinions of the Department of State. Bryan's contribution to the Mexican policy of Wilson thus seems to have been one of almost unquestioning support.

V

In the twentieth century, unfortunately, the ultimate test of the statesman has been his understanding of the uses—or misuses—of the instruments of coercion. In a half century of global conflict, the leaders of nations have all too often had to face the issue of whether to resort to force or to find avenues for compromise, conciliation, or appeasement. Bryan's instinctive reaction was to shun coercive methods and to search for peaceful solutions. During the controversy over the Panama Canal tolls, Josephus Daniels recorded the following entry in his diary: "England is willing to arbitrate. Mr. Burleson said he did not believe in arbitration. Mr. Bryan said he would arbitrate anything." The Secretary of State, on another occasion, resolutely opposed all suggestions that the United States provide armed protection for its citizens who had remained in Mexico to protect their own private business interests. These Americans, Bryan was convinced, were staying of their own volition in a country where they were not welcome; military protection could be tendered them only if the United States first recalled all its citizens from Mexico, requested the Mexican government to grant them safe conduct, and then learned that Mexico could not guarantee such safe conduct. Then, and then only, could the United States legitimately consider the use of force. Likewise, after he had resigned from the administration, Bryan refused to endorse the plans of the League to Enforce Peace because they called for the use of force to fight force. At times Bryan could be virtually unreasonable at the mere suggestion of the possible use of coercive methods. During the 1913 dispute with Japan, Bryan "got red in the face" when the Secretary of War merely stated that, in his opinion, officers of the Army and Navy were competent to decide whether or not naval vessels should be moved to other stations as a precaution. "He thundered out," one witness later recalled, "that Army and Navy officers could not be trusted to say what we should or should not do . . . that we were discussing not how to wage war, but how not to get into war."

This is not to imply that Bryan was always consistent, for he obviously tolerated military moves against Mexico and he utilized the Navy in the Caribbean. And he was willing to go to war if the United States itself was attacked. He remained convinced, however, that there would always be sufficient time to create a nation in arms out of the millions of Americans who would volunteer to defend their country after it had been attacked. Like many Americans of his time, he felt that military preparedness was wrong, that it was a cause rather than a symptom of international tension, and that, in any event, the United States could establish a force capable of repelling any enemy after the crisis occurred.

It is not surprising, therefore, that Bryan believed at the time—and long continued to believe—that his greatest accomplishment as Secretary of State was the successful negotiation of the series of treaties whereby the United States and the signatory nations agreed to submit their disputes to an investigating panel and refrain from going to war during the period that the issues were under investigation. These cooling-off treaties, as previously noted, did not represent any original contribution on the part of Bryan and—aside from a clause which permitted disputes involving that greatest of all intangibles, "the national honor," to be investigated—were not dissimilar to various arbitration and conciliation treaties submitted to the Senate by William Howard Taft. To Bryan's credit, however, the Senate, which was normally provided with built-in mechanisms to resist such proposals, readily endorsed his treaties and subjected them to little adverse criticism. This occurred in part because Bryan carefully explained his purposes to the Senators and kept them well informed and also because the chairman of the Foreign Relations Committee, being himself a Democrat of the Bryanite faith, needed little persuasion.

What was even more noteworthy was Bryan's continuing faith in the validity of his treaties. His convictions remained unchanged despite the fact—and it is, indeed, one of the central ironies of his career—that the first great holocaust of the twentieth century broke out in Europe just at the moment when his treaties were being signed. He rejoiced in the British signature, although a more suspecting Secretary of State, noting that Britain's final approval came less than a month after that nation had gone to war with Germany, might have concluded that the British had an ulterior motive and were, by signing the treaty, trying to convince the United States of England's abiding love of peace. Indeed, Bryan even convinced himself that Imperial Germany endorsed his treaties "in principle." Therefore, although he never obtained the German signature on a cooling-off treaty, he regarded the German attitude with perfect equanimity and thought that Germany's agreement "in principle" provided a viable basis for German-American negotiations designed to break the stalemate over the submarine issue. The frequently told story about Bryan and the plowshares is revealing of both the naïveté and the sincerity of his hopes for peace: After the signing of several of his treaties, Bryan obtained a surplus army sword from the War Department and had it melted down and recast into miniature plowshares; these he distributed personally to his colleagues at special Departmental ceremonies. On each was inscribed the Biblical quotation about beating swords into plowshares and, in addition, two maxims: "Nothing is final between friends," and "Diplomacy is the art of keeping cool."

VI

For William Jennings Bryan, as for Woodrow Wilson, the European conflict was the greatest challenge of all. Here again the basic policy was that of the President, and Bryan was the consultant whose ideas were given careful attention but, in the last analysis, were never decisive.

At the outset of the war there was no fundamental disagreement between the two men. Bryan's desire for absolute impartiality between the belligerents was matched by Wilson's insistence that his fellow countrymen should remain neutral in thought and deed. But not far beneath the surface were genuine differences. Wilson insisted that the belligerents must respect America's rights as a neutral, and as the war continued, he began to see a relationship between the issues of the war and the broader, more vital interests of mankind. But the matter of rights was never crucial to Bryan, certainly not when their enforcement seemed to demand American involvement in the conflict. Although Bryan, too, was concerned about the fate of mankind, his humanitarianism tended toward emotionalism, and he was always moved to personalize the great issues of the war and to view them in terms of the fate of individual human beings. Thus his instinctive reaction to the news of the sinking of the *Lusitania* was to declare that the British were trying to use women and children as a shield to get illicit armaments across the Atlantic. British policy, Bryan contended, was like putting women and children in front of an army. His particular brand of humanitarianism led him to believe one of the great hoaxes of World War I: the German charge that the civilian population of the *Reich* was being starved by Britain's "food blockade." And because he believed that the problem of food was crucial to Germany, he was led into a number of false moves which attempted to relate the British blockade to the submarine question.

Bryan was always certain that the European war was both unnecessary and wicked. From the very beginning of the conflict he

begged Wilson to offer American mediation and to use all his influence to attempt to restore peace in Europe. He never cared
about the issues which had led the powers to war or the underlying causes of the conflict. All that mattered to Bryan was the
restoration of peace and the end of bloodshed. Indeed, he firmly
believed that the onus of continuing the war was as great as the
responsibility for initiating hostilities.

This is not to say that Bryan's ideas were entirely dissimilar to
those of Wilson. The President, after all, was himself to propose
mediation and on several occasions to express his opinion that the
causes of the conflict were both obscure and irrelevant. But Bryan
never showed any sophistication or sense of timing in his many
calls for mediation; his mind never seemed to encompass any concept more complex than that of the virtue of peace and the wickedness of war; and he never suggested any feasible terms or programs
whereby the blessed state of peace could be achieved. His ideas, in
short, stopped at the point where Wilson's began.

In regard to American neutrality, however, the Secretary of
State did offer some common-sense proposals which were not lacking in his usual ingenuity. There was, for example, his attitude on
the famous issue of whether or not loans could be granted to the
European belligerents—an issue whose importance was later
swelled out of all proportion by the "revisionist" historians who
believed that these loans were responsible for the American entry
into the war. To a Bryan who had fought for free silver and who
had never wavered in his hostility toward the "money power" of
Wall Street, it was obvious that money was the great contraband
which controlled everything else. The tenets of international law
notwithstanding, there should be no loans. This outright prohibition
was actually unneutral; it was founded upon distrust of the financiers rather than upon any understanding of the economics of
modern war; and, as time was to prove, it was an unrealistic policy
for a nation emerging from an economic recession and anxious to
participate in wartime trade. Yet it had a common-sense appeal
which was lacking in many of the more urbane arguments which
were put forth to justify financial dealings with the Allies. There
was also cogency in Bryan's contention that Americans who know-

ingly booked passage on Allied passenger vessels were, after Germany's formal announcement of submarine warfare, guilty of "contributory negligence." Therefore, if the ships on which they traveled were torpedoed, they were not entitled to the full protection of their neutral rights under international law. The doctrine of contributory negligence, so frequently employed in civil suits, could hardly be plucked out of Anglo-Saxon common law and applied to the more complicated structure of international law; and Woodrow Wilson, with his broader sense of the interests of both the United States and humanity, could not accept it. Yet, in retrospect, it too seems to have offered a leaven of common sense to the submarine controversies that was missing in the Wilsonian argument based on higher principle.

The split between President and Secretary became virtually inevitable when Wilson insisted upon treating German violations of American rights as more serious than those of Britain and, above all, as demanding immediate resolution. Bryan, whose concept of neutrality still demanded absolute impartiality and who wanted to avoid even the slightest chance of involvement, felt compelled to oppose Wilson at almost every step. He insisted that protests against German policy should be linked with protests against Great Britain. He could never understand the logic behind Wilson's argument that such an approach might lead the German government to temporize and to think that there was no urgency, since Anglo-American relations were also in a state of disarray. Bryan insisted that Germany must be given every opportunity to understand that Wilson's protests did not foreclose the possibility of peaceful settlement and that, indeed, the American government confidently expected a favorable response from William II. Bryan was never convinced that this would weaken the force of the American demands and perhaps convince Germany that Wilson's notes were not to be taken in deadly earnest. Above all, Bryan was afraid of any American step which could be interpreted as an ultimatum, any measure which would put the final decision for peace or war in the hands of William II and his advisers. It is true that Bryan's arguments did at least sway Wilson momentarily from his course and forced him to examine his own arguments in detail (though it is also true that

Bryan weakened his own position by mishandling an interview with the Austrian Ambassador in such a way that he gave the impression of desiring peace at any price). But, throughout the weeks of the controversy, Bryan showed himself essentially unsuited to the rough-and-tumble of serious diplomacy and completely unable to be tough-minded in dealing with fundamental questions of national policy. Although his proposals had their usual quality of common sense, they were always too simple for the complexity of the issues and too liable to misinterpretation by those who would have received them.

By the time of the second set of *Lusitania* notes, there was clearly no alternative for Bryan but resignation. Wilson was absolutely determined that Berlin must realize the seriousness of the American protest; Bryan was equally determined that a conciliatory attitude must be preserved. There was a period of intense emotional strain during which the Secretary of State bluntly accused his colleagues in the Cabinet of harboring pro-British sympathies and accused the President of treating him as a mere figurehead. Unable to comprehend the attitude of the President, he went home night after night with the unanswered question, "Why can't he see that by keeping open the way for mediation and arbitration, he has the opportunity to do the greatest work man can do!" His resignation was an act of conscience, an act made necessary by his conviction that Wilson was unintentionally, but irrevocably, committing the nation to unnecessary war. He resigned to take the issue to the people.

The rest was anticlimax. Few understood the reasons for his resignation, and many a newspaper shrieked desertion. Moreover, when the second set of *Lusitania* notes did not produce the war which Bryan had feared, it was the President and not his former Secretary of State who appeared vindicated. Bryan developed no great following, and Wilson, ironically, was re-elected in 1916 as "the man who kept us out of war." But in a very real sense Bryan's failure to convince the American public was a sign not only that he had misread the popular temperament but also that his ideas were unsuited for the age in which he lived. Bryan had always assumed that, if "the people" had time to study the issues of international affairs and reflect upon them, they would always prefer peace to war. But after the election of 1916 was over and after the Germans had resumed unrestricted submarine warfare, the American public did not so react. The passage of time merely increased the sentiment for war. Thus, when April, 1917, came, Bryan was virtually a leader without troops.

VII

William Jennings Bryan left no permanent mark upon the Department of State. The significant ideas of 1913–1915 were those of the President, and it is the foreign policy of Woodrow Wilson that is studied by historians. Bryan was a stubborn man who could compel another stubborn individual, Wilson, to pay heed to his opinions, and the President valued his advice precisely because he realized that Bryan often reflected instinctively the attitudes of the average American on the farm or in the small town. But the great ideas which made these years memorable in the history of American foreign policy originated in the White House and not in the Department of State.

A Secretary of State can be too consistent. The record of Knox, for example, could have been improved by a few moralistic binges to counterbalance the drab sameness of his reliance upon dollars, investments, and marines. But Bryan's record was the worse for his inconsistency. He wanted to avoid the evils of dollar diplomacy in Latin America, but his lack of knowledge about that part of the world and his assumption that American standards of political behavior could be exported combined to produce a moralistic brand of imperialism which was even less appealing than the blunter practices of his predecessor. He wanted to stem the tide of imperialism in the Far East, but the foreign policy of morality became ridiculous when it was based on the assumption of the Christian character of the Chinese revolution and positively dangerous when it failed to discover any way to deal with the rising power of Japan except to insist, as did the Open Door tradition, that all nations must respect the rights of China. Finally, it is impossible to reconcile Bryan's attitude toward Mexico with his insistence upon neutrality toward the war in Europe.

Bryan's most severe critics have been those who believe that America's greatest failures in diplomacy have resulted from a national inability to comprehend the role of power in international relations and from a tendency to shrink from its application. The "realists," to be sure, have often painted an exaggerated picture. They have drawn too sharp a dichotomy between realistic and idealistic approaches; at times they have conveniently overlooked the fact that precise calculations of the national interest were announced in idealistic terms in order to convince a skeptical public that the United States was really concerned with justice and morality; and they have frequently failed to realize that the ideals of a Woodrow Wilson might in fact be a form of "higher realism." But with respect to Bryan, the realist critique is unfortunately substantiated by fact. He did think that "power politics" was inherently wrong; he did believe that coercion and force were immoral; and he was convinced that American democracy was not only a unique achievement but also something to be taught to backward peoples and held up as an example to the snobbish societies of Europe. His, in short, was an essentially negative reaction to anything that can be described as "realistic."

But Bryan's greatest failure was his lack of analysis, for he approached all issues in terms of simple blacks and whites, of right and wrong, of "good" and "evil." He apparently never had command of the facts in a given situation or was aware, in advancing his own solutions, of the sharp complexities of the nettle he had grasped. Had he understood the causes of the European war or the forces which were prolonging that conflict, he could scarcely have advocated the simple remedy of mediation or have based his entire program on a foundation no stronger than the Christian belief that peace is always preferable to war. His greatest virtue, to be sure, was his love of peace—for, even in the twentieth century, the peacemakers have sometimes proved to be blessed. But his desire for peace, expressing itself in an insistence on strict American neutrality in a world at war, was also one of his greatest defects. World War I demonstrated that the world of the twentieth century is an interrelated world in which no country, let alone any individual, is an island. Bryan's simplistic conviction that America had no interest but to remain at peace was a personal attitude, not a viable policy.

It is exceedingly difficult for the historian, writing almost half a century after the event, to argue that there is much in Bryan's experience that is meaningful for America's present concerns. In an era in which intercontinental missiles can arrive on target in twenty minutes and in which the great danger is war from miscalculation, what is to be learned from a man who believed that the solution to the problem of war was to have the United States sign treaties promising to turn all its disputes over to impartial investigation and to forswear conflict for the twelve months during which the facts were being ascertained? The historian is tempted to conclude either that the lessons of Bryan's career in diplomacy are merely lessons in errors to be avoided—on the grounds, as Santayana wrote, that those who do not know the past are condemned to repeat it—or that the history of recent American foreign policy is essentially a repudiation of the principles for which Bryan is remembered. As a nation, the United States has grown, if not more sophisticated, certainly less innocent; by the seventh decade of the twentieth century, it had acquired sufficient experience to play the game of power politics in a manner to suggest that it had exorcised any Bryanesque ghost of the past.

Bryan was a representative of the old America which had to succumb before the age of steel and oil. His was essentially the outlook of rural, Middle Western America, of the small town and the small farm; it was an outlook which could not withstand the demands and pressures of the twentieth century. His career in domestic politics was itself an illustration of the fact that the agrarian, populist virtues for which he stood were rapidly becoming outmoded. In Wilson's Cabinet, Bryan represented a point of view in domestic affairs that had already been superseded. It was the same in foreign policy. His ideas were anchored to a provincialism which rendered them even less applicable than Wilson's to the world in which he lived. Shortly after he resigned, Bryan returned to Nebraska and, in delivering an oration on the farmer's interest in

peace, congratulated his cheering audience on living west of the
Alleghenies. These mountains, he said, still served as a dike to
keep out the heresies of the Eastern press. But Bryan was wrong.
It was not the Eastern press that was corrupting the prairies from
which he came. It was rather the twentieth century—with its wars
and revolutions, its new weapons, its interrelated economies, its
instantaneous communications, its global political issues—that was
beginning to press in upon the towns and farms of his America.
And, as time would eventually reveal, against these forces the
Alleghenies were no barrier. In the twenties and thirties, to be sure,
there would be a temporary return to many of the older, isolationist
concepts, but the events of 1913 to 1915 had already indicated that
the traditions which Bryan represented were unable to meet the
new challenges that confronted the United States.

War and Peace

The torrent of abuse which Bryan had experienced ever since his resignation as Secretary of State had by accumulation made him feel lonely and apart. It was to be expected that the press of the great Eastern cities would be as vindictive as possible; it was to be expected, too, that political foes like Roosevelt should spare no words of condemnation.[1] Nor was it a surprise when former European associates in the international movement, such as d'Estournelles de Constant, turned against him.[2] But it was a blow indeed to find his honored religious associates indicating they must disapprove of his action.[3] And it was likewise hard when old political supporters like Richard Metcalf and Senator Tillman repudiated his campaign against preparedness and openly accused him of being obsessed with the idea of "peace-at-any-price." [4] Threats to assassinate him unless he ceased talking "peace" did not of course sway him from his course, though they may well have made him uncomfortable.[5] In Baltimore an antipacifist mob yelled, "We'll hang Bill

[1] For example see *The New York Times,* July 20, 1915.
[2] *Ibid.,* July 2, 1915.
[3] For example, Rev. Dr. Len G. Broughton, *The New York Times,* July 19, 1915; and a letter from Bryan to Professor W. P. Trent, March 27, 1917, Bryan Papers (Manuscript Division, Library of Congress).
[4] *The New York Times,* Dec. 14, 1915.
[5] Anon. to Bryan, Johnson City, Tenn., Mar. 1916, Bryan Papers.

Reprinted from Merle E. Curti, "Bryan and World Peace," *Smith College Studies in History,* XVI (Northampton, Mass., 1931), pp. 244–254. Reprinted by permission of Octagon Books, Inc.

Bryan on a sour apple tree!" [6] But all this was nothing in comparison to the bitter and excessive denunciations on the floor of Congress: in February, 1917, Miller of Minnesota and Gardner of
Massachusetts practically accused him of treason. He was compared to traitors and copperheads, Gardner insisting that he was
tearing apart the country itself by playing politics in the midst of a
national crisis.[7] Bryan's friends in the House refuted this charge by
pointing out that war had not yet been declared, and that it was the
right of every citizen to exercise free speech. Even a Nebraska Republican, a political enemy, rose to defend him in the interest of
justice and fair play.[8]

In mid-February an effort was made to prove Bryan a violator
of the Logan act, which forbids a private citizen from negotiating
with a foreign power, and to denounce him as a near-traitor. In
an editorial *The New York Times* more than implied that he had
inspired the dispatch of a cable, drawn up by Dr. George W.
Kirchwey and Dr. George Bartholeme, to the German press, the
purpose of which was to urge further concessions and explanations
from Germany, and to assure its people and government that
America did not want war.[9] Bryan, as a matter of fact, had no
connection with this peace move other than that he had given to
Dr. Kirchwey a note of introduction to a member of the Cabinet,
who approved the sending of the cable message. Yet Bryan was
excoriated and bitterly denounced.

March came. Toward the end of the month Bryan hoped that
his friends in Congress could persuade it to hear him plead against
entering the war. But such consent Congress would not give. It was,
as David Starr Jordan said, "pretty thoroughly hypnotized." [10]

[6] David Starr Jordan, *The Days of a Man* (Yonkers-on-Hudson, N.Y.,
1922), II, 729.

[7] *Congressional Record,* 54, Part 3 (64 Congress, 2 Session), 2648; Part
4, 3358 (Feb. 15).

[8] George Huddleston to Bryan, Feb. 13, 1917; Charles A. Sloane to Bryan,
Feb. 14, 1917, Bryan Papers; *The New York Times,* Feb. 14, 1917; *Congressional Record,* 54, Part 4, 3441; 54, Part 3, 2650 (Feb. 5).

[9] George W. Kirchwey to Bryan, Feb. 10, 1917. The cable is printed in
The New York Times, Feb. 14. See also the editorial of the *Times,* "A
Crime Against the Nation," Feb. 13.

[10] David Starr Jordan to Bryan, April 1, 1917, Bryan Papers.

Bryan wrote to his wife from Washington: "We are so near war that I feel that I ought to stay here—at least until tomorrow. It is distressing to see so many men afraid to act. I am needed to give them courage and help and plan." [11] And he did urge Congressmen to resign rather than to vote for war if they sincerely opposed it and yet believed it to be favored by their constituencies.[12] Beyond that he could do little save to make a final appeal to the country and desperately to plan for a great, silent parade as a concrete demonstration against entering the war. The plan was for crowds to parade simultaneously in cities the length and breadth of the land. But there was no organization, either pacifist or pro-German, adequate to carry out such a project.[13] Helpless before irresistible events, he must have shared the views of his friend, Senator James Vardaman, who wrote him on March 31, 1917:

The prospect for our country is gloomy. The advocates of preparedness have won their fight. The metropolitan newspapers have created a sentiment that seems to be sweeping the White House like a cyclone. God alone knows what will be the outcome. Your appeal is of course unanswerable and ought to have some weight—and would have great weight under different conditions. But the world has gone crazy on the subject of war and pecuniary profits. . . . (two days later) Things look gloomy. God alone can now save this Republic, it seems to me, from the horrors of European slaughter. If the newspapers are to be believed . . . the President has made up his mind to have Congress declare war, and Congress will do his bidding.[14]

On April fifth Congress did declare war. David Starr Jordan reminded Bryan of what Norman Angell had told a group of internationalists in Europe after the cataclysm had broken out in 1914 —"We were not successful, we were merely right." [15]

Right or wrong, the battle had been fought, and lost. One of his sympathetic political associates, Senator George W. Norris, has expressed the view that Bryan's opposition to the declaration of war

[11] Bryan to Mrs. Bryan (no date), Bryan Papers.
[12] Bryan to H. C. Hilliard, Apr. 3, 1917, Bryan Papers.
[13] George Sylvester Viereck, *Spreading Germs of Hate* (New York, 1930), p. 259.
[14] James Vardaman to Bryan, March 31 and April 2, 1917, Bryan Papers.
[15] David Starr Jordan to Bryan, April 1, 1917, Bryan Papers.

would have been more bitter had the Republicans been in power, and that it would in that case have carried an effect impossible to understand or to measure.[16] Indeed, partisanship certainly weakened his opposition to our entry into the war: it was carried out under Democratic auspices. But it is doubtful whether the forces of opposition, which he conceivably might have rallied, could have stayed the tide. In reality it was another and apparently inevitable victory of the new America over the old.

Once war was declared, Bryan's belief in the necessity of accepting the will of the majority and his patriotism made his course both clear and easy. "Please enroll me as a private whenever I am needed and assign me to any work that I can do" he wrote to President Wilson. In his editorials in *The Commoner* he favored the suspension of criticism and free speech, and he spoke out against conscientious objectors and draft resistance.[17] He contributed to the Red Cross, bought liberty bonds, and aroused patriotism among recruits at military encampments. Some of his former supporters regretted all these actions, clinging steadfastly to their convictions. Not, indeed, the American Peace Society, of which he was an officer: this organization, like Bryan, accepted the war as a holy crusade to end war.[18] But some pacifists did put personal conscience before the obligation to accept a majority decision.[19] One Unitarian minister sorrowed that Bryan could openly say that all his utterances against war, including his statement that Jesus was a pacifist, must be put on the shelf for the duration of the struggle.[20] Others, too, regretted that his peace principles seemed to apply only in time of peace, and only to foreign countries. Attorneys, editors and politicians from the West and South denounced the war in letters preserved in the Bryan papers.[21]

[16] *Current History Magazine*, Sept. 1925, XXII, 865.

[17] W. G. McAdoo to Bryan, Sept. 18, 1917; Josephus Daniels to Bryan, Aug. 29, 1917; Bryan to George Sylvester Viereck, March 15, 1921, Bryan Papers.

[18] Arthur Deerin Call to Bryan, June 6, 1917, *Misc. Letters 1914–1922; Advocate of Peace* (1917–18), *passim.*

[19] George Foster Peabody to Bryan, Apr. 23, 1917, *Misc. Letters 1914– 1924.*

[20] Henry W. Pinkham to Bryan, June 12, 1917, Bryan Papers.

[21] Bryan Papers, *Misc. Letters 1914–1923.*

But Bryan's thoughts turned to peace even when he was talking war. Acting on the theory that he might be honored by an appointment to the peace commission, he spent much time in reading history, studying treaties, and otherwise preparing himself for the place he solicited of Wilson and urged Senators and Congressmen to help him secure.[22] An official of the State Department received his plan for handling the problem of minorities: when a territory was transferred from one power to another, it should be so arranged that nationals might change residence without pecuniary loss. German residents in Alsace-Lorraine, for example, who did not wish to be under French sovereignty, might sell their property to that government. While many would elect not to do so, the mere opportunity would remove much discontent and criticism.[23] But Bryan was disappointed in his hope of being one of the peacemakers.

Bryan's position in regard to the Treaty of Versailles and the Covenant of the League of Nations was in part conditioned by his criticisms of the League to Enforce Peace. We have seen that he denounced this organization and its principles soon after resigning as Secretary of State.[24] The word "force," in his mind, vitiated the plan. Peace, he had written to Bernstorff on December 15, 1916, could not be enforced: the effort to do so had been responsible for most modern wars. It could come only as a result of the establishment of friendship and cooperation. He could not look complacently on any plan by which America obligated herself to take part in the settlement of Europe's quarrels, even though a majority of the Council of Nations in which we were represented determined on the enforcement of its decisions in the interest of peace.[25] He had shared Borah's idea that any participation on our part in enforcing sanctions for peace was inadvisable.[26]

[22] Bryan to Wilson, Jan. 15, 1918; J. B. Scott to Bryan, Oct. 18, 1918, Bryan Papers.

[23] Bryan to J. B. Scott, Jan. 23, 1919, *Misc. Letters 1900–1922.*

[24] *Ante.* 224. See *World Peace,* a written debate between Wm. Howard Taft and Wm. J. Bryan (New York, 1917).

[25] Bryan to Bernstorff, Dec. 15, 1916, Bryan Papers; William Jennings Bryan and Mary Baird Bryan, *The Memoirs of William Jennings Bryan* (Philadelphia, 1925), p. 436; *The New York Times,* June 20, 1915, July 3, 1915.

[26] Wm. Borah to Bryan, Dec. 29, 1916, Bryan Papers.

When the President, in his message to Congress in January, 1917, advocated a league of nations, Bryan did not hesitate to disapprove of the implication that force was to be used to secure peace. He told an audience in Madison, Wisconsin: ". . . the President has sown wheat and tares together. I hope that the Senate will approve of the wheat and reject the tares." [27]

In a newspaper article dated March 12, 1919, Bryan came out in favor of the Covenant of the League, at the same time proposing certain changes and additions. For the contemplated deliberation before war, which he identified with his own treaty plan, for the reduction of armaments, and for the abolition of secret treaties he had nothing but praise. "If the League of Nations did nothing more than provide these three things our nation would be justified in supporting it to the utmost." But he felt that the basis of representation was unfair to the United States; he favored admitting new members by a mere majority, rather than a two-thirds vote; and he advocated a clearer recognition of the Monroe Doctrine. He also desired assurance that America would not be forced to accept mandates without her consent, and that the League would not interfere in the domestic affairs of its members. Above all, each nation ought to decide for itself whether or not it would lend physical support to the undertakings and schemes of the international council. "This nation cannot afford to allow a council in which it has so small a voice to carry it into war against its will." As for the economic boycott, it was to be remembered that even such a weapon might well lead straight to war. Bryan also proposed an impractical scheme by which nations desiring "the waste places of the earth" for exploitation and expansion might acquire them peaceably through the League.[28] Yet, in spite of his objections and qualifications, he concluded that the risks we took in accepting the Covenant were less than the risk we took by rejecting it and turning back "to the old ways of blood and slaughter."

Bryan did not insist on incorporating these ideas in amendments or reservations before ratifying the Treaty and the Covenant. In-

[27] *The New York Times,* Jan. 24, 1917.
[28] David Hunter Miller, *The Drafting of the Covenant* (New York and London, 1928), I, 374–377.

deed, he believed that it would be better to ratify first, and then to secure amendments and changes once we were a part of the League.[29] When, however, it became apparent that ratification could not be secured without reservations or amendments, then he was willing to accept many of those offered by the Republican opposition.[30] At the Jackson Day dinner, January 9, 1920, he advocated abandoning Article X and making a compromise with the Republicans.[31] When the President refused to listen to the idea of compromise, his representative in the Senate, Gilbert Hitchcock, asked Bryan to urge Wilson to make concessions.[32] It was indefensible, Bryan thought, to risk the election on the question of the Covenant without reservations.[33] Yet he did not have his way. Administration leaders in the convention rejected the plank pledging prompt ratification with the majority reservations which he offered, and in turn Bryan withheld his support of the candidate and platform during the campaign. Up almost to the very day of the election pleas came urging him, in the cause of international peace, to speak out for the party.[34] He could not but think that Wilson had erred grievously and actually hindered the cause of peace. It was his disapproval of Wilson's position on the treaty, his endorsement of universal compulsory military training and his opposition to a reduction of the army which led him later to refuse to serve on the Wilson Memorial Foundation.[35]

Disappointed in his hope that the Republicans would redeem their campaign pledge by inaugurating an "association of nations," Bryan still tried to promote machinery for peace. He advocated our adherence to the World Court [36] and held that, since the League

[29] *The New York Times,* Sept. 27, 1919, Jan. 10, 1920.

[30] Bryan to Arthur Dunn, Feb. 1, 1923, Bryan Papers; *The New York Times,* May 11, 1920. Bryan advised Democratic Senators to vote quickly for reservations, *The New York Times,* Apr. 30, 1920.

[31] Arthur Wallace Dunn, *From Harrison to Harding* (New York and London, 1922), II, 385; *The New York Times,* Jan. 10, 1920.

[32] G. M. Hitchcock to Bryan, Nov. 30, 1919, Bryan Papers.

[33] *The New York Times,* June 27, 1920.

[34] R. W. Wooley, Sept. 24, 1920, Bryan Papers. Cox's "wetness" was also, of course, an important factor in Bryan's attitude.

[35] Bryan to Henry Holt, Sept. 17, 1921, Bryan Papers.

[36] Wm. Seaver Woods to Bryan, Mar. 6, 1923, Bryan Papers.

would probably admit us on our own terms we should not hesitate to join.[37] President Harding invited him to consult with him on our international relationships, but we do not know what took place in the interview.[38] Efforts were later made to induce Harding to appoint him a member of the American delegation to the Washington Disarmament Conference,[39] but it was not to be his fortune to contribute officially to the cause of peace. He could only help get the churches behind the conference, and make suggestions as to its program. Fearing that the Four-Power treaty might lessen our independence of action, he urged Borah, Oscar W. Underwood and President Harding to sponsor amendments to insure against such an eventuality.[40] The President did not think it necessary or wise to ask Congress to take such action. "Of course," wrote Harding, "you know, as I do, that there is nothing in any of the treaties which involves us in any way, which commits us to make war, which includes us in any alliance, or otherwise endangers our freedom of action." [41]

In spite of the fact that during the last years of his life his interests were chiefly in Prohibition and evangelical orthodoxy, Bryan occasionally made suggestions in the interest of world peace. He urged on President Coolidge the cancellation of the Allied debts in the interest of better international relations, pointing out that we might use the debts as a lever for limiting armaments.[42] He kept up his connection with various peace and arbitration societies, contributed to a fund for the relief of the impoverished Austrian pacifist, Alfred Fried, and supported a movement for lessening the influence of propaganda in the press through the establishment of an independent news bulletin.[43] But his work for peace was almost over.

[37] Statement dated Apr. 24, 1923, Bryan Papers.

[38] Harding to Bryan, Nov. 13, 1920, Bryan Papers.

[39] Mrs. Harding to Mrs. Bryan, July 28, 1921, Bryan Papers.

[40] Borah to Bryan, Dec. 13, 1921, Bryan Papers; Oscar W. Underwood to Bryan, Mar. 14, 1922, *Misc. Papers 1914–1923*; Bryan to Harding, Jan. 26, 1922, Bryan Papers.

[41] Harding to Bryan, Jan. 31, 1922, Bryan Papers.

[42] Bryan to Coolidge, Jan. 1, 1925, Coolidge to Bryan, Jan. 5, 1925, *Misc. Papers 1923–1926*.

[43] Bryan Papers.

How little his ideas on the subject of war, its causes and cure, had been changed by the titanic struggle which he had seen, is clearly brought out in the essay which he submitted for the Bok prize. His draft distinguished between justiciable and nonjusticiable disputes. The former were to be submitted to the existing international court; the latter, without exception, were to be referred to commissions of inquiry. All legal and moral obligation to use force in carrying out the decisions was repudiated, although nations might, by international agreement, refuse loans and commercial intercourse to governments that began war without first submitting the dispute to the court or commissions of inquiry. And in no instance, save actual invasion, was war to be declared save by popular referendum. In addition to these familiar ideas, the plan emphasized the necessity of developing peace sentiment through meetings, discussion of the causes and cure of war, extension of woman suffrage throughout the world, and the naming of highways in such a manner as to suggest peace. This plan, which was submitted under a pseudonym, failed to win the prize. Deprived of that consolation Bryan sent the paper to President Coolidge and to Secretary of State Kellogg to whom he wrote, by way of an explanation for sending his essay, "As you know, my heart has been in the peace movement for nearly a quarter of a century." [44] This is the last statement of Bryan's interest in peace to be found in his papers. Three months later he was dead.

Long after Bryan's death, and probably long after the passing of all his contemporaries, others will fight his battle for peace. Hard as that fight will be, it cannot but be somewhat easier because of this conscientious and intelligent critic of the war system who was, after all, a pioneer among political authorities in experimenting with concrete machinery for preventing war.

Some will continue to fight for peace in his way; others will find different, and perhaps better, ways. From his mistakes all warriors against war can learn lessons of value. For those who, like him, will continue to emphasize the Christian and individualistic approach, the best lesson he can teach is the weakness of inconsist-

[44] Bryan to Kellogg, May 1, 1925, Bryan Papers.

ency. Pacifists who approach the problem from the point of view of doctrinaire opposition to war under *all* possible circumstances, will attribute Bryan's failure to his willingness to regard war as the last desperate, inevitable means to an end. They will tell us that the fatal weakness in his tactics was his acceptance of war as an exceptional and "holy crusade" once his country opened the gates of Janus. Bryan's tragedy was, in their estimation, due to the fact that he went so far toward the position of consistently refusing to sanction war, and yet, when the time of testing came, attached a higher value to nationalism than to peace. Their warning will be for friends of peace to steel themselves against the kind of rationalizations by which Bryan was able to talk peace in time of peace, and make war in time of war.

Others who would have us learn a lesson from Bryan's failure will insist that those who really want peace must recognize the futility of an individualistic morality in a society so complex and so ordered, economically, as to be blind to the sort of appeal that may still be effective when made to individuals. Those who approach the problem from the socialist point of view will insist that if Bryan's mistakes are not to be repeated, friends of peace must do even more than see some of the connections between capitalism and war; they will do more than denounce the war propaganda of a profit-minded press; they will not stop with criticism of munition-makers and bankers profiting from lending neutral resources to belligerents; they will not even pin their faith to a popular referendum on the question of war or peace. They will realize that the people, influenced by propaganda, are not always right; that they are, in short, the victim of agencies and forces over which they have, at present, no effective control. They will take a more realistic view of human nature. Bryan, these critics will tell us, wanted peace, but at the same time wanted other things which were incompatible with peace, and, in the last analysis, wanted them more than he wanted peace. If enemies of war would learn from Bryan's failures, they must take the profits out of the whole system which has bred so many wars; they must so order society that one class, and one nation, cannot exploit another class, and another nation. For so long as that can be done, may it not be said that the instruments for exploitation will be found? Bryan's tragedy, these critics would say, was that he came so near to seeing these relationships, and was yet blinded, in the time of testing, by a more fundamental loyalty to private property and its legal rights.

Bryan was, in a tragic sense, the champion of lost causes, or, at least, of causes that appear half-lost: free silver, anti-imperialism, effective Prohibition, and antievolution. But, more than any person in his day, he put these causes, together with that of world peace, before the people. It is yet to be decided whether world peace shall be added to the list of causes for which he fought—and which were lost.

✪

Bryan and John Barleycorn

Several months after his resignation from Wilson's Cabinet Bryan had declared that the three great reforms of the age were peace, Prohibition, and woman suffrage.[1] Although Bryan devoted the greater part of his time and energy to the first of these reforms, at least until April, 1917, he managed to find time for the latter two as well.[2] Of the two, Bryan was more devoted to Prohibition, since it constituted a far more bitter struggle and had its roots in the political and moral fabric of the nation to a much greater extent than did suffrage.

In crusading against alcohol, Bryan and many of his fellow prohibitionists thought of themselves as progressives engaged in a reform which would last for all time and eventually engulf the entire world. The inability of the present generation to understand this aspect of the prohibitionists is not surprising, since even Jo-

[1] "Three Great Reforms," *The Commoner*, December 1915, p. 5.

[2] At least two students of this period feel that Bryan's fight for Prohibition and woman suffrage, during the years following his resignation, appreciably weakened his peace crusade since it necessitated a division of time and zeal. See Arthur Wallace Dunn, *From Harrison to Harding* (New York, 1922), II, 297; Merle Curti, "Bryan and World Peace," *Smith College Studies in History* (Northampton, Mass.), XVI (1931), nos. 3–4, p. 228.

sephus Daniels' son Jonathan, who had a unique opportunity to observe at close range such leading advocates of national temperance as his father and Bryan, was baffled by them.[3] But if our failure to comprehend just what it was that the prohibitionists were trying to do is understandable, it is, nevertheless, unfortunate. Focusing upon the later phase of the movement in the 1920's, we have tended to view Prohibition as the austere instrument of a pack of blue-nosed puritans who found life a joyless thing and were determined that no one else should be allowed to squeeze any pleasure out of it, as an aberration produced by the spirit of intolerance and summary action fostered by World War I, as a manifestation of rural frenzy and fanaticism in the postwar era, as a caricature of reform.[4] Thus we have not merely misread the motives and aims of many of the prohibitionists, but have failed to understand as well as we might the impulses and assumptions basic to a large segment of the progressive movement in this country.

The fact is that the temperance movement was nurtured in the soil of reform and remained a genuine reform movement right down to the 1920's. It came into being as a movement in the first half of the nineteenth century amidst a generation that was increasingly concerned with elevating and improving the individual not only for his own sake but also in order to safeguard the democratic experiment and establish a more perfect social order. It was an age which was finding that man was indeed his brother's keeper; an age which began to concern itself with the welfare of women and children; an age in which men built causes around the plight of the slave, the pauper, the drunkard, the mentally unbalanced. Prohibition, with its promise of insuring a more responsible, intelligent, and sober electorate and eliminating the root cause of many of man's greatest problems, fit neatly into the wave of humanitarian reform.[5]

The links that bound Prohibition to the larger reform movements of the day continued to hold fast with the passing of the

[3] Jonathan Daniels, *The End of Innocence* (New York, 1954), p. 44.

[4] A study containing all of these views is Andrew Sinclair, *Prohibition: An Era of Excess* (Boston, 1962), Chap. I–II, and *passim*.

[5] John Allen Krout, *The Origins of Prohibition* (New York, 1925), pp. 297–300.

years. The Prohibition movement was closely allied with the Northern abolitionist crusade and often pointed out that both movements had as their aim the freeing of enslaved men.[6] The Prohibition party, founded in 1869, exhibited a diversity of interests in regard to reform which often makes one feel that its name was a misnomer. In every platform it issued from 1872 to 1924, with but two exceptions, it fused Prohibition to many other reforms which at various times included direct election of Senators, the right of labor to organize, the right of all citizens to vote regardless of "color, race, former social condition, sex, or nationality," liberal immigration policies, the settlement of international difficulties by arbitration, antitrust legislation, initiative, referendum and recall, a graduated income tax, government ownership or control of public utilities, employer's liability laws, the eight-hour day, prohibition of child labor, and government guarantee of bank deposits.[7] While not nearly enough work has been done on the Prohibition movements in the states, a recent study of California has shown that almost every reform movement in that state, from antislavery to populism and progressivism, was closely linked to the antiliquor movement.[8] And finally, with but one exception, every church in which the social gospel played an important role was also officially committed to Prohibition.[9]

An understanding of this affinity between Prohibition and American reform movements in general is essential to a re-creation of the atmosphere that prevailed when men like Bryan, Daniels, and many other progressives joined the movement. More than a few progressives, of course, remained indifferent to the cause and

[6] *Ibid.* pp. 176, 289.

[7] For the platforms of the Prohibition party, see Kirk H. Porter and Donald Bruce Johnson, eds., *National Party Platforms, 1840–1956* (Urbana, Ill., 1956). They may also be found, along with some sympathetic commentary and brief biographies of the party's nominees, in D. Leigh Colvin, *Prohibition in the United States: a History of the Prohibition Party and of the Prohibition Movement* (New York, 1926).

[8] Gilman M. Ostrander, *The Prohibition Movement in California, 1848–1933* (Berkeley, 1957), pp. 102–119.

[9] Paul A. Carter, *The Decline and Revival of the Social Gospel* (Ithaca, N.Y., 1954), pp. 33–34; James H. Timberlake, *Prohibition and the Progressive Movement, 1900–1920* (Cambridge, 1962), pp. 23–24.

some denounced it as an unwarranted violation of individual liberties. A great many more, however, especially in the rural sections of the West and South, regarded it as a necessary and logical reform which differed from other progressive reforms neither in method nor purpose.[10] To Bryan and many of his co-workers and followers, Prohibition was just a continuation of the struggle against the selfish interests that put private profit above human welfare and fed upon the helplessness of the masses. Those who labor for Prohibition, he wrote, "are helping to create conditions which will bring the highest good to the greatest number, without any injustice to any, for it is not injustice to any man to refuse him permission to enrich himself by injuring his fellowmen." [11] The brewers and distillers, he asserted, located their saloons among the poor "knowing full well when they do so that their saloon will absorb the money that their patrons ought to spend on wife and children. They . . . impoverish the poor and multiply their sufferings . . ." [12]

The doctrine of the perfectability of man was one of the secular American political principles that was taken over and given religious connotations by the social gospel and, in this form, was adopted both as an assumption and a goal by many progressives. Bryan, who adamantly believed that "A man can be born again; the springs of life can be cleansed instantly so that the heart loves the things that it formerly hated and hates the things it once loved. If this is true of *one*, it can be true of any number," adopted Prohibition partly because he saw in it a means of liberating and elevating the people, of giving them a new and more perfect birth, and this he insisted was the duty of every progressive and every Christian. "I claim no right to tell any body else what to do," he told the Presbyterian General Assembly in 1916, "but I believe in the Christian doctrine that brethren should commune with each other and that they should seek to help each other."

---

[10] For an exposition of this theme, see *ibid*. Chaps. I, IV.

[11] WJB, "Why I Am for Prohibition," *The Independent*, LXXXVII (July 17, 1916), 89.

[12] WJB, *Prohibition Address . . . Made in Ohio . . . October 25 to 30, 1915*, p. 6.

If I understand what a Christian is, it is not that he is a perfect man,
but that he desires to be perfect. . . . If I understand the Christian's
attitude it is one of openness and willingness, the desire to have his
life censured and his conduct scrutinized that he may get rid of his
bestial sins.[13]

Finally, Bryan championed Prohibition so vigorously because
he was convinced that it was a democratic reform. By 1917 he was
arguing that a majority of the American people lived in dry territory and a majority of their representatives in Congress opposed
the saloon. "The accurst thing exists only because the Constitution,
by its ultraconservative provisions, restrains the majority from immediate and decided action." [14] To Bryan this was the chief consideration before which all abstract discussions of liberty and all
questions of political expediency paled. Once the majority had
spoken he could be concerned with nothing else, for the right of
the people to rule was the one indispensable right which never
could be tampered with.

These were the factors that drew many progressives into the
Prohibition movement and they were the factors that kept them
there even after the movement itself began to undergo changes in
the 1920's.

Bryan's favorable attitude toward temperance reform was shaped
not only by the reform ethos of his age but by his early training
and environment. His parents impressed upon him at a tender age
the evils of alcohol. "Even before I had any clear understanding
of the temperance question," he wrote in later years, "I began
signing the pledge." His first recollections of signing a pledge
dated back to 1872, when he was twelve, but he assures us that "it
had by that time become a habit with me." [15] During the period
when he was practicing law in Jacksonville, Illinois, Bryan de-

---

[13] WJB, *Temperance Lecture Delivered Before the 128th General Assembly of the Presbyterian Church, at Atlantic City, New Jersey, Sunday
May 21, 1916.*

[14] WJB, "Prohibition's Progress," *The Independent*, XC (May 19, 1917),
332.

[15] William Jennings Bryan and Mary Baird Bryan, *Memoirs of William
Jennings Bryan* (Philadelphia, 1925), p. 187.

livered a temperance address in which he endorsed the theory of
Prohibition but asserted that a policy of moral suasion and education was superior to one of legislative proscription. "Our great
work is the work of education," he announced. "The best, the most
effective way to stop the sale of intoxicating liquor is to stop the
demand for it." [16]

Not long after voicing these sentiments, Bryan moved to Lincoln,
Nebraska, and while he remained a steadfast abstainer and privately
opposed the saloon, he now refrained from speaking against it
publicly. Omaha, Nebraska, which was in Bryan's Congressional
district, was the home of the third largest distillery in the country,
and Bryan was evidently not willing to jeopardize his political
future by speaking out on an issue which he felt was more of a
private than a public matter. In 1890 the voters of Nebraska went
to the polls to decide the wisdom of adopting state-wide Prohibition, and Bryan, who was a candidate for his first term in Congress,
not only failed to endorse the amendment, but, as he later admitted,
he voted against it as well.[17]

During his tour of duty with the Third Nebraska Infantry in
1898, Bryan made some small contribution to the Prohibition
cause by excluding intoxicating liquor from his camp canteen.[18]
Still he was reluctant to join the crusade. When in 1902 Carry
Nation toured Nebraska and spent several days in Lincoln brandishing her famous hatchet against saloons, Bryan not only declined to
aid her in her fight but even refused to see her, causing the militant
prohibitionist to remark: "From that time forth I knew that Bryan
was for Bryan and what Bryan could get for Bryan." [19]

Two years after Mrs. Nation's disillusionment, Bryan took his
first cautious step along the road he was eventually to travel, by
coming out in favor of local option.[20] Six more years were to pass,
however, before he joined the prohibitionist ranks in earnest. The
metamorphosis that changed Bryan from a private teetotaler to an

[16] Bryan delivered this address sometime between 1883 and 1887. Bryan
Papers (Manuscript Division, Library of Congress).
[17] *The Commoner,* April 1916, p. 4.
[18] *Ibid.* October 1917, p. 2.
[19] Herbert Asbury, *Carry Nation* (New York, 1929), pp. 260–261.
[20] *Memoirs,* p. 290.

active, militant prohibitionist, followed in the wake of his third unsuccessful bid for the Presidency in 1908. The reasons for the transformation were as personal and political as those which had hitherto kept him on the sidelines. He became convinced that the liquor interests had been instrumental in causing his defeat in Missouri, Indiana, Ohio, Illinois, New York, and had almost defeated him in his own state as well. While he was still fuming over this, the same interests thwarted him in his attempt to induce the legislature of Nebraska to adopt the initiative and referendum.[21] Thus, added to his long-standing personal dislike for alcoholic beverages and his recognition that sentiment for Prohibition was slowly building throughout the country, was Bryan's newborn conviction that the defenders of alcohol were enemies of progressive reform.

Still denying that he was a prohibitionist, Bryan, in the spring of 1910, decided to advocate county option and journeyed to Omaha to open his campaign. Unable to find one Democrat of prominence in the entire city who was willing to introduce him or even sit on the platform with him, Bryan hired a small hall, put his coat and hat on a chair, addressed his opening remarks to that same chair and then launched into his first Prohibition speech before a very small audience.[22] Several months later he attended the Democratic State Convention at Grand Island, Nebraska, where he introduced a minority report in favor of county option. He knew he was precipitating a schism in the state Democracy and he did so reluctantly: "Never in my life have I performed a duty that I less desired to perform; and never have I felt more sure that I was performing a duty." He apologized to the fathers and mothers of the state for not speaking out earlier and ended his address by closing the door on all future compromise: "We never espoused a more righteous cause than that which now appeals to us; we never faced an enemy more deserving of attack. . . If a retreat is to be

[21] WJB, *Speeches of William Jennings Bryan* (New York, 1913), I, 326, 332–333.
[22] WJB to Warren Worth Bailey, September 22, 1910, Bailey Papers, Princeton University, Box 1; *The Commoner,* October 1918, p. 9.

sounded, it must be sounded by another. I shall not do it—never, never, never!" [23]

This dramatic peroration proved more forceful than his subsequent actions. He was not yet ready to champion nationwide or even state-wide prohibition.[24] But though his position was by no means an advanced one, it enabled him to lend his great prestige and his eloquent voice to the movement. Bryan has been frequently accused of entering the Prohibition movement only after its victory was assured, yet his own party in his own state repudiated him for his temperance leanings in 1910, and during his tenure in the State Department the nation's press attempted to use his temperance views as a means of laughing him out of office. In the beginning they ridiculed his substitution of grape juice for alcohol at the various diplomatic gatherings over which he and Mrs. Bryan had to preside. Their jibes turned to bitter scorn when Bryan continued to address temperance meetings even after the European war began. After one such gathering in 1915 in Philadelphia, where 12,000 spectators stood up and joined Bryan in taking the pledge, the *New Republic* commented: "It is easy to laugh at Mr. Bryan for doing things like this in times like these. It is even a little hard not to." [25]

In October 1915, just four months after his resignation, he toured Ohio speaking in forty counties and making sixty speeches in six days to almost a quarter of a million people. Licensing a man to sell liquor and then fining people for getting drunk, he asserted, made as much sense as "licensing a person to spread the itch through a town and then fining the people for scratching." The saloon, he declared, "has been not only accused but convicted of

[23] WJB, *Speeches*, I, 324, 346–347.

[24] When a national Prohibition amendment was before Congress in 1914, Bryan advised against its submission on the grounds that it "would divert attention from other issues pressing for consideration without advancing the cause of Prohibition." *The Commoner*, December 1914, p. 1. During the next two years, Bryan continued to oppose the submission of a national Prohibition amendment. See WJB to Richmond P. Hobson, August 12, 1915, Burleson Papers (Manuscript Division, Library of Congress), Vol. 15.

[25] *New Republic*, II (March 20, 1915), 165.

being an enemy of the race." He dismissed the idea of compensated Prohibition as "superlative impudence," and thundered:

Let the liquor dealer compensate the mother for the son he has taken from her; let him compensate the wife for the husband of whom he has robbed her; let him compensate the children for the father whom he has first transformed into a brute and then driven to suicide. Let him compensate those whom he has wronged by restoring to them the priceless value of homes ruined and lives wrecked, and then society will be glad to compensate him for whatever pecuniary loss he may suffer by the closing of a business which he knew to be harmful—a business which can not thrive save as the community suffers.[26]

Bryan's campaign was well received by the citizens of Ohio, whose cheers helped to ease the memory of the abuse which his resignation had brought him. "The audiences were so attentive and responsive," Mrs. Bryan noted in her diary, "I do not see how he could have failed to convince many. I had some glimpses of what a national campaign on this subject would be—a veritable religious crusade." [27]

Bryan himself could not have failed to perceive the impact that a national Prohibition campaign would have, but he was not yet ready to enter upon one. He was willing to admit that there was but one solution to the liquor question "and that is the nation-wide extermination of the traffic in alcohol," but he was not willing to carry this admission to its logical conclusion. He would not approve the submission of a national Prohibition amendment until a sufficient number of states had expressed themselves favorably upon it. The country, he explained, was not ready for national Prohibition and any attempt to secure it at present would jeopardize the administration's economic reforms and the work of peace.[28]

There was still an element of expediency in Bryan's Prohibition views. Though he condemned the saloon as "the festering source

---

[26] *Memoirs*, p. 433; *Prohibition Address by Hon. William Jennings Bryan Presenting in Substance the Line of Argument Followed by him in the Sixty Speeches Made in Ohio During the Week of October 25 to 30, 1915* (Washington, D.C., 1916), pp. 3–7.

[27] *Memoirs*, p. 433.

[28] *The Commoner*, August 1915, pp. 4–5, 24, December 1915, p. 5.

of political and moral pollution," [29] he was in no hurry to cut it out of the body politic. He failed to give serious consideration to the assurances of one of the leaders of the Prohibition party that he could receive the party's Presidential nomination in 1916 if he desired it.[30] The peace issue still held his immediate interest, and in all likelihood he envisioned the Prohibition crusade as one which might constitute the main issue of the 1920 campaign but not before that. But whatever Bryan's views on the proper moment for launching the Prohibition crusade in earnest, he soon discovered that Prohibition, like the Paris mobs in the upheaval of 1848, was not always content to wait for its leaders. Throughout the first half of 1916 he continued his efforts to keep the Prohibition question out of the forthcoming Presidential campaign. Shortly after the national conventions he wrote: "I hope to see the campaign this year fought upon economic issues, and upon such international questions as it may be necessary to consider." [31]

Though he was to have his wish in this respect he was less successful in his own state. Here the prohibitionists were agitating for the submission of a state-wide Prohibition amendment to the voters in November. Bryan strongly advised against such a move, protesting that it would divert attention from important national issues during the coming Presidential campaign.[32] The more ardent prohibitionists, however, proved victorious and Bryan found himself in a dilemma. His resignation had already impaired his prestige among his fellow Democrats, and he was convinced that a refusal on his part to attempt to secure a place on the Nebraska delegation would be construed as a lack of interest in the campaign and in the Democratic party.[33] He would have preferred to run on a platform endorsing the economic and social reforms of the administration and stressing his own efforts to keep the country at peace. The Prohibition issue was a complication which he felt certain could only diminish his chances of election. Yet it was clear to Bryan

[29] *Ibid.* June 1915, p. 6.
[30] Clinton H. Howard to WJB, June 10, 1915, Bryan Papers.
[31] WJB, "Why I Am for Prohibition," *The Independent,* LXXXVII (July 17, 1916), 89.
[32] *The Commoner,* May 1916, p. 2.
[33] WJB to Albert S. Burleson, March 8, 1916, Burleson Papers, Vol. 17.

that Prohibition was to be one of the leading issues in the not too distant future and that if he repeated his performance of 1890 he would eliminate himself from playing a leading role in the coming struggle.

The factors which led Bryan to his eventual decision were, of course, not all quite so carefully reasoned or politically oriented. By this time he had become convinced that the temperance movement was a righteous one being waged against a contemptible and reactionary foe. It was probably this latter factor that tipped the scales, but, whatever the reasons, Bryan threw expediency to the wind and entered the Nebraska primary campaign bearing the incubus of Prohibition. Once Bryan had made his decision, nothing could dissuade him, not even an offer of $150,000 for a series of lectures, which he turned down because it would have taken him away from Nebraska during the campaign.[34]

Bryan's month-long tour of Nebraska, which began on March 20, was an exciting and gratifying one. He spoke in forty-four counties averaging three speeches a day, and rarely did he have to look at many empty seats. So enthusiastic was the response that after completing his scheduled speech he was often compelled to address an overflow crowd outside the hall.[35] In the face of this reception, even some of Bryan's opponents began to concede that his election was inevitable.[36] The situation, however, was more complex than it seemed. Bryan, essentially, was waging a dual battle in Nebraska; he was determined not only to defeat the anti-Prohibition forces but to destroy the Hitchcock faction of the Democratic party as well. The two groups, unfortunately, were not always identical. Thus Bryan found himself in the uncomfortable position of supporting I. J. Dunn, Hitchcock's opponent for the Senatorial nomination, although Dunn himself was a foe of Prohibition. Bryan

[34] Bryan intimated that "interests" which did not want him to re-enter politics actively were behind the offer. *The New York Times,* March 22, 1916.

[35] For a detailed description of Bryan's primary campaign, see the *Nebraska State Journal* from March 20, 1916 to April 18, 1916. Senator Hitchcock's newspaper, the Omaha *World-Herald,* is valuable for a description of the activities of Bryan's opponents.

[36] *Nebraska State Journal,* April 12, 1916.

attempted to justify his action by claiming that, while Dunn was opposed to Prohibition, he was not a tool of the liquor interests, and would, therefore, follow the wishes of the electorate when Prohibition became a national issue.[37] His rather lame explanation may well have cost him some prohibitionist support without winning over any wet voters.

Aside from this episode, Bryan conducted himself as a good prohibitionist should. "If, after next November, any saloon is ever licensed in Nebraska," he roared at one point, "it will be in spite of all that I can do to prevent it. If any of these young men, who should be the glory of the state, are ever again led into temptation by the open saloon, it will not be my fault." [38] He was completely candid about his past actions in regard to the liquor issue. He admitted that he had voted against Prohibition in 1890 but maintained that he had a right to change his mind in twenty-five years. He confessed also that he had advised against the injection of the issue into the present campaign but quickly added: "it is here, and whenever there is a child born in our family, I take care of it." [39]

Although Prohibition was the main issue in the campaign, the Hitchcock forces brought up Bryan's resignation and his subsequent differences with Wilson.[40] Bryan's response was immediate. "If you think Woodrow Wilson doesn't want me in the St. Louis Convention as a delegate from Nebraska," he shouted to a crowd of over 1,500 at Auburn, "just write him a letter and ask him about it, and if he says there is a Democrat in Nebraska whom he prefers as a delegate, I'll gladly withdraw on the spot." [41] Though the Democrats of Nebraska may not have doubted the validity of Bryan's assertion, they proved indifferent to it. On April 18 they went to the polls and defeated Bryan, his brother Charles, who had campaigned for the gubernatorial nomination, and every other

[37] Omaha *World-Herald*, April 14, 1916. Similar circumstances led Bryan to support another opponent of Prohibition, Mayor Arthur Dahlman of Omaha, who was running against Hitchcock's candidate, Arthur Mullen, for Democratic National Committeeman. *Ibid.*

[38] *The Commoner*, April 1916, p. 5.

[39] *Nebraska State Journal*, March 21, 1916.

[40] See, for example, the Omaha *World-Herald*, April 7, 1916.

[41] *Nebraska State Journal*, March 25, 1916.

candidate on the Bryan ticket.[42] Bryan appeared to be neither surprised nor dismayed at the results. He attributed his defeat to the fact that the Nebraska Democracy was a prisoner of Hitchcock and the liquor machine and to the wet Republicans who crossed party lines to vote against him. He claimed that an analysis of the primary returns of both parties showed that a majority of the Nebraska electorate was dry, and he correctly predicted a victory for the Prohibition amendment in November.[43] Breathing what amounted to a sigh of relief, Bryan turned his attention once again to the issues of peace and economic reform.

During the Presidential election Bryan maintained a consistent silence on Prohibition, though he did urge the voters of Nebraska to vote for dry candidates to the state legislature "without regard to party differences on other subjects." [44] Once the Wilson administration was safely elected to a second term, however, all of Bryan's caution departed, and he became as militant and extreme a prohibitionist as was to be found in the country. "The prohibition issue is here, and here to stay until the saloon is driven out of the United States," he wrote in the first post-election issue of *The Commoner*.[45] The election had given Bryan's support of Prohibition additional impetus, for of the 23 dry states, almost all of which were in the West and South, 17 had cast their electoral votes for Wilson. It was evident that the Democratic party had captured the dry vote and Bryan was determined to keep things that way; he was going to turn the Democratic party into the party of Prohibition. "My work during the next four years," he told a group of reporters a week after the election, "will be to contribute whatever I can toward making the national Democracy dry. . . . The Democratic party cannot afford to become the champion of the brewery, the distillery and the saloon. The members of the party will not permit it to be buried in a drunkard's grave." [46]

Traveling to Indianapolis that same month, Bryan launched a

[42] *Ibid.* April 23, 24, 1916.
[43] *The Commoner*, May 1916, p. 2.
[44] *Ibid.* October 1916, p. 5.
[45] *Ibid.* November 1916, p. 1.
[46] *New York World*, November 15, 1916, reprinted in *ibid.* December 1916, p. 5.

movement to force the Democratic National Convention of 1920 to declare in favor of Prohibition. "Prohibition is sweeping the country," he declared. "It will be a Presidential campaign issue in 1920 if a Constitutional amendment is not submitted . . . by that time." [47] He soon had his brother Charles send out circular letters giving the details of his proposal to organize a "Dry Democracy" systematically, precinct by precinct.[48] At the Washington banquet given by leading Democrats in Bryan's honor, Bryan pointed out again, as he had been doing since the election, that Wilson owed his victory to the dry West and South and not to the wet East. "Shall we part with those friends who saved us, in order to ally ourselves with those who would have annihilated us?" He appealed to his comrades to enlist their party "on the side of the mother, the child, the home and humanity," and not allow it to be made the champion "of the most mercenary, the most tyrannical group that ever entered politics for the purpose of debauching party and corrupting government." [49] Bryan was clearly burning all his bridges behind him; there was to be no turning back.

We have already noted that the war which Bryan had fought so hard to avoid was responsible for bringing him unprecedented popularity. No less paradoxical was the fact that this same war was to pave the way for the rapid adoption of national Prohibition; a cause to which Bryan now devoted himself wholeheartedly.

The war, of course, was by no means solely responsible for the coming of Prohibition. The triumph of national temperance was the result of a long and intensive campaign and, judging from the number of dry Congressmen elected in 1916, it would have come had war not occurred.[50] The war, however, did help to expedite

[47] *Indianapolis Star,* November 19, 1916, reprinted in *The Commoner,* December 1916, p. 9; *The New York Times,* November 20, 1916.

[48] Clarence E. Pitts to WJB, February 22, 1917, Bryan Papers.

[49] *The Commoner,* January 1917, p. 19.

[50] Wayne Wheeler of the Anti-Saloon League has written of the election of 1916: "Many hours before the country knew whether Hughes or Wilson had triumphed, the dry workers throughout the nation were celebrating our victory. We knew the prohibition amendment would be submitted to the States by the Congress just elected." Quoted in Timberlake, *Prohibition and the Progressive Movement,* p. 172.

the victory by aiding the Prohibition movement in a variety of ways: it centralized authority in Washington to a greater degree than had been known since the Civil War; it brought into the movement such nonprohibitionists as Theodore Roosevelt and Herbert Hoover who now advocated Prohibition as an emergency war measure; it diverted the attention of the nation from Washington and the state capitals where the battle for Prohibition was raging; and, finally, it furnished the temperance forces with an entire battery of new arguments which enabled them to make Prohibition and patriotism synonymous.[51]

Bryan was one of the first to make effective use of these new points. One almost suspects that he was so eager to speak in behalf of food conservation primarily because from this vantage point he could deal liquor some devastating blows. There could be no argument against the fact that Prohibition was an efficient means of saving grain, and Bryan never tired of reiterating this point. We have had "meatless" days and "wheatless" days, he exclaimed. "Why doesn't someone suggest a few beerless days? . . . How can we justify the making of any part of our breadstuffs into intoxicating liquor when men are crying for bread?" In addition to wasting food, the use of alcohol impaired efficiency "and in this crisis we cannot afford to allow efficiency to be impaired either among soldiers or producers." "Alcohol," he cried, "is an enemy at home scarcely less deadly than the foe upon the field." [52]

But merely citing the pernicious effects of spirituous beverages was not Bryan's main aim; it was their manufacturers he was after. If alcohol was a deadly enemy, what could be said of the man who persisted in producing it. "The liquor interests," asserted Bryan in one of the most savage attacks he had ever made against any group, "are the most unpatriotic and conscienceless groups . . . [the United States] ever knew." "So much greater is their passion for dollars than their patriotism that they would, if they

---

[51] Charles Merz, *The Dry Decade* (Garden City, N.Y., 1931), pp. 25–27; Herbert Asbury, *The Great Illusion: an Informal History of Prohibition* (Garden City, N.Y., 1950), pp. 136–137.

[52] *The New York Times,* January 28, 1918; *The Commoner,* May 1917, p. 3, April 1918, p. 7.

could, make drunkards of the entire army and leave us defense-less before a foreign foe." [53]

Though such extreme attacks were both unfair and untrue, they were characteristic of Bryan's righteous, evangelistic fervor and necessary to his style of argumentation. It has often been noted that Bryan was one of the nation's chief exploiters of the conspiracy thesis; it should be added that he was also one of its major victims. As long as an issue remained on the periphery of Bryan's interests he was able to view it with some degree of realism, to perceive many of its complexities, and often to deal with it relatively and fairly. But once the issue was joined, once he became convinced that the time for resolving it was at hand, his mind clamped shut and became incapable of perceiving subtle distinctions. This oc-curred not because Bryan was an opportunist but because his mind and temperament led him to view all important issues in terms of absolutes. In the uncomplicated world in which he thrived, all decency and depravity were quickly separated and placed into easily recognizable compartments. Good was good and bad was bad and they never joined hands in the Nebraskan's simple uni-verse. Thus he could insist that no man could serve two masters, "he must be on the side of the home or the saloon." "There is only one side to a moral issue," he repeated untiringly, "and that is the moral side." [54]

And if the war accomplished nothing else it made Bryan more confident than ever that he was on the moral side. He not only recited the patriotic arguments in behalf of Prohibition, he *believed* in them implicitly. "I have never taken part in any fight which was as great in its far-reaching influence as the fight in which we are now engaged and my heart has never been so deeply in a cause as in the cause which now approaches its complete triumph," he told an audience in the fall of 1918. Never before was Bryan so certain that the fight which he was waging would benefit all mankind: "Thousands, tens of thousands, hundreds of thousands of men who will vote against Prohibition and who will think we are violating

[53] *Ibid.* July 1917, p. 7, January 1918, p. 5; *The New York Times,* Jan-uary 28, 1918.
[54] *The Commoner,* September 1918, p. 2, March 1917, p. 6.

their personal rights will, when they are released from the habit and relieved from temptation, go down on their knees and thank us for having helped them against their will, and their wives and children will not have to wait a year; they will thank us now for saving their husbands and fathers. . . . I say, my friends, we are fighting a battle where even our opponents will be benefited." [55]

Armed with these certainties, Bryan visited more than half of the states in the Union, speaking under the auspices of the Women's Christian Temperance Union, the Anti-Saloon League, and the Democratic Forward League. Everywhere he went he spoke out boldly and decisively, and at no time was he willing to concede one point to his opponents. All justice and all righteousness were on his side. When it was argued that the Prohibition crusade was undermining individual rights, he answered that the rights of the individual could not be placed above his duty to society, and that personal liberty must often be curbed for the greater good. "A man does not have to be run over by a drunken chauffeur more than twice before he learns that no man's personal liberty includes the right to injure another one." [56] Nowhere in these arguments did he recognize the vast majority of wets who drank moderately and injured no one. It is by no means improbable that Bryan, carried away by his own rhetoric, forgot that this type of drinker even existed. When it was sensibly suggested that beers and wines be treated more leniently than whisky in any proposed legislation, Bryan refused to listen. "Whiskey and beer will stand or fall together; it is the alcohol in both that makes them a menace. . . . The entire firm of 'Barleycorn, Gambrinus and Bacchus' must retire from business—a dissolution of partnership is not sufficient." [57]

Once again, the most serious charge leveled against Bryan, that his Prohibition crusade belied his own professed faith in the people,[58] was one that he did not even bother to answer; indeed, it

---

[55] *Ibid.* October 1918, pp. 7, 9.
[56] *Ibid.* October 1917, p. 3. See also *Memoirs,* p. 292.
[57] *The Commoner,* July 1917, p. 1.
[58] Journalist William Hard, for example, wrote of Bryan: "He has abandoned the rights of man and is in favor of state interference and paternalism and tyranny." *Everybody's* XXXIV (April 1916), 454.

was a charge that he probably failed to understand. Anyone well versed in the Scriptures should have known that you cannot elevate man unless you first remove temptation from his path. This was not an attack upon man's innate wisdom or goodness; it was merely a realistic admission of his weaknesses. In an article in which he praised the farmer's advanced position in adopting and championing Prohibition, Bryan intimated that this precocity stemmed in large part from the fact that the rural population of the country enjoyed the advantage of living "in the absence of many of the temptations which throng about the city." [59] The fault, then, Bryan unconsciously attributed not to man, who could not help his own weaknesses, but to God, who first created a man who was too weak to withstand certain temptations and then placed those temptations directly in his path. "God never made a human being so strong that he could begin the use of intoxicants with the certainty that he would not become a victim of the habit." [60] The remedy was not to attempt to do what God Himself could not do, but simply to remove the temptation. Bryan was going to prevent all the Adams that still roamed the earth from repeating their precursor's mistake, not by making them better or wiser men, but by confiscating all the apples in sight. That these men who were today too weak to resist temptation, might tomorrow begin to cultivate their own illicit apple orchards, was a thought which apparently never troubled him.

With the eyes of the nation and the nation's press riveted upon the battlefields across the Atlantic, the temperance forces concentrated their attention upon Washingon. Despite the fact that Bryan continued to raise the specter of a vast liquor conspiracy which was determined to prevent Congress from complying with the people's wishes, it was the prohibitionists and not their foes who were more efficiently organized and more adept at winning public support. The hitherto well-oiled political machines of the brewers and distillers were by this time thoroughly discredited, and the remainder of the wet forces seemed unable to treat Prohibition as a serious threat.[61] By the time they did it was too late, for on August 1,

[59] "Prohibition and the Farmer," *The Commoner,* September 1917, p. 8.
[60] *Ibid.* May 1918, p. 2.
[61] Merz, *The Dry Decade,* p. 36; Asbury, *The Great Illusion,* pp. 108ff.

1917, the Senate adopted the Eighteenth Amendment and the following December the House followed suit.

Bryan was seated in the press gallery when the House took its decisive vote, and as soon as victory was assured he entered upon the floor and was immediately surrounded by a score of Democratic Representatives. "Bryan Again Party Leader," ran a headline in the next edition of the *New York Sun*: "As a result of the vote in the House today Bryan has made himself a political leader of the Democratic Party and has pushed his new moral issue to the front as a preliminary to the next campaign." [62] The Legislative Committee of the Anti-Saloon League promptly sent Bryan a letter of congratulations in which they assured him that: "Generations yet unborn will rise up to call you blessed. Women and children without number . . . will not cease to thank God that He sent you to help proclaim the day of their deliverance." [63]

During the battle for ratification Bryan was, if anything, even more zealous than before. As far as he was concerned, the majority had already spoken through two-thirds of its representatives in Congress, and the procedures which compelled three-fourths of the states to concur as well was one of the Constitution's "ultra-conservative" provisions which he was to spend much time combating in the coming years. In this frame of mind Bryan was less willing than ever to make concessions or brook interference. Prohibition, he declared, was "the supreme domestic issue" until the amendment was secured. He continued to regard the East as one of the chief obstacles to reform of all kinds. During the winter of 1918, he was invited to testify before a joint legislative committee of the New York State legislature, and in his address which, according to *The New York Times*, "held the vast audience spellbound," Bryan thundered: "New York State, I say to you that it is time you were leading in something good. New York, it is time that you got into this race. The South is leading." [64]

In March, 1918, Bryan was elected president of the National

---

[62] *New York World,* December 17, 1917, *New York Sun,* December 17, 1917, both reprinted in *The Commoner,* January 1918, p. 8.
[63] *Ibid.* p. 3.
[64] *The New York Times,* February 27, 1918; *New York Evening Post,* February 27, 1918.

Dry Federation, an organization consisting of twenty-eight separate national groups including the Federal Council of Churches, the Prohibition party, and the Women's Prohibition League.[65] Despite his new organizational affiliation, Bryan's most important work still was accomplished through his oratory: in addresses to numerous state legislatures, in testimony before Congressional committees, and especially on the platform where he appealed directly to the voters. This was democracy as he understood it—it was what he knew how to do best. As the fall elections approached, Bryan, in his eagerness to have the temperance forces control the state legislatures, made one of his rare nonpartisan appeals: "The voters should lay partisanship aside and vote for the DRY legislative candidate against the WET candidate regardless of party. A Republican legislator who will vote to ratify the national prohibition amendment is better than a Democratic legislator who will vote to defeat the amendment and retain the saloons." [66]

When news of the final ratification of the Eighteenth Amendment reached Bryan on January 16, 1919, he commented: "Let the world rejoice. . . . The greatest moral reform of the generation has been accomplished." [67] He was especially pleased because he felt that the settlement of the Prohibition issue would remove an important source of friction within the ranks of the Democratic party. To Postmaster General Burleson he wrote: "You have certainly been a good fighter and deserve to retain your side arms if not the contents of your hip pockets. The settlement of the liquor question eliminates the only difference between us as the Civil War removed the root of discord between the North and South." [68] Unfortunately, Bryan's analogy proved to be more apt than he knew.

His work, of course, was still not fully completed. Laws, as he well knew from past experience, are not self-enforcing. Accordingly, he inaugurated his long battle for a rigid enforcement statute. His most bitter struggle, however, centered upon the issue of wartime Prohibition. The Eighteenth Amendment was not due to go into effect until January 16, 1920, but in September, 1918, Con-

[65] *The Commoner,* March 1918, p. 2.
[66] *Ibid.* September 1918, p. 1.
[67] *Ibid.* February 1919, pp. 1, 8.
[68] WJB to Burleson, January 22, 1919, Burleson Papers, Vol. 22.

gress had passed an emergency act establishing wartime Prohibition beginning the following July. With the end of the war, Wilson proved reluctant to enforce the act and recommended its repeal pertaining to wine and beer. Infuriated by the President's recommendation, Bryan now indulged in an act which was even rarer for him than mere nonpartisanship: he appealed to a Republican Congress to override a Democratic President.[69] On most questions, he announced during a Chicago address, the President might be assumed to know more than the average citizen, "but on the question of the saloon a mother with a drunken son knows more than he does." [70] In the end, widespread opposition to Wilson's recommendation, even among members of his Cabinet, forced him to back down, and on July 1, 1919, the saloons all over the United States were legally closed. "What a night of sorrow we have passed through," Bryan told a Methodist Conference at Columbus, Ohio, "but the morning is here and joy cometh with it." Nine years before he had not expected to live to see the nation go dry but now, though he was fifty-nine, he was confident that he would see the day "when there will not be an open saloon in any civilized nation on the globe." [71]

Even with the coming of Prohibition Bryan's troubles were far from over. He soon found himself under attack by certain newspapers for having accepted payment for some of his Prohibition speeches. "William Jennings Bryan worked for humanity for $250 a day and expenses, spot cash," commented the *New York World.*[72] It was true that in 1919 Bryan had received $11,000 for making a series of lectures for the Anti-Saloon League, but, as the records of the League proved and as Bryan and League officials hurriedly pointed out, he had been speaking for the League and other dry organizations for nine years without receiving a penny even for his

[69] *The Commoner,* June 1919, pp. 1–2.

[70] *The New York Times,* May 26, 1919.

[71] *The Commoner,* July 1919, p. 5. Bryan went so far as to ask Secretary Lansing to forward all available information relating to the liquor question in other countries. WJB to Robert Lansing, January 20, 1919, National Archives, Washington, D.C.

[72] Quoted in Peter H. Odegard, *Pressure Politics: the Story of the Anti-Saloon League* (New York, 1928), p. 203.

personal expenses. Only after Congress had approved Prohibition did Bryan agree to accept any compensation for his work and, as he himself maintained, had he been the money-grabbing opportunist pictured by the newspapers he could have earned a fortune years before by speaking in behalf of the liquor interests or any number of other interest groups.[73] The newspaper attacks had hurt him, however, and he reverted to his previous policy of accepting no remuneration for making Prohibition speeches and even became wary of speaking under the auspices of such organizations as the Anti-Saloon League.[74]

In addition to difficulties with the press, Bryan also found himself embroiled in a senseless dispute with William H. Anderson, the State Superintendent of the Anti-Saloon League of New York, which was precipitated when Bryan accepted the presidency of the National Dry Federation. Anderson, who saw the new organization as a threat to his own, publicly attacked Bryan for his tardiness in joining the dry forces and asserted that "as a LEADER, as a supposed strategist, as a general, . . . Mr. Bryan is frankly a joke so far as the Prohibition movement is concerned." [75] Bryan had no need to defend himself, for leading prohibitionists throughout the country quickly repudiated Anderson's charges and the National Anti-Saloon League itself eventually censured Anderson for "making an attack of a personal nature upon an outstanding friend of Prohibition." [76]

Difficulties of this nature, however, could not mar the joy Bryan felt when a few seconds before constitutional Prohibition was due to go into effect, at a minute past midnight on January 17, 1920, he paused in the midst of his speech before a victory celebration to recite the Scriptural lines: "They are dead which sought the

[73] See *ibid.* Appendix F, p. 274; *The Commoner,* March 1920, p. 5; Wayne B. Wheeler's statement in *The New York Times,* January 9, 1920.

[74] WJB to Josephus Daniels, December 5, 1922, Daniels Papers (Manuscript Division, Library of Congress), Box 566.

[75] A copy of Anderson's article, dated April 2, 1918, is in the Bryan Papers. See also *The New York Times,* April 14, 1918.

[76] See the following letters to Bryan: Howard H. Russell, April 6, 1918, F. L. Crabbe, April 22, 1918, A. C. Bayne, May 9, 1918, Ella A. Boole, April 24, 1918, Bryan Papers. See also the report of the Anti-Saloon League Committee which investigated the entire affair. *Ibid.*

young child's life." [77] At the same moment in Norfolk, Virginia, Billy Sunday, with his usual flair for turning the sublime into the ridiculous, was holding a full-scale funeral service for John Barleycorn. Despite his unfailing hyperbole, Sunday enunciated the hopes and expectations of many prohibitionists when he cried:

The reign of tears is over. The slums will soon be only a memory. We will turn our prisons into factories and our jails into storehouses and corncribs. Men will walk upright now, women will smile, and the children will laugh. Hell will be forever for rent.[78]

"King Alcohol" was dead; all that remained was the task of burying the corpse; a task that proved far more exacting than Bryan, Sunday, and their fellow executioners anticipated. . . .

[77] The Commoner, February 1920, p. 1.
[78] Quoted in Asbury, The Great Illusion, pp. 144–145.

The Struggle Against Darwin

Bryan came late to the Prohibition movement; he came even later to the antievolution crusade.

From the publication of *The Origin of Species* in 1859, many religious men had opposed Darwin's theories for fear of their impact on morality. If man had developed from lower species of animals rather than having been created by God in His image, what assurance was there that man had a moral sense and could discern and follow God's law? If the Bible lost its authority as explanation of man's origins, how could it retain authority as a standard for his conduct? These fears found ludicrous forms. Just before the Civil War Josiah Nott, a Southern biologist, and Louis Agassiz of Harvard advanced the thesis that God had created each human race separately, that Negroes and whites had been created as separate species by God. This theory was indignantly rejected by fundamentalists of that day because it conflicted with the account in Genesis; the Bible was the bulwark of social order; the thesis of multiple creation, by subverting the Bible, threatened the entire social system. A writer in 1867 complained that the theory of man's evolution would create a chaos of "defalcations and robberies, and murders, and infanticides, and adulteries, and drunkenness, and every form and degree of social dishonor." In the following decades such fears occasionally were expressed in the firing of a

Reprinted from Ray Ginger, *Six Days or Forever?* (Beacon Press, 1958), pp. 27–34, by permission of the Beacon Press. Copyright © 1958 by Ray Ginger.

professor by this college or that, in the expulsion of scholars by various Protestant churches.

During those years also, the years when Bryan was earning his reputation in progressive causes, many reformers were vigilantly fighting the applications of alleged Darwinian theory to social problems. Such social Darwinists as William Graham Sumner, a much respected Yale professor, not only justified the status quo as manifesting "the survival of the fittest" but also claimed that society changed gradually and naturally over eternities of time, and that man's efforts to influence the course of social change were futile or harmful. The lengths to which this attitude could carry are illustrated by an episode involving Henry George and E. L. Youmans, founder in 1872 of the *Popular Science Monthly* and the leading American propagandist for Herbert Spencer. Youmans denounced the political corruption in New York and declared that the rich were indifferent or sympathetic to it because it paid them to be so. George asked: "What do you propose to do about it?" Youmans replied: "Nothing! You and I can do nothing at all. . . . Perhaps in four or five thousand years evolution may have carried men beyond this state of things."

After the turn of the century, explicit social Darwinism died down, and so did the evolution controversy. Then, in 1910, appeared the first of a series of ten small pamphlets, *The Fundamentals,* which expounded as a touchstone for Christians the Five Points: the infallibility of the Bible, the Virgin Birth of Christ, Christ's substitutionary atonement for man's sins, the Resurrection of Christ, the authenticity of all Biblical miracles. On the basis of this creed, *The Fundamentals* declared that Darwinism "can have no possible points of contact with Christianity."

Although fundamentalist activity declined during World War I, the war—by emphasizing the mystical and evil elements in man, by exuding vague anxieties and irrational fears, by equating evolution with "survival of the fittest" and then equating survival of the fittest with "German barbarism," with Nietzsche and the rule of force—eventuated in a postwar climate that proved ideal for fundamentalism. The war also witnessed the creation of a new organization. In 1918 Dr. William Bell Riley, pastor of the First Baptist

Church of Minneapolis, led in the formation of the World's Christian Fundamentals Association.

All this happened without Bryan. He had joined the Presbyterian Church in boyhood, and in 1900 he became elder of his congregation at Lincoln. As the most popular Chautauqua speaker in the country for thirty years, he of course needed some religious talks, so he prepared one about Christ called "The Prince of Peace" and one about Christianity called "The Value of an Ideal." But he was blind to the menace of Darwinism. In 1909 he said blithely: "I do not carry the doctrine of evolution as far as some do; I am not yet convinced that man is a lineal descendant of the lower animals. I do not mean to find fault with you if you want to accept the theory . . ."

Then Bryan was reborn. "When I fall, I shall arise: when I sit in darkness, the Lord shall be a light unto me" (Micah 7:8). One factor in alerting Bryan was a book by Vernon Kellogg, a biologist who had gotten to know some German military leaders in Belgium; in *Headquarters Nights* (1917), Kellogg declared that the philosophy of the Germans was Darwinism applied to international relations. Bryan was alarmed also, as he toured the country giving religious talks after the war, by the many expressions of disbelief, especially by college students. He became convinced that the theory of human evolution was the evil instrument that had undermined the students' faith. It devastated him, at the conclusion of a speech in Atlanta, to be told by a college sophomore that Darwinism and Christianity could be reconciled easily; all one had to do was to discard Genesis. "Only Genesis!" Bryan exploded. "And yet there are three verses in the first chapter of Genesis that mean more to man than all the books of human origin: the first verse, which gives the most reasonable account of creation ever advanced; the twenty-fourth verse, which gives the only law governing the continuity of life on earth; and the twenty-sixth, which gives the only explanation of man's presence here."

Alert to any trace of scurf on the student soul, he publicized the report of a religious paper, based on a survey, that at one large university only 10 per cent of the male students were interested in religion, but 50 per cent gambled and 62 per cent drank. Bryan was especially aroused by James H. Leuba's *Belief in God and Immortality* (1916 and 1920). Leuba, a professor of psychology at Bryn Mawr, reported the results of some confidential polls he had taken. Of the 5,500 names in *American Men in Science,* he chose 1,000 as representative. Over half doubted or denied a personal God and personal immortality. Of the biologists replying, two out of three stated their disbelief. Leuba also got from nine ranking colleges 1,000 answers from students, 97 per cent of whom were 18–20 years of age. Only 15 per cent of the freshmen expressed a lack of belief, but 40–45 per cent of the men graduating did so.

Here, thought Bryan, was absolute proof. He hurled himself into the battle. Not only was the theory of evolution destroying our moral standards, he roared, but it was also poor science; there was no evidence of its validity. When he took this line in his address, "Brute or Brother?," at the University of Wisconsin in 1921, President Birge of the University remarked that Bryan would destroy the students' faith by identifying religion with untenable scientific doctrines. The comment was passed on to Bryan, who immediately started a dispute with Birge that lasted a full year. "The real question is," wrote Bryan in *The New York Times* in 1922, "Did God use evolution as His Plan? If it could be shown that man, instead of being made in the image of God, is a development of beasts we would have to accept it, regardless of its effect, for truth is truth and will prevail. But when there is no proof we have a right to consider the effect of the acceptance of an unsupported hypothesis." Henry Fairfield Osborn, director of the American Museum of Natural History, wrote in reply that evolution had been purposeful, not accidental, and that the evidence of evolution actually proved the existence of God.

Bryan got much encouragement, from both Midwest and South. Louis F. Post, a longtime Chicago liberal, the man who had done more than anybody else to stop the postwar deportation delirium, wrote him a warm endorsement. Post declared that man was separated from the animals by "an impassable gulf." The essential feature of man was that God had breathed life into him so that he became a living soul. Post would accept even Genesis as literally true if "indefinite periods" were substituted for the six days of the Creation. Bryan, much pleased by this support, replied: "I am very much in earnest in my opposition to Darwinism because I have abundant evidence of the evil influence it is exerting. I am trying to protect the students from atheistic professors by showing them that it is not necessary to reject the Bible—that there is no proof of animal origin."

Contrary evidence—what Bryan regarded as contrary evidence —continued to pile up. In February, 1923, he was jubilant about the discoveries in the newly opened tomb of Tutankhamen. "King Tutankhamen," he chortled, "appears to have been a man . . . If ever man came from the ape we must have quit coming before the Egyptian king took the throne. Man seems to have arrived on our earth a good while ago, judging from the fact his civilization of 3,000 years before Christ was in quite a high state of progress." No doubt of it, Darwin was wrong. A newspaper clipping reporting these comments by Bryan was sent to Clarence Darrow, who in no way shared Louis Post's enthusiasm about the religious views of Bryan. Bryan, he thought, was worse than a boor, he was a dangerous boor. And Darrow soon found a way to express his attitude.

When the Chicago *Tribune* editorialized against Bryan's efforts to proscribe the theory of evolution, Bryan replied in a letter to the editor. Here was Darrow's chance. His terse but lengthy letter rated the front page of the *Tribune* on the Fourth of July, 1923, and was reprinted in full by many other newspapers.

Commenting on a questionnaire that Bryan had publicly addressed to those professors who claimed to believe simultaneously in Christianity and in the theory of evolution, Darrow agreed that answers to Bryan's queries might help to clarify the issue; "likewise," he continued, "a few questions to Mr. Bryan and the fundamentalists, if fairly answered, might serve the interests of reaching the truth—all of this assumes that truth is desirable." Then came 55 questions to Bryan about the Bible. Did he believe in the literal truth of every word of it? Was the story of the Creation factual or allegorical? "Did God curse the serpent for tempting Eve and decree that thereafter he should go on his belly? How did he travel before that time?" Darrow asked questions about the Flood, the age of the earth, the origins of man.

Bryan was an artful politician; he would state his case in his own way. This was not it. He didn't answer Darrow's questions, which lay fallow to crop up again, two years later, in an unforeseen context.

Bryan's campaign was meeting opposition. Even in his own Presbyterian Church he had been humbled. A delegate to the General Assembly of the church in 1923, Bryan was nominated to be moderator, the denomination's highest office. In the voting he led on the first ballot, and again on the second. He turned to another candidate, Charles F. Wishart, and said confidently, "I'll win on the next ballot." But he didn't. Wishart did, a man only nine years in the church, the president of Wooster College that harbored a biologist, Horace Mateer, whose religious liberalism had already stirred Bryan's indignation. And Wishart further humiliated Bryan by refusing to name him as vice-moderator. Bryan did not offer the congratulations that the vanquished customarily advances to the victor.

Four days later, Bryan introduced a resolution in the General Assembly that would have denied any part of the church's educational fund to any school that taught, "as proved a fact," any evolutionary theory that connected man with any other species. During the debate, Bryan declared: "I am now engaged in the biggest reform of my life. I am trying to save the Christian Church from those who are trying to destroy her faith!" But his resolution was sidetracked in favor of a milder one. In spite of this personal defeat, Bryan could find considerable solace in the affirmation by the General Assembly of the fundamentalist Five Points. . . .

✪

Denouement at Dayton

A buzz ran through the crowd as I took my place in the packed courtroom in the little town of Dayton, Tennessee, on that sweltering July day in 1925. Seated next to me at the defense table was my chief counsel, the famous criminal lawyer Clarence Darrow. Opposite us, languidly waving a palm-leaf fan, sat the prosecution's star, William Jennings Bryan, the silver-tongued orator, three times the Democratic nominee for President and leader of the fundamentalist movement which had brought about my trial.

A few weeks before I had been an unknown high-school teacher in a little mountain town. Now I was involved in a trial reported the world over. Seated in the courtroom, ready to testify in my behalf, were a dozen distinguished professors and scientists, led by Prof. Kirtley Mather of Harvard. More than 100 reporters were on hand, and even radio announcers, who for the first time in history were to broadcast a jury trial.

"Don't worry, son, we'll show them a few tricks," Darrow whispered, throwing a reassuring arm around my shoulder as the judge ascended the bench.

The case had erupted around my head not long after I arrived in Dayton to teach science and coach football at the high school. For a number of years a clash had been building up between the fundamentalists and the modernists. The fundamentalists adhered

Reprinted, with permission, from John T. Scopes, "The Trial that Rocked the Nation," *Reader's Digest*, 78 (March 1961), pp. 136–144. Copyright 1961 by the Reader's Digest Assn., Inc.

229

to a literal interpretation of the Old Testament. The modernists, on the other hand, accepted the theory advanced by the nineteenth-century English biologist, Charles Darwin, that all animal life, including monkeys and men, had evolved from a common ancestor.

Fundamentalism was strong in Tennessee, and the state legislature had recently passed a law prohibiting the teaching of "any theory that denies the story of creation as taught in the Bible." The new law was aimed squarely at Darwin's theory of evolution. An engineer, George Rappelyea, used to sit around Robinson's drugstore and argue with the local people against the law. During one such argument, Rappelyea said that nobody could teach biology without teaching evolution. Since I had been teaching biology, I was sent for.

"Rappelyea is right," I told them.

"Then you have been violating the law," druggist Robinson said.

"So has every other teacher," I replied. "Evolution is explained in Hunter's *Civic Biology,* and that's our textbook."

Rappelyea then made a suggestion. "Let's take this thing to court," he said, "and test the legality of it."

When I was indicted on May 7, no one, least of all I, anticipated that my case would snowball into one of the most famous trials in U.S. history. The American Civil Liberties Union announced it would take my case to the U.S. Supreme Court if necessary to "establish that a teacher may tell the truth without being sent to jail." Then Bryan volunteered to assist the state in prosecuting me. Immediately the renowned lawyer Clarence Darrow offered his services to defend me. Ironically, I did not know Darrow before my trial but I had met Bryan when he addressed my college graduating class. I admired him, although I did not agree with his views.

By the time the trial began on July 10, our town of 1,500 had taken on a circus atmosphere. The buildings along the main street were festooned with banners. The streets around the three-story red brick courthouse sprouted with rickety stands selling hot dogs, religious books and watermelons. Evangelists set up tents to exhort the passers-by. People from the surrounding hills, mostly fundamentalists, arrived to cheer Bryan against the "infidel outsiders."

Among them was John W. Butler, the genial state legislator who had drawn up the antievolution law. Butler was a 49-year-old farmer who, before his election, had never been out of the county he was born in.

The presiding judge was John T. Raulston, a florid-faced man who announced: "I'm jist a reg'lar mountaineer jedge." At the prosecution table with the aging and paunchy Bryan, sat his son, also a lawyer, and Tennessee's brilliant young attorney general, Tom Stewart. Besides the shrewd 68-year-old Darrow, my counsel consisted of the handsome and magnetic trial lawyer, Dudley Field Malone, 43, and Arthur Garfield Hays, quiet, scholarly and steeped in the law. In a trial in which religion played a key role, Darrow was an agnostic, Malone a Catholic and Hays a Jew. My father had come from Kentucky to be with me for the trial.

Judge Raulston called for a local minister to open the session with prayer, and the trial got under way with the selection of a jury. Of the 12 jurors, three said they had never read any book except the Bible. One admitted he couldn't read. My father growled, "That's one hell of a jury!"

After the preliminary sparring over legalities, Darrow began his opening statement: "My friend the attorney general says that John Scopes knows what he is here for. I know what he is here for, too. He is here because ignorance and bigotry are rampant, and it is a mighty strong combination."

Bryan sat nibbling on his palm fan as Darrow walked slowly around the baking courtroom. "Today it is the public-school teachers," Darrow continued, "and tomorrow the private. Next, the magazines, the books, the newspapers. After a while, it is the setting of man against man and creed against creed until we are marching backward to the glorious age of the sixteenth century when bigots lighted fagots to burn the men who dared to bring any intelligence and enlightenment and culture to the human mind."

"That damned infidel," a woman whispered loudly as he finished his address.

The following day the prosecution began calling witnesses against me. Two of my pupils testified, grinning shyly at me, that I had taught them evolution, but added that they had not been contaminated by the experience. Howard Morgan, a bright lad of 14, testified that I had taught that man was a mammal like cows, horses, dogs and cats.

"He didn't say a cat was the same as a man?" Darrow asked.

"No, sir," the youngster said. "He said man had reasoning power."

"There is some doubt about that," Darrow snorted.

After testimony was completed, Bryan rose to address the jury. The issue was simple, he declared. "The Christian believes that man came from above. The evolutionist believes he must have come from below." The spectators chuckled and Bryan warmed to his work. In one hand he brandished a biology text as he denounced the scientists who had come to Dayton to testify for the defense.

"The Bible," he thundered in his sonorous organ tones, "is not going to be driven out of this court by experts who come hundreds of miles to testify that they can reconcile evolution, with its ancestors in the jungle, with man made by God in His image and put here for His purpose as part of a divine plan."

As he finished, jaw outthrust, eyes flashing, the audience burst into applause and shouts of "Amen." Yet something was lacking. Gone was the fierce fervor of the days when Bryan had swept the Democratic convention like a prairie fire. The crowd seemed to feel that their champion had not scorched the infidels with the hot breath of his oratory as he should have.

Dudley Field Malone popped up to reply. "Mr. Bryan is not the only one who has the right to speak for the Bible," he observed. "There are other people in this country who have given up their whole lives to God and religion. Mr. Bryan, with passionate spirit and enthusiasm, has given most of his life to politics."

Bryan sipped from a jug of water as Malone's voice grew in volume. He appealed for intellectual freedom, and accused Bryan of calling for a duel to the death between science and religion. "There is never a duel with the truth," he roared. "The truth always wins—and we are not afraid of it. The truth does not need Mr. Bryan. The truth is eternal, immortal and needs no human agency to support it!"

When Malone finished there was a momentary hush. Then the courtroom broke into a storm of applause that surpassed that for Bryan. I found myself pounding Malone on the back of his damp jacket. But although Malone had won the oratorical nod over Bryan, Judge Raulston ruled against permitting the scientists to testify for the defense.

When court recessed, we found Dayton's streets swarming with strangers. Pitchmen hawked their wares on every corner. One store announced: DARWIN IS RIGHT—INSIDE. (This was J. R. Darwin's Everything to Wear Store.) One entrepreneur rented a store window to display an ape. Spectators paid ten cents each to gaze at the simian and ponder whether they might be related. "The poor brute cowered in a corner with his hands over his eyes," Westbrook Pegler noted, "afraid it might be true." H. L. Mencken wrote his sulphurous dispatches sitting in his shorts with a fan blowing on him, and there was talk of riding him out of town on a rail for referring to the local citizenry as yokels. Twenty-two telegraphers were sending out 165,000 words a day on the trial.

Because of the heat and a fear that the old courthouse floor might collapse under the weight of the throng, the trial was resumed outside under the maples. More than 2,000 spectators sat on wooden benches or squatted on the grass, perched on the tops of parked cars or gawked from the courthouse windows.

Then came the climax of the trial. Because of the wording of the antievolution law, the prosecution was forced to take the position that the Bible must be interpreted literally. Now Darrow sprang his trump card by calling Bryan as a witness for the defense. Judge Raulston looked startled.

"We are calling him as an expert on the Bible," Darrow said. "His reputation as an authority on Scripture is recognized throughout the world."

Bryan was suspicious of the wily Darrow, yet he could not refuse the challenge. For years he had lectured and written on the Bible. He had campaigned against Darwinism in Tennessee even before passage of the antievolution law. Resolutely he strode to the stand, carrying his palm fan like a sword to repel his enemies.

Under Darrow's quiet questioning he acknowledged believing the Bible literally, and the crowd punctuated his defiant replies with fervent "Amens."

Darrow read from Genesis: "And the morning and the evening were the first day." Then he asked Bryan if he believed that the sun was created on the fourth day. Bryan said that he did.

"How could there have been a morning and evening without any sun?" Darrow inquired. Bryan mopped his bald dome in silence. There were snickers from the crowd, even among the faithful. Darrow tugged on his lavender galluses and twirled his spectacles as he pursued the questioning. He asked if Bryan believed literally in the story of Eve. Bryan answered in the affirmative.

"And you believe that God punished the serpent by condemning snakes forever after to crawl upon their bellies?"

"I believe that."

"Well, have you any idea how the snake went before that time?"

The crowd laughed, and Bryan turned livid. His voice rose and the fan in his hand shook in anger.

"Your honor," he said, "I will answer all Mr. Darrow's questions at once. I want the world to know that this man who does not believe in God is using a Tennessee court to cast slurs on Him. . . ."

"I object to that statement," Darrow shouted. "I am examining you on your fool ideas that no intelligent Christian on earth believes."

Judge Raulston gaveled the hubbub to a halt and adjourned court until next day. Bryan stood forlornly alone. My heart went out to the old warrior as spectators pushed by him to shake Darrow's hand.

The jury got the case at noon the following day. The jurymen retired to a corner of the courthouse lawn and whispered for just nine minutes. The verdict was guilty. Judge Raulston fined me $100 and costs.

Dudley Field Malone called my conviction a "victorious defeat." A few Southern papers, loyal to their faded champion, hailed it as a victory for Bryan. But Bryan, sad and exhausted, died in Dayton two days after the trial.

I was offered my teaching job back but I declined. Some of the professors who had come to testify in my behalf arranged a scholarship for me at the University of Chicago so I could pursue the study of science. Later I became a geologist for an oil company in South America and Louisiana.

Not long ago I went back to Dayton for the first time since my trial 35 years ago. The little town looked much the same to me. But now there is a William Jennings Bryan University on a hilltop overlooking the valley.

There were other changes, too. Evolution is taught in Tennessee, though the law under which I was convicted is still on the books.* The oratorical storm which Clarence Darrow and Dudley Field Malone blew up in the little courtroom in Dayton swept like a fresh wind through the schools and legislative halls of the country, bringing in its wake a new climate of intellectual and academic freedom that has grown with the passing years.

* In May 1967 the Tennessee legislature repealed the law [ed.].

HENRY STEELE COMMAGER

✪

The Great Commoner

The strength and persistence of fundamentalism well into the
twentieth century is one of the curiosities of the history of American thought. That a people so optimistic and self-confident should
accept a theology which insisted on the depravity of man, that a
people so distrustful of all authority should yield so readily to the
authority of the Scriptures as interpreted by men like themselves,
that a people so inclined to independence should take their religious
ideas at second hand, that a people so scientific minded should
resolutely ignore the impact of science in the realm of religion—
all this is difficult to explain, except on fundamentalist grounds.

Other explanations suggest a divorce between religious and secular thought, a dichotomy in the American mind which the student
is reluctant to accept. That, in a world which trembled and reeled
beneath them, where life seemed a matter of endless adjustments
and readjustments to the obscure and shifting facts of science, men
should cling to something that seemed stable and familiar was not
wonderful; that they should find it exclusively in the fundamentalist version of the Scriptures was. They sang Henry Lyte's great
hymn as a prayer:

> Swift to its close ebbs out life's little day;
> Earth's joys grow dim, its glories pass away;

Reprinted by permission of Yale University Press from *The American
Mind*, by Henry Steele Commager, pp. 178–183, 346–347. Copyright ©
1950 by Yale University Press.

> Change and decay in all around I see;
> O Thou who changest not, abide with me.

With Henry Adams, whom they did not read, they were ready to believe that, force for force, the Virgin was as intelligible as the dynamo. With T. S. Eliot, whom they did not know, they cried:

> God is leaving us, God is leaving us, more pang,
>   more pain, than birth or death.
> Sweet and cloying through the dark air
> Falls the stifling sense of despair.
>
> *(The Cathedral)*

As science revealed a mysterious universe, they clung all the more devoutly to their familiar God. They did not wish to inquire into the truth of revealed religion, for that old-time religion gave them assurance of salvation, just as it was. They resented the invasion of religion by science just as many Southerners resented the invasion of race relations by science; they preferred to cling to the doctrine of the inspiration and the inerrancy of the Scriptures, as many Southerners preferred to cling to the notion of white supremacy—as an article of faith. They felt instinctively that to subject the Bible to the test of textual criticism or of the laboratory was both shabby and dangerous.

Yet other beliefs as deeply imbedded in tradition and custom, and almost as sacrosanct, had yielded to the findings of scholarship and science, and even Southerners were forced, in time, to modify some of their notions about the Negro. That religion could be brought into conformity with new currents of thought and fitted to the practical needs of society without consequences fatal to its spiritual content had been asserted by their greatest religious leaders—men like Henry Ward Beecher and Lyman Abbott and Phillips Brooks—and abundantly demonstrated by the modernists. Why were the assertions so widely ignored, the demonstrations so commonly rejected?

Perhaps it was because religion meant, on the whole, so little; because, divorced as it was from the intimate realities of daily life and excused from active participation in the affairs of business, politics, or society, it could be regarded as a thing apart, not subject to the normal tests prescribed for secular faiths and doctrines. Fundamentalists resented a critical attitude toward their religion as they resented a critical attitude toward their mothers. They improvidently ignored religious precepts, just as they ignored the moral axioms inculcated by their mothers, but they did this, as it were, on weekdays and honored religion on Sundays—as they honored their mothers on Mother's Day, that curious American institution. Because they rarely subjected their religion to the test of experience and application, they could cherish it as they might cherish some museum piece which was never subject to such wear and tear as might expose its fragility.

For what is striking about fundamentalism is not alone the zeal with which it was maintained or the general acceptance it commanded but the superficiality with which it was observed. These terms may seem contradictory, just as it may seem contradictory to remark that the superpatriotism of the D.A.R. sometimes constituted disloyalty, but the contradiction is resolved if we keep in mind that fundamentalism came to be, increasingly, a ceremonial attitude, divorced from conduct. The fundamentalists themselves were rarely fundamentalist; they asserted the inerrancy of the Scriptures, but that literal interpretation of the New Testament upon which they insisted would have convulsed their society and economy. It is recorded that the Reverend C. M. Sheldon sold eight million copies of *In His Steps,* but the number who followed its precepts was probably somewhat smaller. Certainly some of the Southern fundamentalists did not act as if they believed in the authority of the Biblical injunction to love thy neighbor as thyself; geographically, fundamentalism and lynching seemed to go together. It was typical of the fundamentalist position that the organized fundamentalist movement, launched in 1909, was financed by two California oil millionaires who had somehow overlooked both Matthew 19:24 and Mark 10:25. Dwight Moody, most attractive of postwar revivalists, gave away all of his fabulous earnings, but his successors in spreading the straight Gospel—men like Bryan and Billy Sunday and John Alexander Dowie—did not display a comparable contempt for money.

After the First World War, fundamentalism lost much of its driving force, its authority, and its dignity, and became increasingly querulous, negative, and histrionic. The fundamentalists were eased out of the colleges and lost control of most theological schools; those which they retained, or founded, lacked prestige and good students. Heresy trials, painfully frequent even in the nineties and the early years of the century, were abandoned, and heretics went their way unmolested if not unrebuked. The contrast between the treatment accorded poor Tom Paine and Col. "Bob" Ingersoll is illuminating; even more illuminating is the fact that the next generation had no need for any devil's advocate and that organized Free Thought, which flourished on opposition and martyrdom, flickered and died out. Except in certain backward areas like southern California and the rural South, revivals petered out, and even Chautauqua, never aggressively fundamentalist or without dignity and beauty, declined sharply in popularity. The champions of fundamentalism in the twentieth century were men and women like Sam Jones, Gypsy Smith, Billy Sunday, John Roach Stratton, and Aimee Semple McPherson, who compared somewhat unfavorably with their predecessors in orthodoxy like Jonathan Edwards, Bishop Asbury, Charles Finney, or even Dwight L. Moody. Under such leadership, fundamentalism appealed, increasingly, to the uneducated and the half-educated; it exploited fear not only of hell-fire and damnation but of Catholics and Jews, and in the South and Middle West it formed an unofficial alliance with the Ku Klux Klan.

Two episodes which came at the conclusion of the first quarter of the new century dramatized at once the tenacious strength of fundamentalism and its intellectual decadence: the fight over the Ku Klux Klan plank in the Democratic national convention of 1924 and the Scopes trial at Dayton, Tennessee, the following year. Fundamentalism was not officially represented at the Democratic convention, but William Jennings Bryan was its unofficial spokesman, and it largely inspired the opposition both to the nomination of the Catholic Alfred E. Smith and to the plank denouncing the notorious Ku Klux Klan. For reasons not entirely connected with religion it was victorious on both issues: it is proper to recall, however, that Governor Smith was nominated in 1928 and that the Ku Klux Klan disintegrated. That fundamentalists should have opposed Governor Smith on religious grounds in 1924 and again in 1928 is a reflection either on their sincerity or their intelligence, for Catholics were extreme fundamentalists, and whatever else Romanism may have threatened, it scarcely threatened either religion or morality.

The issue at Dayton was more clear cut: here was one of the decisive battles in that warfare between science and theology which Andrew Dickson White had deplored more than a generation earlier. The religious question—the wisdom of the state law forbidding the teaching of evolution in public schools—was, to be sure, confused by the legal one—the right of the state to enact such a law. Both public opinion and counsel largely ignored the legal and concentrated on the religious issue. It was appropriate that Bryan should have appeared as counsel for the prosecution, for he was not only the most distinguished and eloquent of American fundamentalists but largely responsible for the enactment of anti-evolution laws in several Southern states. It was less appropriate, perhaps, that Clarence Darrow should have been chief counsel for the defense, for in the eyes of most Americans he represented not modernist religion but irreligion, and his advocacy of evolution and assault upon fundamentalism enabled the prosecution to identify science with atheism.

Bryan at Dayton is a spectacle that cannot fail to command the anxious interest of every student of the American mind, for it marked the end not only of a career but of an era. No one had more faithfully represented the American mind and character than the Great Commoner who had thrice led the Democracy, the Peerless Leader who had championed righteousness and morality with a consistency without parallel in modern politics; but it was the mind and character of the mid-nineteenth, not the twentieth, century that he represented; it was for the America of the Middle Border, of the farm and the village, of the little red schoolhouse and the little brown church, of the Chautauqua tent and the Redpath circuit, of puritanism and evangelism, of agrarian democracy and homespun equality that he spoke. He had spent his boyhood and youth in an atmosphere of piety and was never thereafter able to breathe any other without discomfort. His father had been a Baptist, his mother a Methodist, he himself was converted to Presbyterianism when still a boy; it was characteristic that he should have been attached to the three most numerous and conservative of Protestant denominations. From these fundamentalist churches he derived his religious ideas and habits and he never saw reason to modify them: the old-time religion was good enough for him and for everyone else. His sincere devotion to Jefferson did not embrace that statesman's religious views or concepts of toleration, and the evolution of democracy from Jefferson to Bryan went far to confirm Henry Adams' theory of entropy. History remembers the Cross of Gold, but his contemporaries knew Bryan rather for the oft-repeated eulogy of the Prince of Peace; to them he was the Peerless Leader not only of democracy but of morality, his very vocabulary freighted with the Scriptures, his political campaigns moral crusades. As he had founded his political morality on the Bible, there was no inconsistency in his advocacy of fundamentalism; as he had always been opposed by the rich, the privileged, and the learned, there was some consistency, too, in his hostility to a modernism which found its support in the Eastern cities and seats of learning.

Constitutionally Bryan's case was unimpeachable, for in a democracy, as Justice Holmes never tired of pointing out, the people have a right to make fools of themselves. Bryan, however, did not adopt this logical but embarrassing position. Neither he nor Darrow argued the constitutional issue, and their evasion was encouraged by the court, the press, and public opinion. It was not young John T. Scopes, after all, who was on trial but fundamentalism itself. To the delight of the newspapermen and the chagrin of the devout, the trial degenerated into a circus and a brawl. That was both unfortunate and misleading, but it was perhaps inevitable. It was unfortunate because it made a mockery of the faith of millions of men and women; it was misleading because fundamentalism, for all its glaring intellectual inadequacies, was not to be confounded by arguments which Colonel Ingersoll had already exhausted. If Bryan failed to meet the challenge of science, Darrow failed equally to meet the challenge which traditional religion presented to modern philosophy, and the failure of both illuminated the confusion that permeated the American mind in the twentieth century.

Technically Bryan won his case, for Scopes was convicted and the conviction sustained in the state Supreme Court; actually he lost it, and even his dramatic death could not reverse the decision which public opinion had rendered. It was not that Darrow and his colleagues made fundamentalism ridiculous; actually, by falling back on the arguments of Ingersoll and Brann "the Iconoclast," they made antifundamentalism almost equally ridiculous. It was rather that Bryan, for all his eloquence, was unable to demonstrate the connection between fundamentalism and morality or explain the relevance of fundamentalism to the complex problems of the twentieth century or infuse the fundamentalist cause with vitality or dignity.

Although fundamentalism persisted and the numbers of those who theoretically subscribed to its dogmas remained high, it never quite recovered from its connection with the Ku Klux Klan and the Dayton trial. By the midcentury it had lost power and prestige: the legal crusade against evolution was quietly dropped; the war on Higher Criticism became an anachronism and fundamentalist churches found no religious obstacles to an interest in social welfare. Fundamentalism declined not so much because it was refuted —for its adherents were indifferent to secular refutation—as because it had lost whatever intellectual vitality and moral justification it had possessed.

William Jennings Bryan was not a political philosopher, and many would deny his title to statesmanship. Yet his political creed was born of an instinctive understanding of the meaning of American history, and he pioneered in the advocacy of more and more important legislation than any other politician of his generation. The most representative American of his time, he represented what was, on the whole, soundest and most wholesome in the American character. His democracy was intuitive but none the less rationalized for that; his moral earnestness grew out of religious convictions; his economic radicalism was a product of experience familiar enough to those born and raised along the Middle Border. He spoke for the God-fearing, Protestant, evangelical America, for the rural America that was giving way to the urban, for the South and the West whose resources were being exploited to profit the East, for the homespun, egalitarian America dismayed at the emergence of social classes and exotic standards, and he spoke with the tongue of angels. Less sophisticated than Theodore Roosevelt, less profound than Wilson, not so hard-headed as La Follette, he was neither the simpleton nor the demagogue that his critics pictured and that a later generation, misled by Dayton and Coral Gables, imagined. Without any profound grasp of economics, he knew as much about the tariff or the money question as most contemporary politicians—and rather more than Mark Hanna or the silver-plated McKinley—and as his instincts were sound he managed to penetrate to the nature, though not to the solution, of the economic problems that harassed his followers. Lacking in critical acumen, he had nevertheless a firm grasp on political and economic realities, and, though he clothed all his arguments in trailing clouds of rhetoric, the arguments themselves were logical enough. He was the first major political figure to give articulate expression to the rumblings of discontent that were sweeping the nation, the first to understand that the problems of politics were primarily economic, the first to formulate a broad program designed to translate the hopes of the nineteenth-century democracy into policies relevant to the practical needs of the twentieth. The most astute politician of his day, he never compromised his integrity; the most ambitious, he never sacrificed principle to ambition; three times rejected by the American people, he never wavered in his faith in their virtue or in the essential soundness of their judgment, and he gloried in the name, "The Great Commoner." He had an understanding of the psychology of his own kind that has never been surpassed and inspired such devotion in them as few other American statesmen have been able to command.

Of the new forces transforming American political thought—evolution, pragmatism, economics, and psychology—he was wanting in comprehension of only the second. He knew, none better, that the Constitution had to be adjusted to the needs of a twentieth-century society, and for two decades he led the fight on laissez faire; all his political campaigns were economic—though it was an economics curiously blended with morals; his understanding of popular psychology was shrewd and enlightened. But, unlike his contemporaries, La Follette, Theodore Roosevelt, and Wilson, he was wholly lacking in the scientific habit of mind, and for the expert he had only distrust—a distrust which was generously reciprocated. He is the connecting link between the nineteenth and the twentieth centuries, embodying the best of the American character that was rapidly becoming archaic, anticipating the political program designed to adjust that character to the complex demands of the new day. The people whose battles he so gallantly fought have all but forgotten him; the causes he championed were to be vindicated under new leaders; his reputation has been buried among the ruins of his own triumphs.

Bibliographical Note

Controversial as Bryan was, he became the subject of a great many books and articles during his own lifetime. After his death, and until well into the thirties, the biographical writing about him continued to mount. Little of it was scholarly; blind devotion to the man, or intense dislike for what he symbolized, flawed nearly all of it. The best of the early biographies was Paxton Hibben and C. Hartley Grattan, *The Peerless Leader: William Jennings Bryan* (New York: Farrar and Rinehart, 1929), a book that put the worst possible construction on everything Bryan did. Morris R. Werner, *Bryan* (New York: Harcourt, Brace and Company, 1929) was also hostile, but not so well written. Of the sympathetic early biographies, John C. Long, *Bryan, The Great Commoner* (New York: D. Appleton and Company, 1928) was the most balanced. Others, such as Genevieve F. and John D. Herrick, *The Life of William Jennings Bryan* (Chicago: Grover C. Buxton, 1925), Wayne C. Williams, *William Jennings Bryan* (New York: G. P. Putnam's Sons, 1936), and Charles M. Rosser, *The Crusading Commoner* (Dallas: Mathias, Van Nort and Company, 1937), were uncritical accounts by Bryan partisans.

For over a decade after this initial outburst of writing, curiosity about the Great Commoner seemed to wane, perhaps because of the portentous events in Europe and Asia and the coming of World War II. Anyone seeking objective understanding had to rely heavily, then, on the products of his own pen and effort: *The First Battle* (Chicago: W. B. Conkey, 1896); *Speeches of William Jennings Bryan,* 2 vols. (New York: Funk and Wagnalls Company, 1909); and *Memoirs of William Jennings Bryan* (Philadelphia: John C. Winston Company,

1925). This last, though hastily completed by his wife after Bryan's death, remains both interesting and useful for the attitudes it reveals. Available, to be sure, were studies of genuine merit such as George R. Poage, "The College Career of William Jennings Bryan," *Mississippi Valley Historical Review*, XV (September 1928), 165–182; Estal E. Sparlin, "Bryan and the 1912 Democratic Convention," *Mississippi Valley Historical Review*, XXII (March 1936), 537–546; and Merle E. Curti, "Bryan and World Peace," *Smith College Studies in History*, XVI (Northampton, Mass., 1931). The memoirs of Bryan's friends and associates—Willis J. Abbot, *Watching the World Go By* (Boston: Little, Brown, and Company, 1933) is a good example—were often informative. But of course none of these memoirs, monographs, or articles was meant to take the place of a full-scale biography. Nor were the early, often perceptive, sketches that appeared in Charles E. Merriam, *Four American Party Leaders* (New York: The Macmillan Company, 1926), Walter Lippmann, *Men of Destiny* (New York: The Macmillan Company, 1927), and William Allen White, *Masks in a Pageant* (New York: The Macmillan Company, 1928).

In the years immediately after World War II a revival of interest in the problems of political leadership found expression in Richard Hofstadter's *The American Political Tradition, And the Men Who Made It* (New York: Alfred A. Knopf, 1948), a book that had enormous impact on American historiography and biography. Hofstadter's profile of Bryan, along with James A. Barnes, "Myths of the Bryan Campaign," *Mississippi Valley Historical Review*, XXXIV (December 1947), 367–404, initiated a resurgence of Bryan scholarship. Far and away the most productive of postwar investigators was Paolo E. Coletta; articles flowed from his pen in rapid succession. Among the most important, in addition to the piece reprinted in this book, are the following: "The Youth of William Jennings Bryan— Beginnings of a Christian Statesman," *Nebraska History*, XXXI (March 1950), 1–24; "William Jennings Bryan and the Nebraska Senatorial Election of 1893," *Nebraska History*, XXXI (September 1950), 183–203; "The Morning Star of the Reformation: William Jennings Bryan's First Congressional Campaign," *Nebraska History*, XXXVII (June 1956), 103–119; "William Jennings Bryan's Second Congressional Campaign," *Nebraska History*, XL (December 1959), 275–291; "Bryan, Cleveland, and the Disrupted Democracy, 1890– 1896," *Nebraska History*, XLI (March 1960), 1–27; "Bryan, Anti- Imperialism and Missionary Diplomacy," *Nebraska History*, XLIV

(September 1963), 167–187; "William Jennings Bryan and Currency and Banking Reform," *Nebraska History,* XLV (March 1964), 31–57; and "Secretary of State William Jennings Bryan and Deserving Democrats," *Mid-America,* XLVIII (April 1966), 75–98.

Articles by other authors also began to appear in great profusion. Norbert R. Mahnken, "William Jennings Bryan in Oklahoma," *Nebraska History,* XXXI (December 1950), 247–274, deals with Bryan's influence in a state where he was highly popular. Edgar A. Hornig published three articles on the campaign of 1908: "The Indefatigable Mr. Bryan in 1908," *Nebraska History,* XXXVII (September 1956), 183–199; "Campaign Issues in the Presidential Election of 1908," *Indiana Magazine of History,* LIV (September 1958), 237–264; and "The Religious Issue in the Taft-Bryan Duel of 1908," *Proceedings of the American Philosophical Society,* 105 (December 15, 1961), 530–537. For the results of other investigation see Samuel Proctor, "William Jennings Bryan and the University of Florida," *Florida Historical Quarterly,* XXXIX (July 1960), 1–15; Boyce House, "Bryan the Orator," *Journal of the Illinois State Historical Society,* LII (Autumn 1960), 266–282; D. Jerome Tweton, "North Dakota Editors and the Presidential Candidates of 1900," *North Dakota History,* XXVII (Winter 1960), 35–42; Robert F. Durden, "The 'Cow-bird' Grounded: The Populist Nomination of Bryan and Tom Watson in 1896," *Mississippi Valley Historical Review,* L (December 1963), 397–423; and Roger Daniels, "William Jennings Bryan and the Japanese," *Southern California Quarterly,* XLVIII (September 1966), 227–237.

Several book-length studies exploring particular phases of Bryan's career appeared after 1960. My own *The Trumpet Soundeth, William Jennings Bryan and His Democracy, 1896–1912* (Lincoln: University of Nebraska Press, 1960) is an effort to see Bryan as the product of a rural culture in his opposition to Republican domination of national politics. Norman Pollack, *The Populist Response to Industrial America, Midwestern Populist Thought* (Cambridge: Harvard University Press, 1962) emphasizes radical influences within the agrarian movement, but treats Bryan's relationship to them. Three recent works concentrate on the election of 1896: Stanley L. Jones, *The Presidential Election of 1896* (Madison: University of Wisconsin Press, 1964); Robert F. Durden, *The Climax of Populism: The Election of 1896* (Lexington: University of Kentucky Press, 1965), and my *McKinley, Bryan, and the People* (Philadelphia and New York: J. B. Lippincott, 1964). For an analysis of recent literature on the campaign see Gilbert Fite, "William Jennings Bryan and the Campaign of 1896: Some Views and Problems," *Nebraska History*, XLVII (September 1966), 247–264. The last memorable event of Bryan's life is the subject of Ray Ginger's *Six Days or Forever? Tennessee v. John Thomas Scopes* (Boston: Beacon Press, 1958). And perhaps the most perceptive work yet written about Bryan focuses on his last ten years. That masterful study is Lawrence W. Levine, *Defender of the Faith, William Jennings Bryan: The Last Decade, 1915–1925* (New York: Oxford University Press, 1965).

While historians have written much about Bryan and his times in the years since 1945, no really good biography has been completed. But the first volume of Paolo Coletta's detailed study has been published under the title *William Jennings Bryan, I. Political Evangelist, 1860–1908* (Lincoln: University of Nebraska Press, 1964), and when the second volume appears students will at last have at hand a complete and thorough life of the Commoner. Further research is underway, although the value of another traditional biography at this point is doubtful. Several scholars have, in fact, already shifted their emphasis from individual biography to the sort of behavioral investigation suggested by Samuel P. Hays in "The Social Analysis of American Political History, 1880–1920," *Political Science Quarterly*, LXXX (September 1965), 373–394. Such investigation, with its examination of groups and the underlying patterns of political life, may well open the way for fresh assessment of individual political leaders such as Bryan.

Contributors

THOMAS A. BAILEY, Professor of History at Stanford University, has written widely in the field of diplomatic history. His publications include *Theodore Roosevelt and the Japanese-American Crisis*; *The Policy of the United States toward the Neutrals, 1917–1918*; *Woodrow Wilson and the Lost Peace*; *Woodrow Wilson and the Great Betrayal*; and *America Faces Russia*.

RICHARD CHALLENER, who received his doctorate in history from Columbia, is Professor of History at Princeton University. He has written *The French Theory of the Nation in Arms, 1866–1939*, and he is co-author of *National Security in the Nuclear Age*.

PAOLO E. COLETTA obtained his baccalaureate and doctoral degrees from the University of Missouri. He has taught at the United States Naval Academy since 1946. In addition to numerous articles on Bryan he has published the first volume of a biography, *William Jennings Bryan, I. Political Evangelist, 1860–1908*.

HENRY STEELE COMMAGER, after a distinguished career at Columbia University, became Professor of American Civilization at Amherst in 1956. He has been Pitt Professor of American History at Cambridge, Harmsworth Professor of American History at Oxford, and Gottesman Lecturer at Uppsala. His books include *Theodore Parker*; *Majority Rule and Minority Rights*; *The American Mind*;

Freedom, Loyalty, Dissent; *The Era of Reform*; *Freedom and Order*; *The Nature and Study of History*; and *The Search for a Usable Past.*

MERLE E. CURTI is Frederick Jackson Turner Professor of History at the University of Wisconsin. He has studied and lectured extensively abroad, and he has been a fellow of the Center for Advanced Study in Behavioral Sciences. His book, *The Growth of American Thought,* won a Pulitzer Prize in 1943. Among his other works are *Bryan and World Peace*; *The American Peace Crusade*; *The Social Ideas of American Educators*; *The Roots of American Loyalty*; *The Making of an American Community*; *Probing Our Past*; and *American Philanthropy Abroad.* He is co-author of *The University of Wisconsin* and *Prelude to Point Four.*

JOHN A. GARRATY is Professor of History at Columbia University, where he received his Ph.D. degree in 1948. His books include *Henry Cabot Lodge*; *The Nature of Biography*; *Woodrow Wilson, A Great Life in Brief*; *Silas Wright*; and *Righthand Man, The Life of George W. Perkins.*

RAY GINGER, now teaching at Wayne State University, has had both an academic and an editorial career. He is the author of *The Bending Cross: A Biography of Eugene Victor Debs*; *Altgeld's America*; *Six Days or Forever?*; *American Social Thought*; and *Age of Excess.*

RICHARD HOFSTADTER is De Witt Clinton Professor of American History at Columbia University. He has won the Beveridge Award and two Pulitzer Prizes, and in 1958–1959 he was Pitt Professor of American History and Institutions at Cambridge University. Among his many books are *Social Darwinism in American Thought*; *The American Political Tradition*; *The Age of Reform*; *Anti-Intellectualism in American Life*; and *The Paranoid Style in American Politics.*

LAWRENCE W. LEVINE has taught at the University of California, Berkeley, since receiving his doctorate at Columbia in 1962. *De-*

fender of the Faith is his first book. He is also co-editor of *The Shaping of Twentieth Century America.*

NORBERT R. MAHNKEN is intimately acquainted with the environment of the Great Plains. He did his graduate work at the University of Nebraska, and for several years he has taught in the Department of History, Oklahoma State University, Stillwater.

JOHN T. SCOPES received a scholarship from the American Association for the Advancement of Science shortly after the Dayton trial. He studied at the University of Chicago, and from there went to South America as an oil geologist. He now lives at Shreveport, Louisiana.

WILLARD H. SMITH is Professor of History at Goshen College and the author of *Schuyler Colfax, The Changing Fortunes of a Political Idol.* His article, reproduced in this volume, reflects a long-term interest in Bryan's career.

PAUL W. GLAD was born in Salt Lake City, Utah, in 1926. He attended Purdue University and received his advanced degrees in history from Indiana University. He has taught at Hastings College, Coe College, and the University of Maryland. He has been a Fulbright Professor at Philipps-Universität, Marburg/Lahn, Germany, and a Guggenheim fellow. Now Professor of History at the University of Wisconsin, he is the author of *The Trumpet Soundeth, William Jennings Bryan and His Democracy, 1896–1912,* and *McKinley, Bryan, and the People.*

❂

AÏDA DIPACE DONALD, General Editor of the American Profiles series, holds degrees from Barnard and Columbia, where she taught American history, and a doctorate from the University of Rochester. Mrs. Donald has been awarded A.A.U.W. and Fulbright fellowships and has edited *John F. Kennedy and the New Frontier.* She is also co-editor of the *Diary of Charles Francis Adams.*